Stormbird

Stormbird

One of the Luftwaffe's
highest scoring Me262 aces
Oberst (i.R.) Hermann Buchner

Crécy Publishing Limited

Stormbird
One of the Luftwaffe's highest scoring Me262 aces

First published in Great Britain in 2000 by Hikoki Publications Ltd
Crécy Publishing Limited edition first published in 2008
Reprinted 2010

A CIP record for this book is available from the British Library

Printed and bound in Great Britain
by CPI Antony Rowe

ISBN 9 780859 791403

Crécy Publishing Limited
1a Ringway Trading Estate, Shadowmoss Road, Manchester M22 5LH
www.crecy.co.uk

Most of the photographs in this book are from the author's collection. Others were supplied by Hikoki Publications, Philip Jarrett, Simon Parry, Dick Ward and John Weal. Footnotes have been added by the publisher to clarify certain points.

CONTENTS

The bronze Crimea Shield was awarded to all those who served there for three months or who took part in a major operation against the enemy between 21 September 1941 and 4 July 1942.

Chapter One

Youth

I was born at 2.30am on 30 October 1919 in my parents' flat in Itzling, near Salzburg, the son of Franz and Katharina Buchner. My father had only the previous year returned home from Galicia (until 1918 part of the Austro-Hungarian Empire, nowadays part of Poland and Ukraine) where he had been, and still was, employed as a conductor on the KuK State Railway. My mother, meanwhile, had been fully occupied looking after my brothers Franz and Karl and, throughout the war, had been employed by the military administration as a seamstress.

Salzburg is dominated by the fortress of the Mönschberg and the bell towers of the numerous churches. It is, of course, also world famous as the birthplace of Wolfgang Mozart.

I was baptised into the Roman Catholic faith the following month in the Parish Church of St Anton in Itzling. Things were not exactly rosy at that time: economic conditions were pitiful and my father had come back from the war with tuberculosis. In spite of all this my mother did her best to bring the family through the depression intact, despite my father having to spend the first year after the war in the Crafenhof TB Sanatorium at Schwarzac/St Veit, near Salzburg.

When I reached the age of four I attended the Catholic kindergarten in Itzling. My friend Toni Hemetzbyrger and I had to go from our home in Mozartstrasse to church and from the vicarage to Itzling every day on foot, a half-hour walk. In nice weather it was good fun, but in the snow and ice of winter it was neither nice nor fun. But what were generally good years soon passed and, in 1925, I was enrolled in Volksschule (secondary school). My mother made me go to the Jubiläumsschule in Salzburg St Andrä, where I went until 1929. All my friends went to school in Itzling. Our teacher wanted to make us into good and honest students and was therefore very strict. The friends I made at this school were all very nice but I hardly ever came into contact with my playmates from my time at kindergarten.

During the 1920s the political landscape came to play a part in our family history. The children played 'cops and robbers' against a background that was all too real. The year 1927 brought a huge railwaymen's strike, which we young lads looked on with great curiosity. In the stoking house, right by our flats, the steam locomotives could be seen parked up, immobile, with the drivers and stokers standing in groups, wearing red armbands and conducting vehement discussions. My father was also involved in this strike.

As time passed the economic conditions became worse, with many people out of work. In 1928 my elder brother was just one in this mass of people struggling, in vain, to find a job.

In 1929 I moved to the St Andrä Salzburg secondary school. Now things became somewhat more serious, but they were nevertheless enjoyable times and full of learning. I had good school friends and was regularly able to visit the Salzburg and local gymnastics clubs. Political arguments also pervaded the school, dividing both the teachers and the students, the viewpoint of the children being very much dependent upon the political persuasion of their parents.

During the years 1930 to 1933 my family started to build a single family house. The economic situation was still bad and, against this background, a debate was conducted about my future career that was to determine whether I was to continue my studies or learn a trade. After lengthy consideration, my parents decided that I should learn the trade of a baker. The grounds for this were simple: an apprentice baker received food and work clothes. The evidence was clear; I was a burden on the family budget.

In 1933 my schooling ended and, in July of that year, I began my apprenticeship under master baker Martin in Salzburg-Griesgasse. I was not particularly overjoyed at this but accepted the situation for what it was; I had an apprenticeship and my parents had one less drain on their resources.

The business was a good one and was well respected in the area. It had one master baker and twelve journeymen. Most were very good colleagues, but there were also some really malicious people among them. The worst was the relatively young master baker's wife. The master baker, the owner of the business, was hardly ever present as he was heavily engaged in politics. I, not yet 14 years of age, had to start work daily at 4.00am; work ended in summer at 8.00pm, or 6.00pm in winter. At the same time I had to attend the trade school twice a week. Nevertheless, I found the time to involve myself in mountain climbing and became a member of the Austrian Alpine Association youth team. I went away to the mountains with my friends on every available Saturday and Sunday. The trade school itself presented no problems and I quickly learned my trade.

In 1934 my parents finished building their house and moved from 3 Mozartstrasse to 11 Maxstrasse in Itzling. Their dream had been fulfilled – they had their own house, although this was a bit of a disadvantage for me since I had further to go to my workplace in town.

The political environment now became more and more frantic. In February 1934 the 'rebellion' of the 'Reds' took place in Vienna, the effects of which gradually spread to encroach on all the people of Austria and Germany. During the morning hours, the police controlled and monitored the movement of people on the streets. As a result I was often stopped when riding my bicycle to work early in the morning and subjected to a search, which included having my flask of coffee emptied – such was the atmosphere in which we lived. Early in the same year the National Socialists began to carry out bomb attacks. Our master baker was one of their illegal leaders and was only very seldom at the business. Many of the employees were also illegal Nazis, although we apprentices were largely spared from politics. Nevertheless, the police often entered the business

premises and made searches, but without any success. I am
convinced even today that Herr Martin had nothing hidden at the
business. At this time, both my brothers were serving in the Austrian
Army with the Pioneers in Salzburg and Vienna/Korneuburg.
Knowing this, the master baker's wife was very suspicious of me,
believing me to be a supporter of the anti-Nazi Dollfuss regime.

One of the main paramilitary organisations that emerged in Austria during the
turbulent 1920s and '30s was the ultra-conservative Heimwehr (Home Army). Many
members were committed to Austrian independence, while others were sympathisers
with their rival Austrian National Socialists. The Heimwehr was loyal to the Austrian
chancellor, Engelbert Dollfuss, who, until his assassination at the hands of German
SS agents, was a fierce opponent of Hitler. Here members of the Junior Heimwehr
parade their flags.

In July 1934 the Putsch of the National Socialists took place. In
Vienna, the Federal Chancellery was occupied by the Nazis and in
Lamprechthausen there was a shoot-out between the police and the
National Socialists. There were dead and wounded everywhere and
my boss was present at the scene. After the clash was suppressed he
was imprisoned and charged with murder and high treason. As a
consequence, he was sentenced to life imprisonment and was
incarcerated in Garsen (upper Austria). From then on a bleak
atmosphere pervaded the firm. To make matters worse, the
apprentices had to be dismissed and I was left jobless.

After several weeks without work, I was brought under the wing of
the Productive Unemployed Welfare Services and worked as a labourer

at a settlement being built in Sam/Itzling. Then, in 1935, I found a baker's apprenticeship with the Doppler firm in Salzburg. This business had fourteen employees and only one apprentice, who was about my age. The operation was more modern than I had been used to and the pursuit of politics was thankfully much less prevalent. An additional benefit was that the master baker's wife was a good deal more affable.

The master was a somewhat older man and was seldom present at the business. The work also suited me better, with the apprentices starting at 6.00am and able to finish at 2.00pm. For those times it was a very socially conscious business! Also, with my parents' house completed and therefore my help no longer required, I had considerably more time to pursue my leisure interests than I had enjoyed before. In addition to my mountain climbing, I took up gliding from 1935, which took place on the Zistel airfield, conveniently near work.

In 1936 I took my journeyman's examination, passing with a grading of 'very good', and was paid my first wage of Ös35.00. For board and lodging I had to pay my mother Ös20.00. The rest belonged to me, and I was able to start to save a little; thus I was in a position to finance my gliding. This was wonderful because, through the medium of flying, I was able to draw myself away from the pressures and tensions of the unsettled political situation of the period.

At the beginning of 1937 the other apprentice was taken by the 'Stapo' and subsequently imprisoned. I carried on with my work as a console operator in the business and spent all my spare time gliding and in the mountains.

My friends and I were a group of like-minded people and nearly every Saturday we would ride our bicycles the 40km to Tennek and from there climb to the Wimmer-hutte/Tennengebirge (around 2 hours). We were all the same age and always had great fun, climbing and picking edelweiss. At the mountain huts we would regularly overhear people saying that many of the Austrians no longer agreed with the borders of the Fatherland. Nazi songs were sung and most people were convinced that the 'Austrian Legion'[1] would soon march into Austria. In spite of all this, the time that I spent in the mountains was very enjoyable and I can honestly say that, in general, it was a very happy time for me.

In March 1937 my gliding activity became much more regular, and I was able to obtain flying lessons at the Gaisberg Alpine Gliding School. There were around twenty boys in the flying group, including

Swedes and English, and we all managed to find accommodation with the local farmers of the area. Now we were able to become familiar with the aircraft, in this case an SG 38. Our flying instructor, Herr Robert Munz, was a very strict man, who always wore a beret and leather jacket. He was the sort of figure who immediately instilled respect and, with him, and a good spirit of comradeship, we made steady progress. Our first flights lasted just 10 to 20 seconds and crashes occurred often enough that part of our flying duties came to include repair work in the workshop. After four weeks the course came to an end and I returned home, having passed the 'B' examination[2].

This SG 38 glider is typical of the rudimentary aircraft in which many future Luftwaffe pilots such as the author had their first experience of flying. Flights rarely lasted for more than a few moments and crashes resulting in damage to both pilot and machine were commonplace.

After my extended leave, I returned to the business and continued with my work. The political situation was now becoming increasingly tense. The Nazis were firing their weapons and the majority of the population waited for the invasion by the Austrian Legion.

In June I reported to the Gasthof Mödelhammer in Salzburg to volunteer for the Austrian Air Force. To my joy I was accepted! Now, as the illegals became ever more active, and gunfire crackled on the streets, with many acquaintances fleeing to Germany, I waited for the possible call-up. Swastikas were daubed on every wall, and even on rock faces in the mountains. No one knew what was going to happen and rumours abounded. I, meanwhile, had my work to do and I continued to devote my free time to the gliding club and to the mountains.

In Easter 1937 I crossed the Tennen mountain range with four comrades, fathers and sons named Höftberger and Zucherstätter. It was a two-day trip: Werfenberger to Söldenhütte, where we spent the night, then Tauernkogel to Happisch-Haus, followed by the descent to Suklzau. The plateau was in fog and we had to carry out the crossing and the descent secured by avalanche lines. It was a beautiful eight-hour tour, only marred by the poor weather conditions on the plateau. The older Zuckerstätter led in an exemplary fashion and we young lads received good training from him. Several weeks later we did the Göll Heights over the Alpl Valley, again a colossal tour. Once more, we went by bicycle from Salzburg to Berchtesgaden, with our rucksacks on our backs. We left the bicycles at a pub in Berchtesgaden, for which the landlord got a few Virginias – 'smokes', which were very much in demand at the time. From there on the same day we then had a three-hour climb to the Alpl Valley Hut, which we found to be overflowing with climbers, many of them from Salzburg. As in all huts, and especially in Germany, the climbers declared themselves open to the 'Anschluss' (Annexation) and sang the best-known Nazi songs. All were of the opinion that the Austrian Legion would soon be marching into Austria.

Sleeping was a laborious matter there; not everybody had beds or mattresses and many slept on the floor. We left early the following morning, after a good breakfast. It was time to get on with the business of tackling the mountains, which meant passing over the ditches to the Göll ledge and onwards towards the summit. Our efforts were fully rewarded, however, and after a short rest we made a marvellous descent back to the All Valley. It was a splendid day, made all the more rewarding by being able to get to know some people at the hut who had completed their military service with the 'Reichenhall 100th Jägers'. We discussed the political situation together, but time was unfortunately far too short and we had to think of our descent, so that we could return to Salzburg with the bicycles. We had a lot of laughs but the funniest part of the whole journey was at Berchtesgaden when we greeted the Customs men with 'Heil Hitler'.

I continued with my flying whenever my finances allowed. At the club, we began preparing for the 'C' Grade Examination[3], which involved flying the Falken from the Zistel-Alm, with soaring flights in the updraught from the slope, and landing on the crematorium field in Salzburg (about 5-8 minutes flying time). Unfortunately it did not all work out the way I had imagined it. On one day we had no flying instructor and on another there was no wind. When the wind was good it was mostly the old pilots who were flying, with us youngsters having to look on. But we said to ourselves that it would be the same anywhere else – small consolation for us beginners!

We volunteers had still not heard anything from the Österreichischen Luftstreitkräfte (Austrian Air Force). In August we were visited by a delegation of air force officers who were carrying out flying duties on the Zistel mountain. But my colleagues and I wanted to go to the air force to become pilots. A major promised us that we could join and, if we were found to be suitable, we would then be placed on a pilot training course. We were all very confident about this, with thoughts already of military flying service.

Prior to a trip along the Danube at Linz, Hermann Göring is greeted by Luftwaffe Generalmajor Wolff (centre) and the commander of the Austrian Luftstreitkräfte, General-major Alexander Löhr. Löhr is wearing the Austrian field grey uniform with the Austrian breast badge replaced by the Luftwaffe eagle. The uniform bears a close resemblance to the Italian model, in particular by the use of rank insignia on the cuffs and the style of the cap.

There was lots for us to do at this time, since the 'ISTUS 37' flying competition was just about to take place and the Austrian Aero Club was tasked with running it. There were many foreigners expected including English, Swiss, French and Germans. I and my comrades were assigned to the team of helpers.

During this time the German glider pilots Hanna Reitsch and Heini Dietmar, who were then engaged, made the first glider crossing of the Alps. I, meanwhile, was assigned to the team of Dr Erich Aigner, an Austrian pilot from Salzburg. During this week he made the first 60km overland flight to St Georgen in Attergau. It was a great week for us helpers, for which I had taken a week's holiday. The gliding was sensational and dominated all the newspapers, with the German glider pilots getting the most prizes. They had at their disposal six gliders and an additional six towing aircraft, the likes of which we Austrians could only dream.

As time passed I continued to wait, somewhat impatiently, for my first flight from Zistel. For me, the 'C' Examination still seemed a long way off. I did not have any money and, to add insult to injury, I had still not been called up for the air force. As a means of escape I was again often to be found in the mountains, in particular the Tennen and Hagen range, with the Utersberg, Trattberg and the Hochkönig again my main areas of recreation. I passed many a lovely day in these mountains in some excellent company.

One particularly fine day I returned home from work to find my father outside waiting for me. He had a letter in his hand, which he was waving about. From some distance he called out that I had received a registered letter from the military. When I reached him, I immediately and eagerly opened the envelope to find that I now, at last, had what I had been waiting for. The official document that I excitedly held in my hand told me that I was called up on 1 October 1937 to the Ausbildungs-bataillon der Fliegertruppe (Air Force Training Battalion) at Bruck an der Leitha. I had only fourteen days to put my affairs in order!

My parents were astonished: they had no idea that I had volunteered for military service. My father was of the opinion that it would be better for me to stay with the bakery at home. He had no enthusiasm for my immediate future in the military. My mother was also unenthusiastic about my intentions. My employer, too, knew nothing of my intentions and was surprised by this news. He said that he thought it would be more sensible for me to stay at the factory. My boss, as well as my work colleagues, tried to influence me to ignore the call-up orders. But, for me, the die had been cast and I was happy that I had received orders to report to the military. In addition my friends had all joined up; there were six of them from the gliding club.

We went into the Tennen mountains one last time, up to the Wimmerhütte to 'Resl', the landlady of the hut, to celebrate our departure. I also convinced the people at work that I was serious and said my goodbyes. My boss was reluctant to let me go and once again informed me that I could return at any time. My parents also still did not approve of my being called up to the air force; my father felt that, sooner or later, war was inevitable and it would be better for me if I were to stay at home in the bakery.

Chapter Two

Life in the military
October 1937-May 1938

Early on the morning of 1 October 1937 I said my goodbyes to my parents and my younger brother and headed for the railway station. There were two other Salzburgers at the station, both with the same destination as me. I knew both of them since we were all friends from the Salzburg Gliding Group. We were all in a good mood since our wish to join the military was being fulfilled, and we could at last report for duty.

Arriving in Vienna, we had to change trains onto the Ostbahn (Eastern Railway) where we headed towards Bruck an der Leitha. We finally reached our destination at around 4.00pm and disembarked from the train, waiting on the platform to be picked up. Soldiers in uniform soon took us to a parked vehicle, which then took us to the Neudorf Camp. We were now part of the military machine, awaiting our first orders.

On arrival at the camp we were given a short greeting by an Unteroffizier, were divided into groups of nine men and sent to the barrack blocks. Here, in our groups of nine, we met with our first surprise: sparsely filled rooms with just three to six beds, empty straw sacks and a table. No other furniture was provided. A Gefreiter appeared and explained to us how the straw sacks should be filled. If we wanted somewhere to sleep, it had to be done. Still dressed in our civilian clothing, we therefore embarked on our first military task and set about filling the sacks with straw. The fuller the sack was filled with straw, the better one would be able to sleep. No one found it funny – we just quietly got on with it.

We then waited for what was to happen next, until finally a whistle sounded; it was time to eat. A soldier duly arrived and we were led to the kitchen. Once there, we were told to queue up and wait our turn!

Our first meal was known as a 'Grenadier March', a dish with potatoes, noodles and beef, all roasted together. It wasn't bad; in any case it was a novelty for us Salzburgers. We were also hungry, so the meal tasted excellent. Afterwards, we returned to our accommodation alone where we started to become acquainted with our future comrades. All had the same desire, to become pilots. We then learned of our sleeping hours – lights out at 10.00pm and reveille at 6.00am – rather a shock for us civilians.

For many of us the first night, spent sleeping on a straw sack, was something of a novelty. I noted dryly that the mattresses at the ski huts had been rather more comfortable.

Our days were extremely varied: wake, clean the room, parades, exercises and sport. We soon became a firm group of friends and accustomed ourselves to the military way of life. An interesting addition to the daily routine, however, was presented by the large number of gypsies present in the area; many of us from the western part of Germany/Austria were unaccustomed to these people. The gypsy women always brought us fruit, such as grapes, in our exercise breaks, for very little money. They would also read palms for a fee of two schillings. As the first volunteers, we were also tasked with preparing the accommodation for more newcomers, and all was ready for them when they arrived on 5 October.

By and large the officers and directing staff were all decent superiors and very good sportsmen. Our company commander, for example, was not only a very good officer but also a former Olympic athlete. All of the staff demanded a great deal of us but always personally showed us how to carry out difficult tasks and often did them with us. Night manoeuvres and daytime marches were interchanged with each other and we were 'brought on' very efficiently. Marching and singing was also practised, in anticipation of our swearing-in ceremony, which would take place at Kaisersteinbruch Camp in November. We practised our parade again and again until our superiors were completely satisfied. Slowly but surely we were being turned from ordinary civilians into useful soldiers.

The ceremony was finally scheduled for 14 November 1937. We were to be sworn in by His Highness Archduke Eugen, with General Löhr[4] also present. Our wake-up call for the day came at 4.00am and at 6.00am we marched out of Brucker Camp and over the fields to Kaisersteinbruch. It was pouring with rain, and we trudged across the sodden ground towards our destination. We nevertheless arrived punctually at our positions, the others already having arrived. We were then presented to Archduke Eugen. At the entrance to the camp an artillery battery was firing, despite the pouring rain and low cloud. The bad weather prevented us from seeing what they were shooting at, but His Highness was nevertheless satisfied with the gunners' performance. The rain, however, refused to stop and we marched to the sports ground, where we were formed into squares. Then the ceremonies began. General Löhr made a speech to us soldiers, which was followed by others from several civilian men.

After the ceremony we had to march all the way back to Bruck, leaving at about 2.00pm. We returned in equally heavy rain to our barracks. When we arrived, soaked through and very hungry, we were given a meal of Wiener Schnitzel and salad. We were now fully fledged soldiers and ready to be used in the field.

Just before the Christmas break we were assigned to Geschwadern. It was rumoured that we would be engaged in operational full tours; every day there was some bit of news. In any case, some were posted from Bruck to the training unit FLR 2 at Kaisersteinbruch, of whom I, Fliegersoldat Buchner, was one. We made it just in time for an outbreak of typhoid in the camp, which, after several days, resulted in the whole camp being quarantined. As a result our forthcoming transfer to Kampfgeschwader 1 at Aigen, in Ennstal, was delayed.

At the beginning of December our time to move finally came. We would travel by train via Vienna, St Pölten, Amstetten and Hieflau to Aigen. We were to move into a new Fliegerhorst (air base) and would be the first Austrian soldiers in this region.

When we arrived, the countryside already had a powdering of snow over it. We soon settled in, finding the local people, who were about seventy per cent Nazis, or at least sympathisers, to be very friendly to us soldiers. Only the local vicar remained unconvinced about our good character. At High Mass in Wörschach he announced to his congregation, 'Mothers, lock up your daughters, the wolves have moved in.' The sermon didn't have much effect, however, and most people found it highly amusing.

I was assigned to the technical personnel of Bombenstaffel 1. My Staffelkapitän was Oberleutnant Rauer, a red-haired man from Linz. He was to serve to the end of the war as Horstkommandant of a Fliegerhorst in the Ruhr, only to be shot in the camp by the US occupying forces in 1945. But my time spent at Aigen holds many happy memories for me. I learned a lot of technical things and filled the rest of my time with skiing. We also had plenty of opportunity to go flying with trained pilots, usually in the Caproni Ca 133, a three-engined bomber. This was the type that was deployed by the Italians in Abyssinia. We also flew in the Focke-Wulf FW 44 'Stieglitz', a training machine.

We were allowed to return home for Christmas 1937, my first leave as a soldier in uniform. My parents were very pleased that I was able to come home for the holidays and my father was keen to find out what it was like in the military, having himself served from 1903 to 1906 with

This is Focke-Wulf FW 56 '101', construction number 2013, the first of a batch of nine bought by the Austrian Air Force for 800 Reichsmarks each in February 1938. The overall finish is aluminium dope.

At Aigen in 1937, Austrian Air Force officers stand in front of one of the three Junkers Ju 52/3m aircraft acquired by the service. This is most probably serial number '3', OE-HKA, which was used as a staff transport. The other two, Nos 36 and 37, were bombers.

The Austrian Air Force acquired six Focke-Wulf FW 58s (serial numbers 301-306) for the sum of 1,600 Reichsmarks each at the same time as it bought the FW 56 light fighters. The FW 58s were entered into the Austrian inventory as bombers. These two are over Vienna in 1937.

This is FW 58 No 302, apparently finished in German light grey paint overall, with the red and white Austrian cockades.

Two unidentified senior Austrian Air Force officers stand under the wing of a Focke-Wulf FW 58. Note that they are wearing the dark blue dress uniform.

the Rainers in Salzburg. But Christmas passed all too quickly and I had to return to Aigen before the New Year. My father took me to the train and we said our short goodbyes. In my later times as a soldier, my father would often take me to the train to say goodbye.

I was back with my unit on 30 December, and for New Year's Eve I was assigned to guard duty, my first with the army. The night was frosty, the snow crunched underfoot and the fir trees were filled with ice, but I remember it being a lovely night with a full moon. It was one of many regular duties in the army that we were slowly becoming acquainted with.

The arrival of the New Year brought the normal routine of work and, in addition to our technical duties, we had more mundane duties in the kitchen and in our accommodation to perform. But our routine was regularly interrupted by numerous alarms and curfews as the political situation was now becoming extremely precarious and rumours were the order of every day. Throughout January and February we were allowed to go into the neighbourhood only once, being almost continually confined to barracks.

Nineteen-year-old Fliegersoldat Buchner in a formal studio portrait taken in Salzburg on 16 February 1938. He wears the grey-green service uniform common to all branches of the Austrian Army with the wings on his right breast indicating membership of the Air Force. For officers the wings were gold, NCOs wore silver and for other ranks the wings were blue.

At the beginning of March the Geschwader was inspected by the Kommandant of Fliegerregiment 2 at Graz, Oberst Ilam. After the inspection the troops were allowed out for an afternoon's leave. Naturally, we soon spruced ourselves up and left the barracks as members at the air force. The inhabitants of the Aigen neighbourhood asked us why we had not been allowed out of barracks for so long. We didn't know why ourselves, but they were pleased to see us and were very friendly towards as. They told us that radical changes would soon effect us all. They were very enthusiastic about this as many were either Nazis or Nazi sympathisers.

On the evening of 11 March 1938 we saw our first serious trouble in front of the barracks main gate. A mob of civilians with swastika armbands had formed a gang and were demonstrating noisily. In response, soldiers with machine guns and equipped with live ammunition had been deployed from Lien to guard public offices. Our Unteroffiziere (NCOs) were very nervous about the whole thing, particularly since the officers were nowhere to be seen. But we did nothing except raise our readiness state. At around midnight, bonfires were lit and soldiers started cheering and shouting 'Heil Hitler!'[5].

The next morning, yes, as usual, daily watch. An assembly had been ordered at 7.00am in the canteen. All Geschwader personnel were there and some soldiers were wearing a swastika armband. The most senior officer present announced the arrival of the Barracks Kommandant, Major Feldpilot Marenkowitsch. The Kommandant gave a rousing speech for Austria, stating that 'our Fatherland is in danger'. 'He was no German,' he declared. 'No, he was an Austrian.' At the end he asked all soldiers present to sing the national anthem. Everyone in the room joined in and sang the old national hymn from Haydn. After the last note had faded away, some SA men stepped onto the stage and arrested him.

From that time onwards the majority of the station staff wore the swastika armband on their uniform. We were not allowed out for the next couple of days, but the local people and the majority of the soldiers celebrated. Even so, with the German Luftwaffe now in command of the Austrian Luftstreitkräfte, we continued to perform our normal duties, with only flying duties having been discontinued. Towards the end of March the first German Luftwaffe troops arrived and took over the military airfield.

At the beginning of April Adolf Hitler came to visit Graz. I, together with a number of my colleagues, was filled with curiosity

German mountain troops with their pack mules are given a warm welcome as they enter Salzburg on 12 March 1938.

and was keen to see the Führer in person. We took leave and caught the train to Graz. In front of the main railway station, a guard of honour had assembled to greet him. We were in the uniforms of the old Austrian Air Force, so we hid ourselves among the assembled companies, in order to see him as closely as possible.

On his arrival Hitler and his entourage walked along the front of the honour guard. He passed about ten metres in front of us, close enough for us to see his eyes; it was as if he was looking directly at us. For us it was an historical moment. We returned to Aigen, later the same day, happy and contented; we had seen the Führer.

Hauptmann Behrend and other Austrian Air Force officers give the Nazi salute as the Germans take over at Aigen in March 1938. Note the orders tucked into the turned-back cuff of his overcoat.

German units gradually arrived to take over the duties of the Austrians. By April things had become serious enough for us to be asked by the Kommandant whether we would serve in the new German Luftwaffe or whether we would rather disarm. Every single person was asked and I don't think more than four or five soldiers removed their uniforms and left the air force. The officers, as well as the NCOs, all chose to serve in the Luftwaffe.

We were sworn in on the name of the Führer, the Commander-in-Chief of the Wehrmacht, on 20 April 1938[6]. The Austrians had been allowed to fly again for a while now and I was allowed to take a flight in a 'Stieglitz' into the mountains with one of the pilots, a man called Fanowitz. As we passed above the Planner Alm, at about 1,800 metres altitude, he did a bit of stunt flying, during which the engine suddenly stopped. He reacted by trying to glide towards the valley exit and thereby make an emergency landing. We flew, all the time losing altitude, in the direction of Donnersbach until, struggling to maintain height, we hit the top of some fir trees near the

Schrabach pasture. The result was that we were forced to make a difficult and dangerous landing on an avalanche slope, unable to see the lie of the land. As a result we struck the ground with a frightening crash, then all was dark and still. We had crashed through the snow as if we had gone down a bowling alley. After a few moments, the pilot became visible. He asked me whether I was all right and whether anything had struck me. Happily nothing had, and although neither of us was able to move we were unhurt. As we struggled in vain to free ourselves, we could hear voices in the distance. The voices became louder and we could soon make out the first rays of daylight through the layers of snow. Thankfully, rescuers had arrived to get us out of this awkward situation.

A cold and morose Hermann Buchner (right) stands by the wreck of the Focke-Wulf FW 44J in which he crashed as a passenger in the spring of 1938.
Although not clearly visible in this view, this military aircraft carried a civil registration, OE-TCI, as was customary with training aircraft in the Austrian Air Force. No 4015 was Austrian licence-built but did not survive to feature on the 18 May 1938 list of aircraft transferred to the Luftwaffe.

Another view of the wreck of Focke-Wulf FW 44J OE-TCI. As can be clearly seen, the aircraft was in almost brand-new condition before the crash. All that was salvageable was the engine and a few components, much of the wooden structure being burned by local SA men who were supposedly guarding the aircraft during the bitterly cold night on the Planner Alm in Steiermark.

After some time the men's shovels finally reached us and we were freed. The men, who were skiers, told us that we had been lucky, but I was still in shock and probably looked pretty dopey. Initially our rescuers wanted us to climb up to the Planner hut, but after enquiring they found that there was no telephone there. The pilot then decided that I should descend to Donnersbach, in the valley, and make a phone call from the Gendarmerie to inform our commanders at the airfield of the crash. So, as I was alone, without a coat or scarf, I walked through the snow into the valley, cutting through woods as I went, always heading downwards. About halfway down to the valley it began to get dark until I only had the stars for company. After about 2 hours walking, I reached the Gendarmerie at Donnersbach. As I entered it from the darkness, the local police greeted me with great enthusiasm, seemingly overjoyed at my appearance. Our machine was already being searched for by this stage, since it was overdue. I explained that I needed to telephone my unit and, after a short time, the connection to Aigen airfield was made and I was able to report to Kommandant Hauptmann Behrend, a captain on the staff of the Geschwader. He immediately asked where our crash position was and whether or not we were injured. He was naturally very relieved when I told him that we were both OK. He then instructed me to climb straight back up to the crash site and to arrange for the Gendarmerie to guard the wreck. He ordered us to remain on the Planner until we had been picked up by our troops.

The Gendarmerie commander gave me four men (SA brownshirts) to guard the wreckage, and at about 10.00pm we commenced the long climb back up to the Schrabach pasture. I, poor devil, had to climb the mountain again.

We finally reached the crash site at around midnight and the SA men took up position in the Schrabach pasture and guarded the remains of our aircraft. I then went alone further on to the Planner hut, arriving at around 2.00am, to discover the skiers and my pilot still celebrating our escape. After I informed Fanowitz of our Kommandant's orders, I was finally given food and drink. This was, naturally, more than welcome and before long I began to feel quite exhausted after the day's exertions. My desire to find a bed was not fulfilled, however, but I did manage to find a mattress and before long I was fast asleep.

The next day the skiers recounted what they had seen of our accident. It sounded like a fairy tale, such that at round midday Fanowitz and I went down to the accident site to view the wreckage for ourselves, this time in peace. Some of the remaining parts had already been destroyed. The guards had, for example, burned parts of the wings during the night to keep themselves warm. Of the fuselage, only the metal parts remained. When our mechanics arrived from the airfield, they lifted the engine from its mountings and removed the instruments. By the time they had finished, only fragments of the former training aircraft were left there. That evening we climbed once again to the Planner hut, where we exchanged views with the skiers and celebrated our forthcoming departure before settling down for the night.

The next day we bade the skiers farewell and made our descent with the mechanics. The truck driver had his hands full in trying to get the truck and its load back to Donnersbach in one piece and we did not reach our airfield until about 2.00pm, when we reported to our Kommandant, who greeted us heartily. Surprisingly, very little was said about the incident. We had actually expected to be bawled out, but in the excitement of the German take-over our accident was largely forgotten.

The first flying unit, a reconnaissance Staffel from Stargard in Pomerania, bearing the designation 2(H)/18, had just moved its aircraft into Aigen. Meanwhile, for the time being we had to carry out our duties under the command of German officers and NCOs. The old soldiers of the Austrian Luftstreitkräfte were quite unenthusiastic about this and were visibly sullen. They were not prepared to accept pig-headed exercise orders from outsiders. In any case, it was not a particularly pleasant time for the rest of the Austrians.

At the beginning of May 1938 our officers were posted away and no replacement Kommandant had been designated. Then, in mid-year, the remainder of the Geschwader was divided up and I went with part of it to the bomber unit, KG 158, at Wels.

Chapter Three

In the German Luftwaffe
May 1938-May 1940

On arrival at Wels, another wind was blowing. We were picked up at the railway station, bundled off into cars and taken to a school in the town. A former commercial school across from the parish church was to become our lodgings for the next three months.

Our Austrian uniforms were handed in and we were given new clothes. Everything seemed new, particularly being clothed in these smart new uniforms. Work was also going to be different from that in Aigen, now that we were away from our old familiar Austrian NCOs.

After all the formalities had been taken care of, we were ready to start work. But to get there we had to march from our accommodation to the airfield and back every day, no transport being provided to collect us. Once there, we carried out our duties on a rotational basis. We were fed at midday from field kitchens, with breakfast and the evening meal being taken at the school. The three months we spent like this passed very quickly and, at the end, we were divided up to report to a number of different units. I went to Fliegerhorst Kompanie Wels, where my duties included guard and kitchen duties, training as a fireman, and a whole list of other unexciting tasks. I was not particularly pleased about this since it was not helping me to become a pilot. At least they could have posted me somewhere as aircrew.

I did my best to get myself posted out of there and, in September 1938, I was posted to Fliegerhorst Kompanie Wien-Aspern. Here I again met up with Austrians, this time from Aigen and Bruck. They also wanted to became pilots and were not at all happy with having to do guard duty. The soldiers from the airfield company, of which I was one, were employed on guard duty for the Flottenkommando (Fleet Command) and the Luftgaukommando (District Air Command) in Vienna. This was somewhat better work and definitely more varied.

Most of the Austrians already had a year's military service behind them and should have become Gefreiter (junior NCOs), but we had to complete the junior NCO cadre course again before we could be promoted. So we were taken off guard duty and were again detailed to do exercises and sport. In the meantime we had to provide the flag company for Luftwaffe parades in Vienna. It was all extremely varied and, fortunately, our Kommandant, Hauptmann Brustelin, was happy with our general performance.

At the same time I started to meet with some success towards my goal of becoming aircrew, and spent a week at the Pilots' Medical Examination Establishment at Rossauer in Vienna. Together with a number of local soldiers I passed the necessary military tests without difficulty and was granted another period of leave to go home, which gave me the opportunity to spend another Christmas with my family. I also spent several pleasant days with old friends in the wintry conditions around Salzburg, where I did some climbing using my new ice-axe.

Christmas leave passed quickly and in January I was again on guard duty, this time as temporary guard commander. On 1 February 1939 my promotion to Gefreiter (lance corporal) came through, with seniority backdated to 1 December 1938. Things were starting to pick up now and a transfer for pilot training soon followed.

We were sent to the Stabs Kompanie of Jagdgruppe 76 at Vienna-Aspern. A long, difficult period had at last come to an end. We now had new teachers, including Lt Hans Philipp[7] as Gruppe Flying Instructor, five flying instructors and around thirty-six flying students. I was in a class with three colleagues, all with the rank of Gefreiter, named Gill, Steinbatz and Hammerl. Two were from Vienna, one from lower Austria and myself from Salzburg. Our flying instructor was an Unteroffizier (corporal).

After the first introductory flights, we went daily to the Deutsch-Wagram airfield near Aspern to practise our flying. It was good work and the teachers took great pains to school us properly. Unfortunately, the course was broken off in March due to the outbreak of the Czechoslovakian crisis.

Reservists were called up and we, the flying students, were detailed to be 'Gruppenkommandants' (ie section leaders). Our reservists were all older than us, but we became their Gruppe Leaders[8]. They had last carried arms in 1919 and were mostly Unterofftziere, but they had no experience of German operating procedures. Needless to say, this presented a not inconsiderable challenge for us young soldiers in our new command appointments.

Heavy goods vehicles were requisitioned and many still had the names of their companies on them. We had some from the Schwechater Brewery. They were driven by big fat brewery truck drivers who wore trouser belts made from two single ones joined together. But by and large everything went very well. The reservists made our work easy and soon a good spirit of comradeship prevailed.

After about ten days of preparation, we realised that things were serious when we were issued with live ammunition. Then, very early one Monday morning, it started. Our column moved away along Brunner Street in the direction of the Czech/Austrian border town of Nickolsburg. Only days previously many of the drivers had still been travelling around the streets of Vienna in taxis or cars, yet here we were, an invasion force that, in the space of just a few weeks, had been conjured up from virtually nothing.

The weather conditions were treacherous and the streets were overcrowded with army vehicles. In the surrounding hilly countryside of Nickolsburg, Znaim and in the general direction of Brünn, everywhere was covered in snow and the roads were desperately slippery. As a result, many vehicles left the road and ended up in the ditch[9].

In the evening we reached Brünn in Czechoslovakia, and drove in the direction of the airport. The area was still occupied by the Czechoslovakian Air Force, so our units had been sent in to seize the area and to capture their attack positions. It was a tense situation, with no one knowing what was going to happen next. Suddenly, a group of officers, with a spokesman carrying a white flag, appeared at the entrance gate. It was a moment of great tension, but the Czechoslovakian major was prepared to hand over the airport and the aircraft parked there. The task assigned to our unit had been completed.

Czechoslovakian aircraft on an unidentified landing field. Most are Letov S-328 light bombers or reconnaissance types, still in their Czech markings, except for the nearest machine, which is a licence-built Bloch MB200 bomber, the largest type in the Czech inventory at the time. It has already received a swastika on the fin.

The area was handed over without a struggle and our unit was despatched in the direction of Iglau, Deutsch-Brod. In Pryvislaw there was an airfield with a flying school that we look over, together with its installations, and set up our headquarters in the local hotel. Our advance had been completed. About twenty of us then set about guarding the installations and the aircraft on the airfield.

After fourteen days we were stood down and the flying students were detached and ordered back to Vienna-Aspern. For us young Gruppe Commanders, it had been a very interesting and educational period.

Luftwaffe Focke-Wulf FW 44 'Stieglitz' trainers in November 1939: the number, '3', is in an unusual position.

On our return there was equipment to repair and leave due to us. We resumed our schooling in April, with everybody happy that we were once again on our flying course. In the meantime the FW 'Stieglitz' had been taken away and replaced by the Klemm Kl 35. The Klemm was more responsive to fly, such that one had to be more sensitive on the controls. Personally I was very enthusiastic about the Klemm and our course progressed very positively. For us

Another all-silver Focke-Wulf FW 44, some time in August 1939, still wearing a civilian registration.

young people it was a great time with plenty of flying, and guard and parade duty in Vienna for the NCOs. Whenever we paraded in Vienna we were cheered by the local people. Our Kommandant was as pleased with us as we were with ourselves.

By the middle of July I was ready to go solo, the first in our flying group. It was the best day of my life – the dream of my youth, to fly, was being fulfilled. Within a week all of my colleagues had also made their first solo flights. Afterwards we held a huge party to celebrate.

We continued to train until, by the end of the course, we had done between forty and fifty solo flights each, including all the dangerous manoeuvres such as engine-off landings and cross-country flights. With the course ended, the flying Gruppe was divided into two and posted to two separate schools in northern Germany.

Our operational fighter Gruppe, Jagdgruppe 1/76, was transferred to Oppeln in Silesia and with the transfer we lost our flying instructor. The remainder, the flying students, followed after several days. One group, numbering fifteen men, including myself, went to the A/B School at Neustadt-Glewe (Sch/FAR 22). The other group went to a similar A/B School in Hageno-Land.

We travelled to our new airfield by train, via Passau, Nuremburg, Berlin and Ludwigslust. Neustadt-Glewe was a small town on the

Mecklenburg plain but it had an airfield with barrack room accommodation. On arrival we were enthusiastically greeted by the flying pupils already there. After reporting officially and receiving the Kommandant's address, we were assigned to flying 'Gruppen' (ie classes). Here the flying instructors were still civilians, something of a novelty for us. There were also large numbers of aircraft of a number of different types.

Gotha Go 145, WL-ILAQ, somewhere in the vicinity of Neustadt-Glewe in November 1939.

A Heinkel He 46 in service as a trainer with Fliegerausbildung Regiment (FAR) 22 at Neustadt-Glewe in August 1939. The aircraft appears to be finished in a well-worn RLM Grau scheme. The 'WL' registration indicates that it is a military trainer in the markings required in January 1939.

Another Heinkel He 46, WL-IGHN (possibly the same aircraft as in the previous photograph), taxies out for take off. The barely legible Werk Nummer on the fuselage appears to be 367. The man in the foreground wears the summer overland flying suit worn by almost all flying students in the Luftwaffe.

We Austrians were divided up among two flying classes that had already been formed. Ours was fresh from training school, whose members greeted us in a very friendly manner, giving us whatever help we needed. In any case there were no problems between the people from the different areas. In terms of actual flying, we Austrians were more advanced, but the Germans were a bit ahead of us on the theoretical side.

To our joy our training was now advancing swiftly. A part of the Gruppe was converting to the B1 licence and the other was receiving overland instruction. Some were beginning instruction in acrobatic flying. Our training was very intensive during this period since we Austrians had some catching up to do to be on a par with the other flying Gruppen. We would be ready in five months, a schedule that was to leave us somewhat exhausted.

In aerobatics, particularly in spins, my flying instructor had his work cut out. The machine would spin ever faster and I would forget the number of spins we had made. Thankfully the instructor had a great deal of patience and would repeatedly help me until I could do it for myself. After a while the penny dropped and it all went like clockwork.

In October we did a night flight for our B1 certificate with the Arado Ar 66. We went to Perleberg for this, as the airfield in Neustadt was not authorised for night-flying. During this 30-minute night flight my comrade, Gefreiter Franz Gill, from Vienna, crashed and was killed. He was the first of our flying group to be killed. His body was transferred to Vienna, and his flying instructor, Gefreiter Steinbatz, and I were allowed to go there for his funeral. After staying in Vienna for eight days, we took the train back to Neustadt-Glewe. The flying otherwise proceeded at a good pace and I, as well as my comrades, had few problems with the course.

The Gruppe Flying Instructor, Oberfeldwebel (staff sergeant) Möhring, took a liking to me and it soon became clear that, together with two other colleagues, I would remain at the school as an assistant flying instructor. Slowly my future in flying was becoming apparent. Also, those of us who were to remain as teachers at Neustadt-Glewe would be given preferential training; that is, we would be more intensively trained, flying more hours than the others, in preparation for our work as flying instructors.

The B2 training was a real joy for us as we were able to fly all over Germany. From time to time I took a Junkers W34 to Salzburg. My parents were more than a little astonished the first time I landed one of these at Salzburg airport. During the last few weeks we also flew to such places as Vienna, Klagenfurt and Prague. Our theoretical knowledge was also brought on in double-quick time. Everything was directed towards passing the forthcoming exam for the Military Pilots Licence, which I was ready for by the middle of December.

The winter of 1939/40 now started to show its teeth. The countryside quickly became covered by a great deal of snow and temperatures fell to bitterly cold levels. In our barracks it was uncomfortably cold and the allocation of heating material for the pot-bellied stove was minimal. As a result, for most of the time we simply froze. As luck would have it, we were nearly always on guard when a delivery of coals arrived at the barracks, and as far as it was possible to do so we would help ourselves to some to burn. Everybody knew about it, but none of our superiors said anything. Thus, we spent our first winter shivering in barracks, with everybody worried that we would be too late to get into operations. We all wanted to get to a front-line unit and we all wanted to do so as fighter pilots. Yet only myself and my two colleagues knew where we were going; our postings as Assistant Flying Instructors had just been made official.

With Christmas nearly upon us, the entire flying group was allowed leave to go home.[10] I was able to spend fourteen days with my parents in Salzburg, during which time I got my skis down from

Gefreiter Hermann Buchner presents arms as he is inspected by Feldwebel Wilke at Vienna-Aspern in 1939. Both wear Luftwaffe uniform, while Wilke wears a sword for some kind of ceremonial duty.

the attic and again headed for the mountains. My parents were especially pleased that I was able to go home again.

My older brothers were also in the military; Franz was stationed near Koblenz and Karl was serving with the coastguard in Engerau. My younger brother Walter, however, was still an apprentice at a firm in Salzburg. My father was very interested in my duties as a prospective flying instructor but, on the whole, he remained unconvinced about the wisdom of my having joined the military. I think he was probably afraid for his sons, although Franz had already taken part in the Polish Campaign as a Pioneer and I was now a trained pilot. My confidence remained unbroken, however; I wanted to be a fully trained fighter pilot and to be posted to a front line unit. Before that, I had to swallow the bitter pill of being a flying instructor. But I would not remain a flying instructor for ever!

After my holiday I said my goodbyes and took the train back to Neustadt-Glewe. Everybody had returned from their leave and we all swapped stories from our holidays. Rumours again abounded about postings. Enviously, we instructors-to-be listened to our comrades when they told us about their supposed new jobs. In the middle of January the flying group was finally divided up: the largest part would go to fighter pilots schools, some to 'C' Schools, to be posted to reconnaissance duties, and three had to remain as assistant instructors in Neustadt-Glewe. My friends Karl Hammerl and Leopold Steinbatz went to Jagdfliegerschule 3 at Zerbst.

In customary fashion we had a great celebration for the departure of our colleagues since we had been together for over a year both in Vienna and at the Pilots' School. We three assistant instructors continued with our instructors, ready for our first course, Fluggruppe 3/40, which was to begin on 1 March 1940. By the time they arrived, we were fully fledged instructors.

Fluggruppe 3/40 consisted mainly of former members of the army and officers who had been handed over by the army to the Luftwaffe. My students were Leutnants and Oberleutnants. They were somewhat older than myself, but that did not present a problem. We spent the whole day teaching and, to my surprise, things actually went well for me as a young flying instructor. At the end of March the students did their first solo flights, and I became extremely proud of my new occupation.

With effect from 1 April 1940 I was promoted to Unteroffizier (corporal) since not only were my students doing well, but the

Hermann Buchner awaits his next student in front of Gotha Go 145, WL-IOBA.
Belonging to Sch/FAR 22 at Neustadt-Glewe in March 1940, the aircraft appears
to be finished in overall RLM 63 and is illustrated in colour elsewhere in this
book. The author wears the summer overland flying suit.

Gruppenfluglehrer (chief instructor) was very happy with his newly
qualified flying instructors and with himself – we young teachers
were his discoveries, after all.

In May our school was assigned to Kommando Ostsee. At the
same time a teachers' exchange took place between the Sea Pilots
schools and the Land Pilots schools. Flying instructors from the
land schools had to be given up, with postings mainly restricted
to single men. So myself and three other comrades went to
Flugzeugführerschule See 2/Pütnitz in Pomerania. With little
enthusiasm, I said goodbye to my fellow instructors and departed
for what was to be an equally happy time. The other instructors
were all very helpful, but the married instructors had their homes
and their families in Neustadt and therefore it was mainly they
who remained behind.

Chapter Four

With the Coastal Command pilots
May 1940-November 1940

We were flown to Pütnitz, a large, newly built coastal airfield in Pomerania, in a Junkers W34. The barracks were set in a square-shaped clearing in the middle of a lovely pine forest, with water on two sides, trees on another, and the remainder fields. After checking into our accommodation, we reported to the Course Leader and were then divided up. We newly arrived land pilots were looked over, questioned and finally pitied since we had only the B2 Certificate with an Instructor's Classification. The sea pilot instructors were all older and had C2, blind flying, Sea 2 and ship training; many had already done world trips on the *Deutschland*[11]. But we were just young instructors with much to learn so it was probably just as well that the exchange was taking place. After being questioned, the Course Leader, Oberleutnant Gässler, decided that we new instructors should immediately begin the C2 training. This would be in addition to our regular duties as B2 Land Instructors and we were actually quite pleased that our level of training was going to be extended. So, in the mornings, we were instructors, and in the afternoons we were students on the Ju 52/3m, later moving across to the diesel-engined Junkers Ju 86.

The Sea and Land School was very large, with eighteen flying classes in training at any one time. This was once again the start of a new period for me with the Baltic Sea, the 'C' grade training, the lovely summer and, in our free time, instruction in sailing and cutter rowing on the Bodden See[12]. In addition, we instructors had single-room accommodation, such were the standards to which the coastal pilots were accustomed.

My flying Gruppe spent the first four weeks working near Triebsees, accommodated on an estate. Meals were the responsibility of the flying Gruppe and we had been provided with one cook. At that time the first fields had just been harvested and the girls were still working in them. We had four FW 44 'Stieglitz' training aircraft with which to train and, from the air, while doing circuits of the airfield, one could make out the field girls with their blue dresses and red headscarves. We got to know these girls when we were doing emergency landing practice, and some became good friends. Their accommodation was in Triebsees, which was only a few kilometres from our estate, so from time to time we would go to visit them, along with our student pilots, after evening colours. The girls were happy about this, but their leaders were less so. After a while our Group Leader issued a reprimand and we were told not to visit them any more. I don't think he really had anything against these visits – after all, he had surely been young once himself.

When our time at the lovely estate of Bassendorf came to an end, the 'Fluggruppe' was transferred back to Pütnitz. By this time all of our students had gone solo and had made several flights alone. In most cases the friendships that we had cultivated with the young field working girls came to an end.

The next Fluggruppe transferred to Bassendorf and we began training in formation flying and aerobatics. At the same time I continued with my 'C' training. I had already done the solo flight around the airfield with the Junkers Ju 52/3m and Ju 86 and now I had to do the mandatory cross-country flights. My Gruppe flying instructor, Oberfeldwebel Eckstein, was favourably disposed towards me and we had become good friends. I seemed to fit into the whole environment very well and, on the whole, had a really good time.

One of the phases of my training that I particularly enjoyed was aerobatic training. I simply loved throwing the aircraft about the sky with gay abandon. The other instructor, Eckstein, was older than me and had probably taught far more aerobatics than I had. One day he asked me if I would take over his aerobatics students and he would train my students in formation flying. I naturally eagerly agreed, and for the next six weeks I taught nothing but aerobatics. At the same time I made my examination flight right across Germany in the Ju 86.

Shortly afterwards I again returned to Salzburg for a weekend, this time in a Heinkel He 70 'Blitz' bomber. My parents were absolutely amazed that I, a mere Unteroffizier, had actually arrived with an aircraft and my own crew in Salzburg for nothing more than a weekend's holiday. My friends, who had not yet joined up, were equally agog. On the Sunday afternoon they all turned up at the airport to say goodbye to me. The 1,200km return trip to Pütnitz took three hours and took us via Nuremberg, Brocken, Stendal and Perleber, a scenic route that got us back to the Baltic coast shortly before sunset.

Of course, as a member of Coastal Command I also had to do sailor training and get a Sailing Certificate on dinghies. On our free Sundays and holidays we would sail to Gral-Müritz for coffee and dancing. We arrived with our dinghies, dressed up to the nines as if we

Aircrew undergoing training in the cabin of a tri-motored Junkers Ju 52/3m, one of the stalwarts of the Luftwaffe advanced training system. Beyond the men, who are wearing the special winter flying overalls (the so-called 'Bulgarian' suits), is the pilots' cabin with the three throttle levers clearly visible on the central console.

were lords. The girls were all very impressed and quickly turned to us, much to the disquiet of the locals. We instructors had a great time!

Yet, despite all the advantages of a Coastal Command instructor's appointment, I still really wanted to get to a unit at the front. Unfortunately, the Course Leader explained to us again and again that each had his duty to do, wherever he was assigned. The school needed teachers and therefore I had to remain at the school. Nevertheless, while my students were on their 'B2' training with we instructors just doing the cross-country instruction, I took the opportunity to visit the 'C' as well as the Fighter Pilots' schools, in order to meet my former colleagues from the A/B school and swap experiences. As a result of this my resolve was absolutely firm – I would get to an operational unit one way or another.

So I proceeded to make my approaches but my official interviews were unsuccessful and I was again rejected. I was given the same old line once again: each had his duty to do in the place in which he was posted. I therefore now tried other ways. One of my friends was a Feldwebel and Staff assistant with the Course Administration Wing. One day he told me that the higher-ups in the 'Schools Command' were looking at the school for a flying instructor with good aerobatics experience. Suddenly a way out had presented itself to me, and I begged my friend to put me on the list. I added that, should he not be able to do so, he should let me apply independently. Thankfully he complied with my request and I sat back and waited to see what result, if any, it would bring.

In November 1940, just fourteen days after my application had been submitted, a posting order arrived instructing me to report to Jagdfliegervorschule 1 (Pre-Fighter Pilot School No 1) at Kamenz, in Saxony, as a flying instructor. My Course Leader was surprised about the posting but I was overjoyed that my goal, to be in a front-line unit, had finally moved one step closer.

I once again celebrated my goodbyes to colleagues of whom I had grown fond in the customary fashion, but I was nevertheless happy since I was getting what I wanted at last. My friends Zitt, Hammerl and Steinbatz were already with front-line units and already had front-line patrols and enemy encounters behind them. Somewhat nostalgically I therefore left FFS See/2, having learned a great deal and having also imparted a good deal of that knowledge to my young pupils. In any case, I left a good flying Gruppe behind for my successor to continue where I had left off.

Chapter Five

Jagdfliegervorschule 1
November 1940-October 1941

I travelled to Kamenz, Saxony, by train, the pilots' true companion. The journey took me via Strahlsund, Dresden and Berlin. When I arrived at the airfield it was still under construction, with a huge area cleared and makeshift hangars erected around the edges. For the troops there was the usual barrack accommodation – the same as that in Neustadt-Glewe. We instructors were now four to a room – no longer the luxury of a room each, as we had enjoyed during our gliding days! The school itself had been newly set up in November, and all the personnel responsible for running it had arrived within fourteen days of its completion. The new Course Leader was a Hauptmann with recent operational experience from the Western Campaign, during which he had received a spinal injury that rendered him unfit for combat operations. As Senior Flying Instructor, he had a team of fifteen officers and NCOs at his disposal.

After the official take-over by the staff, and getting to meet the leaders in each of the flying specialties, we were made aware of the problems facing us. In particular, we were told by the Commanding Officer that the school was to be fully operational by the New Year, which left us with little time to get everything ready. We therefore set about our task quickly and eagerly, beginning by taking over the aircraft assigned to us and flying them over from where they were parked or from their repair hangars. We worked very long hours to get our Bückers, Arado Ar 96, Focke-Wulf FW 56 and North American NA 57[13] aircraft ready for use, and thankfully we made it in time for the Christmas holidays. But the month had not passed without incident.

In mid-December I was completing a training flight in an Arado 96 when, just before I was due to land, I suffered a loss of fuel supply and was forced to make an emergency landing in a field. The fuel starvation had been caused by a failure of the fuel tank transfer system and the subsequent crash left the machine thirty percent damaged. This emergency landing earned me my first, and last, board of enquiry. I was subsequently court-martialled at the Dresden Air Administration Court, where I was found not guilty. This experience left a deep impression on me and left its mark on my flying experience. In future I would adopt a more mature approach to my flying in order to reduce the possibility of such a thing happening again.

I proceeded on leave for Christmas, once again visiting my parents in Salzburg and spending time skiing with old friends in the mountains. I also made some new friends during this break and, when we discussed our circumstances, we found that we all had basically the same problem: we wanted to go to the front. We did not want to remain flying instructors, or the like, at home.

We began our first course, as scheduled, on 1 January 1941. The course aims were clearly defined: formation flying, schooling on various types of aircraft, aerial warfare manoeuvres, and tactics. The tasks were very interesting and also very enjoyable for the instructors. We had three months in which to prepare our students for a Zerstörer (Messerschmitt Me 110) or fighter pilots' school.

My first flying Gruppe was a course solely for sergeants. Although most would pass the course, there were always some students who should not have been there; they could fly all right but not all of them were suitable as fighter pilots. However, during my time there I would get to know such men as Theo Weissenberger[14], Armin Köhler[15], Albert Brunner[16] and Söffing, all of whom would later become well-known highly decorated fighter pilots.

By the third month of the course we were practising group aerobatics, formation flying, and aerial gunnery. The students developed well under this instruction, but the instructors benefited too, with their own skills improving with every practice. The students were being prepared solely for their forthcoming fighter pilots' training. The course was very demanding but it forced them to overcome their own reservations. Those pilots who could not do so were dropped from the course and went on to the 'C' grade flying training, for less demanding duties.

During my time at Kamenz I made some good friends among the instructors and made friends with a number of students with whom I would later meet up again on the Eastern Front. This included names like Unteroffizier Rossmann, Feldwebel Söchting and Ohm Krüger. In addition the inhabitants of Kamenz were very fond of the soldiers and we got to know plenty of pretty girls from Saxony, where the girls have such lovely long legs!

In May 1941 I was promoted to Feldwebel (sergeant). In order to celebrate my promotion a party was organised, with even the flying students appearing with gifts. But despite the tremendous spirit and comradeship at the school, I still wanted to be with an operational unit at the front. We all felt that we were somehow wasting our time at a school in Germany. The Course Leader was aware that we felt this way and explained that, at the end of the course, four flying instructors would be posted to the fighter pilots' school. We were delighted at this news and threw ourselves back into the job with renewed enthusiasm, with my Gruppe now conducting aerial shooting practice on the military training area at Hoyerswerda near Kamenz.

At about that time a Lufthansa Junkers Ju 90[17], crashed near Kamenz due to icing. The machine was en route to Vienna from Berlin with German radio employees on board. We witnessed its fall as it plunged from the clouds, pulled up once, then fell vertically to the ground and broke apart. The pieces of wreckage still had 3-6cm of ice on them a full 30 minutes after the crash. For those of us who were curious, it was not a very comforting sight.

Easter 1941 was nearly upon us and Heinz Rossmann and I wanted to take an Arado 96 to Salzburg for our holidays. The Course Leader was very generous and authorised the flight for the holiday period. Everything was organised, we had the leave papers in our pockets, we had arranged to stay with my parents in Salzburg, and my friends had already drawn up a programme of things to do. We took off on Easter Saturday and headed south. After a while the weather began to deteriorate and things started to get difficult near the Erz mountains. The weather was now quite bad with the clouds hanging over the mountain tops right down to the valley floor and we were forced to pick our route wherever it was reasonably clear. After about 90 minutes flying we became aware that the weather conditions were going to prevent us from reaching our destination of Salzburg, especially in an Arado 96. Under the circumstances the best we could do was to turn around and go home. Having decided to do this, we turned around and, after a total flying time of around 2 hours, we reached the airfield we had departed from at Kamenz. Our Easter holiday in Salzburg had gone down the drain. We hadn't pushed it since we had not wanted to abuse the generosity of the Course Leader. In terms of flying experience, however, we had again learned something worthwhile that would stand us in good stead for the future. We changed our plans for Easter and spent the holiday in Dresden, taking in the culture. Neither of us knew the city very well and we spent a few happy days there, getting to know our way around.

Our Course Leader kept his promise and, on 1 June, the flying Gruppe and four flying instructors, one of them being myself, were transferred to Jagdfliegerschule 1 (Fighter Pilots'

School 1) at Berlin-Werneuchen. Again, as so often before, we had a leaving party to celebrate, then packed and took the train to Berlin for our new assignment.

Now I had reached my goal. I was at a fighter pilots' school and there could surely be no more hindrance. In a few months I should definitely be assigned to a squadron at the front!

During the assignment process, I learned that I was to join No 1 Staffel at the school. After being allocated accommodation and carrying out the usual administrational formalities, the training began quickly. We were thirty students in all and had Arado Ar 68 and Messerschmitt Me 109Bs on which to learn. In addition to theoretical training, which included aircraft recognition, we carried out formation flying, aerial fighting tactics and shooting. Survival training and sport were also given a place of importance in the programme. Our flying instructors were largely pilots who had come from the Channel to the school for regeneration. The Kommandeur of the school was General Theo Osterkamp, a holder of the Pour le Mérite[18]. Now we could confirm how important our training of the young pilots at the JFVS had been. In effect we had carried out all of the minor preparatory work so that the fighter pilot instructors could concentrate on the essentials. After a short conversion course, we went on to the Me 109 (more correctly the Bf 109).

Messerschmitt Bf 109Ds in service with JFVS 1 in Werneuchen early in the war. All carry the 'S2+M' code of the school, followed by the number of the individual aircraft. The fourth machine back may be '23', an aircraft flown by the author several times in July 1941. It is also possible that '23' may have instead carried the number on a fuselage band – no conclusive proof exists either way.

Oberstleutnant Theo Osterkamp in characteristic pose in front of Arado Ar 68E-1
'21' of JFVS 1 at Werneuchen. The markings are apparently undergoing change
as the earlier 'S2' school code can be seen under the yellow (?) band on the
fuselage. Clearly the last number on the previous code does not end in '1'.
Likewise the camouflaged aircraft behind, 'S2+J51', carries a new number '29'.
How the system for allocating the new numbers operated is not known.

Groundcrew manhandle an Arado Ar 68 into position. Believed to be at JFVS 1 at
Werneuchen, this machine wears a white fuselage band and the remnants of an
earlier four-letter code. Other aircraft in the background all wear the number on a
band so typical of machines used by the school at Werneuchen. Most of the
Arado Ar 68Es found their way to the advanced training schools, their design
having been made obsolete by the newer Messerschmitt 109. Note the number
repeated on a panel on the upper wing centre section.

A busy scene at Werneuchen as Focke-Wulf FW 56s are prepared for the day's
work. The time is probably early in 1940 as the quasi-civil 'WL-' registrations
officially used from January to October 1939 have been superseded by a fuselage
band and a number. From the evidence of this picture it appears that the Arado
68s, the tail of one being seen in the foreground, used a yellow band with white
numbers, while the FW 56s wore a white band with a black number.

As Bf 109E production got into its stride the earlier models were sent to the
fighter schools. These Bf 109Ds are with JFVS 1 at Werneuchen, probably in
late 1939/early 1940 as the aircraft all wear the 'S2+M' code of the time. Note
the oversize crosses under the wing on the nearest aircraft. The Bf 109s later
used by the school probably carried a fuselage band with a number, as on other
types at the school.

In handling the Me 109, some people had difficulty with take
offs, and others ground-looped it when landing. A pilot who was
reasonably careful, however, had no real difficulties with the 109.
We flew two or three training flights per day, and they were really
difficult and demanding. Excuses for our own inadequacies were not

Another Bf 109 line-up, this time of E-4 or E-7 versions (noted the capped spinners) in service with 5.(S)/LG 2, whose 'bear' emblem can be seen on the second aircraft in line. All are finished in the camouflage scheme first introduced during the Battle of Britain, with red (the Staffel colour) tips to the spinners.

readily accepted and show-offs soon found themselves back on the ground. The instructors did not know the meaning of leniency: they had been tasked with making the students into efficient pilots, capable of flying at the front.

In addition to our flying training, we also learned how to play the three-handed card game skat, and chess. There were some squadrons that would not accept you if you couldn't play cards! Also, sports such as boxing and clay-pigeon shooting were useful to know. It was a real pleasure to step into the ring with one's tutors to measure their strength. There were no excuses – it was you against him, each having to stand up to the other man.

Naturally, the difficult training also claimed its victims. Some crashed their Me 109s and others were removed from training. We were sorry for them, but not everybody could become a fighter pilot and at the front certain criteria were absolutely demanded. For those who made it through, it was a good time.

Also, our private life was not too badly curtailed, for we would head to Berlin at the weekend. In time we were also allowed to frequent the local pubs. I got to know a girl from Berlin, a nice young thing who looked after me but wanted to turn me into a man of culture. As soon as I had free time, she wanted to take me to the Berlin theatre. This, however, was too much for me and I tried to get out of going as much as possible. Other than this, she was a really nice girl. There were also a lot of nice regulars at the 'Fatherland' pub. In any event, we flyers were always well looked after in Berlin.

Our course was progressing and we were soon doing 'Schwarm'[19] formation flying. Our Gruppe was designated to carry out bomber escort duties for a bomber pilots' school on the Baltic. Sometimes we acted as 'targets' for a Croatian bomber school flying from there. In our free time there we went to the beach at Gral-Müritz and got to know many more girls. As pilots we were always in great demand with the local girls. We had a wonderful time and were able to have anything we wanted. This enjoyable four-week period eventually came to an end, however, and we returned to the school at Werneuchen, to once again be taken under the wing of the military, with its associated discipline. But all this no longer had much effect on us, as the course was nearly at an end. Preparations for the going-away party were running at full speed and I was tasked with making up a comic newspaper.

In June 1941 the war with the USSR began and our remaining time at Werneuchen became very turbulent. A number of Spanish pilots of the Blue Division[20] arrived for training. They were great pilots but they were totally undisciplined and flew like wild men through the area. Hans Wilmerdinger, a flying instructor, was rammed in the air by one of these men and had to take to his parachute. Meanwhile we were fully occupied with aerial shooting practice, bomb dropping and the preparations for our going-away party.

Our course came to an end and we were now fully fledged fighter pilots. The rumour machine now worked overtime about our postings. Each day we were going to go to a different Geschwader (wing). In preparation for my new, very serious role, I was now in the process of selling off all my personal effects that I had acquired in my time as an instructor, which would be of no use in a front-line unit. I had a really lovely red bicycle, a Triumpf, nearly new, and I sold it for the princely sum of 50 Reichsmarks to my Gruppe Flying Instructor, Feldwebel Scholz. He was a relaxed instructor and kept his Gruppe well in hand, and we had got on very well together. Scarcely fourteen days before our postings, Oberleutnant Franz von Werra[21] arrived at our squadron as a flying instructor. Von Werra had been shot down over the Channel in 1940, captured by the British and sent to Canada as a prisoner of war. He had subsequently escaped imprisonment in Canada and had returned to Germany via the USA, South America and Spain. He was a perfect example to us prospective fighter pilots and would give lectures to the squadrons about his impressions in English and Canadian captivity. It was all very interesting and, in any case, we wanted to follow in his footsteps and prepare ourselves for all possible eventualities. We continued to frequent Berlin in our free time and regularly visited our 'Fatherland' pub in Friedrich Strasse, where we were regulars.

Now it was time for us to find out our postings. My entire class, J9, was to be transferred to 1 Staffel of II Gruppe Lehrgeschwader 2 (Schlacht) at Lippstadt, Westphalia. At the time this was another training unit, which we were a bit disappointed about as we had really wanted to go to a fighting unit. But we were nevertheless on our way to the front so we couldn't really complain. Going with me were a number of comrades who had been trained in the same Gruppe as myself in Kamenz: Ernst Kruger, Helmut Katzerowsky, Jürgen Schultze and a corporal from Vienna. I was soon to discover how effective my training had been.

Chapter Six

My new home: LG 2 (Schlacht)
October 1941-March 1942

When I arrived the Staffel was in the process of being newly set up. The Staffelkapitän was a Viennese Leutnant named Etzl. He was a small but very ambitious man whom I did not find to be a very pleasant type at all. Some of the officers from the operational section of II./LG 2 (Schlacht), who had so far been fighting at the front and had up to then been stationed near Dogino (USSR), functioned as instructors. Their Gruppe had been operational from the beginning of the Russian Campaign and had already been considerably reduced in numbers. There were between fifteen and twenty aircraft still at the front, but many of the now surplus mechanics had been sent back to Germany as the unit was going to be re-equipped.

The instructors taught us schlachtflieger (ground-attack) tactics since our main occupation was now the business of dropping bombs, flying our attacks from low level, and staying as far out of the way of enemy fighters as possible. We could still fly Schwarme and the circus formation[22], but the ground attack role had its own characteristics and we had to recognise the differences and apply the right tactics for our role. We had no problems at all with this new role, as we were the first replacements who had come to Lippstadt as fully trained fighter pilots. It would have been better had we been posted to a fighter wing, as we felt that we were actually too good for this posting. We nevertheless carried out our tasks slickly: a combination of general flying practice, small formation flying, shooting, dropping bombs, limited navigation and more circus. Rumour had it that our training Gruppe was to form the basis of a new Geschwader.

Our training in Lippstadt enabled us to become familiar with the Me 109E, Henschel Hs 123 and the new Henschel Hs 129, with its much improved radial Gnôme-Rhône engines. This made it more powerful and, in our opinion, good to fly. It had an armour-plated fuselage, which the old hands from the front were enthusiastic about, and was well armed, with four 20mm cannons and additional bomb-carrying capacity. I also had the opportunity to carry out a test flight in a Ju 52/3m.

I was now no longer working towards my 'C' grade qualification on account of my rushed posting from Pütnitz to Kamenz, but, according to my flying log, I had fulfilled all the flying conditions necessary for active service. In any event, those of us with the

Loaded with four 50kg bombs, a Henschel Hs 123A-1 of II.(S)/LG 2 is somewhere over Russia in 1941. Like many ground-attack aircraft, it carries the infantry assault badge, a reflection of the close links between the Luftwaffe Schlachtflieger and their army comrades. One of the most fearsome weapons used by the Hs 123 was the appalling noise of its engine, which often panicked men and horses.

A retouched picture of Henschel Hs 129A-0 GM+OG. White numbers on the cowlings relate to the Werk Nummer, 3010. The first fourteen aircraft were all finished in similar fashion, including the 'pike's head' nose marking. The author flew the very similar No 13 while undergoing training at Lippstadt. Problems with the Argus in-line engines seen here led to their replacement by the French-built Gnôme-Rhône radials.

A Henschel Hs 123A of 8./SchG 1 on an airfield somewhere in Russia. When the author joined the same Staffel early in 1942 the Henschel was already in the process of being replaced by the Bf 109E. Many, however, soldiered on for long afterwards as their ability to absorb battle damage and fly in conditions that grounded more sophisticated aircraft meant that eventually they were worn out in service and gradually just faded away. The aircraft appears to have a yellow rudder as well as the Eastern Front fuselage band.

Lippstadt Staffel were already stuffed full of tactics and had a large number of flying hours to our credit. Nevertheless, every day we still had our flying and other duties, just to keep us busy. In terms of actual flying, my training had been significantly better than that experienced by the other flying students, which made me particularly well trained.

Christmas 1941 was just around the corner and there was to be a Christmas party. As the oldest Unteroffizier (NCO) of the Fluggruppe I was tasked by the Staffelkapitän with organising the festivities. Most probably word had got around that I had organised such a party in Werneuchen, but now at least I had a task that could get me off the official duties. I therefore began by looking for colleagues who would be prepared to help me with the organisation. Volunteers were not hard to find and we soon had a programme put together regarding how we were going to play it. We thought that, while Christmas is a contemplative time for friends, the troops who were, after all, away from home should have a bit of fun as well. Our Kapitän wanted to be kept informed about how we were getting on, which was a bit tricky since we also wanted to surprise him. In any event, my co-workers threw themselves heart and soul into the plan and we made excellent progress. With ten days to go before the event, we had got our programme into pretty good shape and felt that we could now inform our Kapitän of our progress; we did, however, withhold just a small part of the programme – that would be the surprise. Leutnant Etzl was happy with our plans and gave us his blessing.

Despite all the fun over the Christmas festivities, time was still dragging since we really wanted to be at the front and, consequently, we felt that we were again wasting our time. We had also not had a holiday for a long time, which was a far cry from the good old days when I was a flying instructor and could fly home for my holidays. But I wanted to get to a Staffel at the front and was therefore prepared to accept such inconvenience. I had often spoken with my friends about this – whether or not it had been sensible to give up my nice position as a flying instructor – just to be waiting around here now, doing everything but what I wanted. I often thought back nostalgically to my time at Pütnitz, flying, sailing and flying back to Salzburg on Sundays.

Preparations for the Christmas party were now finished. The troops' dining room had been appropriately decorated, a stage had been temporarily erected, and the people who had volunteered to do the serving were ready to start. It was very festive to look at. All the soldiers were in their best uniforms and the chef and his entourage of officers, NCOs and other ranks had distinguished themselves, laying the tables with white tablecloths and lighting the candles on the tables. We had also laid on a small band, provided by some of our soldiers, someone to introduce the acts, and our highlight of the evening, a 'Number Girl', who was actually a soldier dressed as a woman, who would precede each act by walking across the stage displaying the number appropriate to that act. With all preparations complete, we were given the green light by our Kapitän.

The party began with the music 'Änchen von Tarrau', sung by the band. Later on Leutnant Etzl gave a stirring speech in which he reminded us of our comrades on the Eastern Front. The administration had also provided a number of small presents, so there was a surprise for every member of the Staffel. The soldiers took the party very seriously, so that when the Christmas tree was lit up against its backdrop, they all joined together and sang 'Silent Night, Holy Night', which completed the festive atmosphere. We then had tea and punch to drink as we opened and admired our gifts. The festive atmosphere was completed by the sight of happy, smiling faces everywhere. This more formal part lasted for about 40 minutes, then came the funny part.

Our Master of Ceremonies, a Gefreiter from the orderly room, opened with some witty words, thanked Father Christmas, the Staffelkapitän, the flying instructors, the technical personnel and the permanent staff for the gifts, for their outstanding care, for the standard of training and for the high serviceability rate of the aircraft. Our pride and joy, the 'Number Girl', then paraded across the stage displaying a large number '1'. Those who didn't already know who our 'Number Girl' really was were somewhat surprised by this, not knowing that she was really one of the pilots, Unteroffizier Fürst from the Lower Danube. He was well dressed up and did his act brilliantly. For quite a while the young soldiers really believed that it was a real girl, only they couldn't figure out where we had found one. The numbers introduced the acts, which were a snake-charmer, a one-act play, a magician and plenty more; we had everything, even a ballet. Also included were gymnastic exercises, which were carried out for a good hour, and our Kapitän, who took part in this, wanted to be absolutely brilliant. As a result, he broke his left forearm doing a somersault. This was unfortunate and we felt rather sorry for him, even though he had overdone it and it was therefore really his own fault.

So, our Christmas Party 1941 came to an end. It had gone down a treat, in spite of our Kapitän's mishap, and had proved to be a worthwhile as well as fun. Long afterwards our soldiers would talk about the party and the 'Number Girl' – that had been our crowning glory. At the end, we removed 'her' disguise to reveal her true identity, much to the astonishment of everyone there. As far as our Staffelkapitän was concerned, we had surpassed ourselves.

We did not get any leave, continuing with our flying duties, shooting and normal duties. But we seemed to spend most of our time loafing about as we had already completed all of our exercises and tests, which meant that the staff no longer knew what to do with us. Our Kapitän did not dare send us home on leave, but we had a lot of freedom and could do what we wanted as long as we informed our superiors. Ohm and I celebrated the New Year in town with the locals. We did not have a party, although there was one for the recruits in the barracks.

By January our future had been decided. The pilots would be posted to Schlachtgeschwader 1 in Werl, Westphalia.

Chapter Seven

Schlachtgeschwader 1
March 1942-April 1942

The long, hard road to a front-line unit had come to an end – it was now a reality. When we eventually arrived at Werl we found ourselves to be nearly the first there. Having reported our arrival, we were each allocated to a Staffel, with Ohm, Helmut Katzerowsky and myself going to 8. Staffel. Our new Kapitän was to be an Oberleutnant Dills.

Most of us joining the Staffel had had no previous combat experience, although there were some among us who had already served at the front. In particular, Oberfahnrich Beutelspacher, Leutnant Stollnberger and Otto Dommeratzky were old hands. One of us was going to have to fill the appointment of Staffel Senior Sergeant until a more suitable candidate arrived, and without delay Oberleutnant Dills decided that I was the right man for the job and promptly informed me that I was it until further notice. I had no previous experience of this sort of role but, looking back now, I feel that I didn't do the job too badly at all.

The initial period for us pilots was all very pleasant. We listened to and learned from the old pilots who told us of their experiences and the lessons they had learned in such skills as aerial gunnery and bomb dropping, as well as the various characteristics of the aircraft. One of our main tasks at that time was the ferrying of aircraft to build up our Geschwader strength. This started when six men from our Staffel were ordered to go to Vienna-Atzgersdorf to take over six Me 109Es. Once collected, they were to fly them back to Werl via Vienna, Wels and Würzburg. Such trips, particularly through scenic and interesting routes, or to somewhere interesting to stay overnight, soon became very popular and there was never a shortage of willing volunteers. Therefore when machines were subsequently assigned to us from the repair units at Erla-Antwerp we were all eager to make the trip. I made several.

Antwerp is a beautiful city, with lots of attractive old architecture and such interesting attractions as the Rubens memorial. At the airport there was also a good canteen that we were to frequent on our numerous visits and the staff became very fond of us. We always stayed at the Antwerp Tourist Hotel, near the railway station, a comfortable place where the pilots were always well taken care of. Leutnant Lange, Otto Dommeratzky, Ohm and I spent several good

Leutnant Lehmann and Oberfeldwebel Kruger of 8./SchG 1 enjoy a visit to
Antwerp in March 1942. The pilot's badge worn by both is clearly visible.

days together in Antwerp, always on the go and partying at every
opportunity. We would then fly back to Werl as a group, with our
return route taking us over Holland, the Rhine and the Ruhr.

In Unna, not far from Werl, Ohm and I soon got to know two
rather nice Flemish girls, who had just visited a driving school.
They told us that, among other things, they would unfortunately
have to return home to Antwerp in the next few days. Since we
were about to head in that general direction in the next few days
ourselves, on one of our ferry trips, this gave us an idea that would
make our trip more interesting. We therefore told them that we
would also be travelling to Belgium and that on our way to
Antwerp we would change trains in order to be able to meet them
in Brussels. They laughed, but didn't believe us. We nevertheless
persisted, explaining that it was quite easy for us to do this, as long
as they wanted us to. A few days later we were again on our way to
Antwerp. Looking at our timetable we had time to get to Brussels
before going on to our destination. With a fast train, it would add
barely 50 minutes to our journey.

The two Flemish girls mentioned in the text and seen here were members of the VAvV, the Volunteer Labour Service for Flanders, a Belgian counterpart of the German RAD. Their brown uniforms have the ear of barley and bell heather badge of the organisation on their breast pockets. Antwerp was the location of the HQ and housed the female leadership training school.

On the day they were due in Brussels, we changed trains, as we had planned, and arrived punctually, with time to find a florist, buy some flowers and still be back at the railway station in time for the arrival of their train. This done, we waited in anticipation to see if they were on the train or if they had just been pulling our legs. So we stood on the station platform among crowds of people who had assembled to meet the incoming train, straining to catch a first glimpse of it and to see if our girls were on board. But lie they hadn't; after the first of the arrivals, the lights came on and we soon recognised some of the Flemish girls in their uniforms, as they were being greeted by officers and relatives. Our friends were also there and we waited in the queue to greet them. The girls recognised us straight away, appearing to be very surprised that we had kept our word and had appeared for their arrival. They seemed to be very pleased about our welcome and were delighted with the flowers we gave them.

Since they had no relatives in Brussels, we took the fast train to Antwerp and spent another lovely afternoon with them in their home town. But unfortunately the day went all too quickly and the following day we had to return with our aircraft to Werl. So we said our goodbyes after a memorable day and went our separate ways, vowing to keep in touch. We never saw those two girls again, and although Ohm and I corresponded with them for some time afterwards, our afternoon diversion had been thoroughly worthwhile.

The good times of picking up and ferrying aircraft soon came to an end. By now the Geschwader had enough personnel and materiel, which meant that I would soon be able to hand over my duties as Staffel Senior Sergeant, or 'Spiess', as the appointment was more commonly known. My successor was to be an old soldier with twelve years service under his belt, and whose flying career was almost at an end.

We now had the whole Geschwader in one place – 120 Me 109Es and all the vehicles and personnel. The place was a hive of activity, with us spending a lot of time in the air and also plenty of classroom instruction. We studied tactics, conduct in captivity, aircraft knowledge and recognition, and combat flying. In good weather the whole Staffel would take to the air to practise bombing manoeuvres and general airborne tactics. During one such practice bombing trip to the Sauerland, in an area to the south of Werl, an Unteroffizier of the 6. Staffel crashed and was killed. He was regrettably the first fatality from the Geschwader – but preparations to go operational carried on regardless. As our anticipated deployment date drew near, rumours about our likely posting abounded as usual. Then, at the beginning of April, we were told it was to be Russia.

Somewhere in Russia in 1941 a groundcrewman guides a Messerschmitt Bf 109E-7/B of II.(S)/LG 2 out to its take off point; it is loaded with four AB23 anti-personnel bomb containers on the fuselage rack. The 'Mickey Mouse' Gruppe emblem is clearly visible, while the yellow spinner tip suggests that it is from 6. Staffel, which in December 1941 became 3/SchG 1.

The famous cigar-smoking 'Mickey Mouse' emblem of both II./SchG 1 and II./SG 2.

As we waited for our transfer to become reality, we pilots again had parties whenever we could. We could usually be found in Hamm or Hagen, where we would part with our last penny without hesitation. Then, finally, with all our money spent, we were given our pilot allocations. I was to be the 'Katzmarek' (wingman) to our Staffelkapitän, Oberleutnant Dills. Beutelspacher and Dommeratzky would be Schwarmführer (swarm leaders) and Leutnants Stollnberger and Rohnstock were to be Rottenführer (leading pairs). Our Staffel was finally complete. For my last task as Spiess, after a good deal of searching I found another batman for the pilots. He was an old reservist by the name of Obergefreiter Held, an armourer who originated from Karlsruhe in the Rheinland. He was happy to take on the job and promised me that he would be a good, true and assiduous batman for 8. Staffel. The boss and the pilots were extremely happy about this, for we now had a man who would take care of our personal matters and our provisions. The pilots already held him in high regard; he could now show them whether their praise had been justified.

A classic in-flight shot of an Henschel Hs 123A, probably of 8./SchG 1 early in 1942 as it still retains the wheel spats. 'Blue 8' wears both the Schlachtflieger black triangle and the infantry assault badge.

Chapter Eight

Russia: my dream is fulfilled
May 1942-Autumn 1943

On 25 March 1942 we began loading the ground elements of the Geschwader onto railway goods vehicles. By the following day the fully loaded rail wagons were ready to begin the move eastwards, into Russia. The remaining aircrew were then briefed on our flight plan, all the details of which had been planned days earlier. We were to fly from Werl to Gramatiko, on the Crimea. Our route would include a number of overnight stopovers taking us via Leipzig, Dresden, Breslau, Krakow, Lemberg (Lvov), Zhitomir, Uman, and finally Nikolayev.

We left Werl on the morning of 26 April and, after an intermediate stop in Leipzig, landed at Breslau/Gandau in the afternoon. This proved to be the end of our first leg since bad weather to the east of Breslau prevented us from continuing our journey on that day. We therefore had little choice but to secure our aircraft ready for an overnight stay. Once we had obtained some suitable accommodation, we naturally drove immediately into town to blow our money on what we hoped to be a good night out. At the end of the evening, we returned to Gandau by taxi.

The following day we took off in poor weather for Lemberg, but as we headed further eastwards the weather continued to deteriorate, forcing us to land at Krakow. Further progress to Lemberg was not possible at that point in time. In such conditions of poor visibility it would have been madness to attempt to move a unit of the order of 120 aircraft as a unified body as it would have been nearly impossible to maintain any degree of control thus making the trip extremely dangerous. The Geschwader was therefore divided up into groups (by Staffel) and the transfer to our destination proceeded in these groupings, with each Staffel taking off at hourly intervals. This method proved to be much more workable with the units now more controllable in the air. The rest of the trip then proceeded without incident and we eventually arrived on the Crimea three days before the start of the offensive at Gramatikowo.

The airfield we moved into already contained a Gruppe of fighters, a Staffel of reconnaissance aircraft and a number of Stukas. With the addition of our complete Geschwader, the airfield was filled to the point of overflowing. Such was the pressure on the airfield facilities that there was no accommodation available to us

A typical dusty take off from a Russian landing ground for a Bf 109E of SchG 1.
The aircraft flown by the author and his colleagues would have looked very
similar to this, although in this instance it is being flown by Georg Dörffel of
the 5th Staffel. Note the white background to the unit badge.

actually on the airfield so our pilots were put up by some of the
locals in their cottages.

On the afternoon of 6 May, our Geschwader, together with the
other units on our airfield, was paraded on the dispersal area and we
were told that we were shortly to be visited by the Commanding
General of the VIII Fliegerkorps, of which we were now part,
General Wolfram Freiherr von Richthofen. We were then informed
that he would be carrying out an inspection of all of the units on the
airfield. This left the officers to ponder over the old problem of what
to do with the mechanics, the 'black men' as we called them on
account of their black coveralls and generally oil-stained
appearance. Our Kommodore wanted the troops to present an
appearance of smart uniformity, which would have been spoiled by
the mechanics in their black coveralls.

Making a snap decision, the Kommodore ordered all of the
'black men' to 'fall out' of the assembly and to take up position
behind the bomb stores, where they could not be seen. Our
mechanics then duly departed, leaving the remainder of the
Geschwader standing smartly on parade in uniform, ready for our
imminent inspection. We all then just stood there, waiting
expectantly for the arrival of our general, cousin of the famous First
World War fighter ace, himself also carrying the title of 'Baron'. We
were expecting him to arrive by car when suddenly a Fieseler Storch
roared over the assembled units on the airfield, turned into wind and

Although subordinate to Löhr, who commanded Luftflotte 4, the man who had direct control of the Schlachtflieger units in the Crimea and Caucasus was Generaloberst Wolfram von Richthofen. Seen here on the right, he was a very capable officer who made highly effective use of the units available to him. On the Russian Front these were never enough. Next to Richthofen is his chief of staff, Oberstleutnant Christ, who was obviously a long-term committed Nazi as he wears the ribbon of the 'Blood Order', awarded to those who had taken part in the abortive putsch of 1929.

immediately landed. Dismounting from his aircraft, the General was announced and proceeded directly towards us to commence his inspection. Everything went like clockwork, until the General asked to whom the men behind the bomb stores belonged. That rather let the cat out of the bag and left some of our officers looking rather embarrassed at the awkwardness of the situation. On being informed that they were part of our Geschwader and of the other flying units, Richthofen ordered that the men be returned to the ranks of their units on the parade square, where they belonged.

With the mechanics returned to our ranks, the troops then stood together, looking colourful and mixed, but as formed units nonetheless. The General then addressed us, beginning with a greeting then drawing our attention to the battle that we were to face over the weeks that were to follow. He concluded by wishing us pilots lots of 'soldiers luck' and much success in the air. He then departed for his aircraft, escorted by the various officers commanding their respective units, including our Kommodore. Everything then settled down to normality with the troops having a good laugh about the unsuccessful ploy to maintain uniformity on the parade square. The mechanics praised the General for not allowing them to be sidelined but it was an important acknowledgement of the invaluable contribution that the 'black men' made to the fighting effectiveness of an operational aviation unit. We would soon learn that lesson for ourselves.

The next morning, 7 May 1942, the pilots were ordered to the command post to be briefed about the enemy dispositions and likely moves. We were then told to prepare for our first operational sortie against the enemy; our departure time was to be 1500hrs. The thought of what was to follow filled me with a sense of apprehensive excitement. Our task was to bomb the railway station at Kerch, then, using the remainder of our on-board weapons, we were to hit any worthwhile targets of opportunity that presented themselves on the return journey. With the briefing over, we then busied ourselves with preparing for our first sortie – planning our route, map-marking and double-checking everything. We then settled down to wait for our departure time to arrive.

Before the attack can commence the pilots must be briefed on their targets. Here members of the intelligence section dismount from their Kubelwagen laden with the latest situational maps.

Once the target has been identified the next step is to select the appropriate ordnance. Here a Bf 109E-4/B of an unidentified unit is bombed up by the 'black men'. The bomb being fitted to the ETC rack is probably an SC250. In the conditions prevailing on the Eastern Front sophisticated equipment like the hydraulic bomb dolly seen here was not always available and improvisation was the order of the day.

Despite all of our fears and expectations, in the event our sortie turned out to be something of an anticlimax, with us neither catching sight of the enemy nor encountering any effective anti-aircraft fire from the ground. We simply dropped our bombs as instructed and departed for home; it could just as easily have been one of the many training flights that we had carried out back in Germany. When we returned to our airfield we were immediately debriefed, learning in the process that all our aircraft had returned safely and that there were no major incidents to report. In the meantime the mechanics worked on our machines to prepare them for the next sortie, which we expected to follow soon. They did not toil in vain since, at around 1900hrs, we took off again for a second attack on Kerch; our afternoon reconnaissance aircraft had recently returned to inform us that we had only been partially successful with our first attack.

For our second sortie the Staffel put up eight aircraft, which formed into two Schwarme, one led by the boss, the second led by Otto Dommeratzky. In front and above us, at an altitude of about 1,200 metres, was a layer of tall cumulus cloud reaching up to about 1,500 metres. The cloud pattern was such that it was filled with gaps – ideal concealment for making an attack. Once again we reached

Railways were a primary target in Russia on account of the enormous distances involved and the dreadful quality of the Russian roads. The very first operational sortie undertaken by the author was against the station at Kerch. This particular locomotive was attacked at Tschir in August 1942.

Wrecked rolling stock and broken tracks in the rail yard at Tschir, August 1942.

A close-up of two of the most useful general-purpose bombs used by the Luftwaffe, namely the SC500. With a thin casing and weighing 500kg, the weapon was capable of penetrating 40mm of armour plate. It could also create a crater almost 10 metres deep and 16 metres across in normal earth, sending out shrapnel over a radius of 190 metres. No armoured vehicle then in service with the Russians could withstand a direct hit or near miss.

Typical of the havoc wrought by the marauding Luftwaffe fighter-bombers ranging ahead of the advancing ground troops is this column of smashed Russian vehicles somewhere near Kerch. The nearest truck appears to be a ZIS 4x4 2½-tonner.

German troops advancing cautiously into Kerch in the summer of 1942.

There was no more tenacious enemy – for both sides – on the Eastern Front than mud. Most Russian roads were unsurfaced and soon turned into quagmires when subjected to rain and military traffic. This is a typical main highway near Kerch. Horses and tracked vehicles were often the only means of moving supplies.

our target without encountering enemy fire and dropped our bombs. The bomb strikes were good and, satisfied, we began the return leg home. This also passed without incident until, with about 30km to go before reaching our airfield, the boss sighted a two-engined machine and declared it to be a Petlyakov Pe 2 (a Russian reconnaissance aircraft). The Staffelkapitän gave the order to attack – just as in the flying school – and led us in from a position to the rear of the hostile aircraft. As we grew nearer, Otto soon felt that this was an error of judgement on the part of our leader, believing the aircraft to be a friendly Messerschmitt Me 110. Convinced that he was right, he promptly came on the air and brought it to the boss's attention. At that point I was on the right-hand side of the battle formation and had already armed my weapons. This was to be my first real encounter with an enemy machine and I was charged with excitement and expectancy.

In spite of the warning that this machine was probably an Me 110, the Staffelkapitän stuck to his opinion and did not break off the attack, flying into extreme firing range of the suspect aircraft and opening fire from a distance of several hundred yards. He had opened fire too early and was too far away to see whether or not he had scored any hits. He hadn't. I myself did not open fire, as by this stage I was not at all sure whether the twin-engined machine flying along in front of us was a Pe 2 or one of ours. But as we flew by I was able to confirm that Otto had been right – it was indeed an Me 110, a reconnaissance aircraft, probably operating from a nearby airfield.

Russian Petlyakov Pe-2 light bombers, whose resemblance to the German Messerschmitt Bf 110 caused such embarrassment for the author and his comrades after a mistake by their Staffelkapitän. The Pe-2 was an extremely capable aircraft and served with the Russians and their allied air forces until long after the war had finished.

Oberfeldwebel Otto Dommeratzky early in 1943 shortly after he had received the Knight's Cross for 425 missions and twenty air victories.

We still had a reasonable amount of fuel, and had plenty of time before we were expected back, so we remained with the Me 110, offering it protection until it reached its own lines, which, embarrassingly, turned out to be our own airfield. After we had landed, Otto walked directly and deliberately over to the boss and, from where we stood, there seemed to be a somewhat heated debate about what had taken place. The Kapitän naturally wanted to play down his mistake, particularly since no one had been hurt and the aircraft was undamaged. But Otto stood by his convictions and declared that he was going to be unambiguous in his report concerning the facts as he had witnessed them. The discussion was ended by a call from the command post, telling the boss to report.

The 110 had meanwhile landed and its crew had reported to their own staff for debriefing. Included in their operational report was an account of the incident that had taken place involving themselves and some 'friendly' fighters. They were naturally most indignant that a German fighter had actually tried to shoot them down and left out none of the details of what had happened. What made matters worse was the fact that the Me 110 and its crew belonged to the reconnaissance Staffel that was at that time operating from the same airfield as us. Needless to say, the whole affair did not place us on a very good footing with the other Staffels on the airfield and we became something of a laughing stock for a while. There was nothing to be done about this except to live with the stigma we had brought upon ourselves, the associated laughter of the other fighter pilots on the airfield and the suspicion with which we were viewed by the reconnaissance boys. Only time, and proving ourselves in battle, was going to improve things.

On the third day after we had begun operations in the Crimea, Leutnant Lange did not return. He had received a hit to his engine from ground fire and, rapidly losing power, had been forced to carry out an emergency landing behind Russian lines. The boys who had been on the mission with him had just returned from debriefing. Visibly upset, they poured out the details of the tragedy that had unfolded before them while a group of Staffel pilots and I listened with increasing horror to what they had to say.

When he had radioed that he had been hit and would be unable to make it back they were still some way behind the German front line. The remainder of his Schwarm therefore stayed with him as he struggled to get nearer to the front line until he could no longer stay airborne. They then watched him pick a suitable field to land in and were relieved to see him put his aircraft down safely and without apparent difficulty. He then opened his canopy and waited for capture by the Russian soldiers who were quickly closing in all around him. When the Russians reached his machine, however, it was clear that they had other, less restrained, ideas in mind. As his comrades circled above, watching the whole grisly scene unfold, the Russians clambered onto Lange's aircraft, surrounding his cockpit, and unceremoniously dragged him from his machine. They then, without any apparent restraint, began to club him with the butts of their weapons, forcing him down onto his knees. Watching with increasing anguish from the cockpits of their aircraft, it quickly became apparent to his comrades above him that poor Lange was doomed. Because of the hopelessness of the situation, our pilots peeled off from the loose formation that they were flying and, one by one, attacked the group of men with cannon and machine guns, mowing them down until they all lay dead around the by now burning aircraft that only minutes earlier had belonged to their former comrade. As the spine-chilling story was recounted it suddenly became abundantly clear that the tales we had been told by our older Staffel comrades from the first year of the war had not been made up or exaggerated. This was a cruel war without chivalry, where no quarter would be given by the enemy, and none was expected.

Lange was the first of our Staffel to fall. It was a sad loss as he had been a popular member of our group, but the brutal manner in which he had died made his death all the more tragic. As I walked away, sickened and stunned by what I had just heard, I began to think about the good times that Ohm, Lange and I had spent, only weeks earlier, in Antwerp. Those happy times suddenly seemed an age ago.

We continued our hectic pace of operations for fourteen days, until the fall of Kerch. Now, with the first two weeks over, we young pilots had completed an average of twenty to thirty operational sorties. By this time the other Staffels had also lost pilots, many under tragic circumstances. The strain of constant sorties and the experience of repeatedly staring death in the face gradually took its effect on us. As a result we who had once been so happy and cheerful had now become much more serious and reflective, no longer the carefree youths of our training days.

With the fall of Kerch, our Geschwader was transferred north to the Kharkov region. The Russians had broken through on the south side of the city and had to be stopped at all costs. Our new base was to be Kharkov-Rogan, from where we were to fly an unbroken succession of operations against the large numbers of tanks that had broken through the German lines. Arriving at our new airfield, we went into action immediately, finding ourselves on the go from dawn to dusk, briefing, planning, flying, debriefing, briefing and so on. Hardly anyone had time to eat and we survived on a diet of coffee, bread and butter. Our mechanics achieved the near impossible, always returning our damaged or unserviceable machines to us on time for the next or subsequent mission. The Army was in difficulty and now needed us constantly. It seemed that we had become their daily bread, without which they would not survive. As a result, we had now become a valued and respected part of the ground troops' effort. We had also become successful fighter pilots, destroying huge concentrations of enemy armour in our attacks. It was partly due to the success of these missions, particularly in breaking up the momentum of the enemy attacks at the spearheads of their armoured effort, that the enemy lost the upper hand and was forced to swing his attack in a westerly direction. This gave our troops a welcome breather, allowing them to reorganise with the intention of surrounding the Russians.

In order to support this and other moves, we were sent to Slaviansk in the Donets Basin. Our own troops then went on to the offensive and we supported their ground movements by continuous and massive low-level attacks. During this period we also experienced our first aerial battles with the Russians. Things often got pretty hot, but our Schwarm was never in serious trouble and we returned several times daily to our airfield in good order. Despite the toughness of the aerial battles and the weight of the enemy defensive fire, we escaped from this particularly intensive period of fighting unscathed. This was a remarkable achievement and word started to get around the Geschwader that we had an exceptionally good Schwarmführer leading us.

For some time now I had been flying as Katzmarek (wingman) to Otto Dommeratzky[23]. The boss didn't fly a great deal so I was able to do this on a pretty regular basis. This was good for me, as there was much for me to learn from Otto – he was an exceptional pilot who flew his aircraft with great skill and refinement. He also put a great deal of thought into the method by which he carried out his attacks. It was a constant challenge for me, however, since he did not seem to worry at all about his Katzmarek. I therefore had to be extra vigilant if I was to avoid becoming another statistic. He was nevertheless an excellent fighter pilot with a number of aerial victories to his credit. Whenever he saw enemy aircraft in the sky, he went at them, having jettisoned his bombs and manoeuvred himself into a favourable attack position, always higher than that of the enemy. He was a real fighter – he had it in his blood. Initially, it was all I could do to recognise his manoeuvres in good time and stay with him, but for the first time I was gaining first-hand experience of how to achieve aerial victories, the sort of action I could only have dreamed about at the fighter pilots' school. I was determined to make the most of it since my boss never searched out aerial opponents, concentrating almost exclusively on the mission in hand. The Gruppenkommandeur was not particularly happy when it became clear that Otto was looking for aerial battles at the expense of jettisoned bombs. Our task was to hit the ground targets and to support our own ground troops, not to engage in aerial combat, except when circumstances dictated it. In spite of this, and frequent lectures from the Kommandeur, Otto couldn't help himself – he was a born fighter and was passionate about it. For my part I had protected Otto's tail and had learned a great deal in the few weeks I had flown with him.

On a subsequent and fairly typical operation to support our own infantry north of Slaviansk, the elation of the recent successes I had been part of took a knock that was to leave a deep impression on me. In accordance with our orders, we had just bombed a number of enemy mortar positions when, as we departed, we were bounced by between fifteen and twenty Russian LaGG 3 fighters. At an altitude of about 1,500 metres, Otto immediately took up the fight and a wild turning battle ensued, despite the overwhelming numerical superiority of the enemy, their altitude advantage and the element of surprise they had achieved. We simply hadn't seen them coming, the blame for

A Messerschmitt Bf 109E-7 loaded with 10kg anti-personnel bombs starts its take off run. It is believed that the aircraft is being flown by Alfred Druschel, Gruppenkommandeur of I/SchG 1 from 1942 until March 1943. The engine cowling is yellow, but the tailband could be either yellow or white.

which was largely mine – I hadn't seen them at all. Otto circled wildly and it was all I could do not to lose him as all around me there seemed to be nothing but 'red stars' threatening to destroy us both.

The aerial battle lasted about 5 or 6 minutes until something lit up in Otto's machine and his aircraft began to burn. He immediately took to his parachute, but that was the last I saw of him as it was then as much as I could do just to get out of that mess, which, thankfully, I somehow managed. I then concentrated on reaching my own airfield. Flying low, I headed south towards my own territory, periodically pulling up to orientate myself. As I navigated myself back, I reproached myself for having lost Otto, largely the fault of my poor lookout. It seemed that I had been lucky – the Russians had let me go, perhaps content with their aerial victory over Otto.

Without further incident I eventually landed at my own airfield at Slaviansk, shaken but unhurt. When I made my report my boss was not at all happy to learn that Otto had taken to his parachute. I was not able to say whether he had landed on friendly or unfriendly ground, as I had had enough to do to keep myself from being shot down. But whatever Otto's fate turned out to be, I knew that I had learned a valuable lesson. We had been totally surprised by the LaGGs, due to my own loss of concentration. I resolved in future to keep my eyes open for enemy aircraft for the whole flight, every moment of it.

The whole division, including the Army unit we had been supporting, was immediately informed of Otto's loss, in the hope that he may have landed behind our own lines. We then waited for any news about his whereabouts. We fortunately did not have long to wait since, after about an hour, we received the news that Otto had landed uninjured and was with our own troops. He could be picked up at an alpine infantry unit about 40km north of us. Everyone was overjoyed at this news, but for me it was especially welcome. I now felt an enormous sense of relief that Otto was safe.

I now started to wonder what Otto would say to me when he got back and how he would describe the aerial battle. I had not given any warning of the enemy attack and continued to brood over how and why I had not seen them until too late. Recognising my mood, my comrades consoled me, generally feeling that, in the heat of a battle of that nature, it is every man for himself. I therefore could have done nothing else but get out of there as quickly as possible. Their support was appreciated, but it did not make me feel any better about my initial mistake.

As evening drew in, Otto returned in one of the alpine unit's trucks to an enthusiastic reception. Dismounting from the vehicle, he immediately walked towards me, with a serious but reassuring look on his face. He then told me that he too had seen the LaGGs too late. We had had no chance of winning an aerial battle from this situation and we were both lucky to be alive. He was pleased to see that I had got away from the enemy fighters after his forced departure from his aircraft and he did not blame me for what had happened. That evening we had a little celebration and chewed over the battle again, wondering how the Russians had succeeded in surprising us. In any case, we were one more experience richer and resolved to watch the sky more thoroughly in future.

The Isyum battle of encirclement developed quickly and was soon in full swing. In support of our ground troops we once more flew continuous sorties, from dawn to dusk. I continued to fly as wingman either to the boss or to Otto Dommeratzky, mounting low-level attacks against enemy positions or carrying out reconnaissance missions behind enemy lines. I only ever found myself embroiled in aerial combat with Otto, the boss concentrating exclusively on the missions we had set out to complete. If there were enemy fighters to be seen, with Otto we would soon be in amongst them.

Towards the end of the battle we moved to an airfield south of Isyum. Only a short while earlier there had still been Russian infantry stationed there. The place bore all the scars of the recent fighting, which now took its toll on us. As we took our turn to land on the cratered airfield we watched Leutnant Rohnstock land safely then taxi away to make room for the next aircraft to land. All seemed to be well when suddenly he hit a trench with his undercarriage wheels. We then watched the momentum of the aircraft carry it forward causing it to pitch onto its nose, then invert, trapping its pilot beneath it. Rohnstock, who was badly injured, then had to be rescued by our own infantry. When they eventually removed him from the badly damaged airframe, he was taken to the main airfield where he could receive medical attention. His injuries from this accident were bad enough to keep him out of the fighting for several weeks.

Operating from our new airfield, we now flew low-level attacks against the Russian supply lines. Partly as a result of our efforts, the Russian attacks slowly ground to a standstill, visible evidence of the effectiveness of our attacks. We then received orders for a deep penetration mission to escort a Schwarm of armed reconnaissance aircraft along the Isyum railway line, 100km to the north. Otto led the Schwarm, I was wingman, Ohm was the Rotte leader and Leutnant Schliefeldner was number four. The weather was good, with cumulus at about 1,500 metres and 4/8ths cloud useful for our task. We flew at around 3,000 metres altitude heading north and scanned the railway stations for supply trains. We were mainly looking for tanks, which could be moved south. After reaching the 100km deep penetration point without seeing anything of any significance, we turned and flew in battle formation, just underneath the cloud base, to Isyum. Throughout the entire flight we could make out no enemy aircraft, nor were we pestered by any enemy ground fire. We were being very prudent, flying in a wide battle formation all the time, and had nearly returned to our airfield when there was a shout over the radio: 'Indians, behind us!'[24]

Already my number one was diving steeply towards the ground, with me directly behind him, heading towards our own lines. We had been bounced, with Schliefeldner having seen the LaGGs only at the last moment. It was a last-minute flight evasive manoeuvre that was totally successful, all of us making it home safely without damage. The attacking Russians had been so sure of their kill that they had left it too late to open fire, waiting for a point-blank-range kill. As a result the attack was a complete washout for them. For our part, many of us owed our lives to Schliefeldner, who, as number four, had carried out his duties brilliantly. Many years later we old pilots held a reunion and Schliefeldner described this particular exploit in lively detail. Again, he was praised for his deeds on that day.

Allegedly victims of a Luftwaffe air attack, these Soviet T-34 tanks were caught at their most vulnerable as they attempted a river crossing. The nearest vehicle has had its turret blown completely off and has also sustained two heavy-calibre hits on top of the driver's compartment. The terrain seems hardly suited for tanks.

Easter 1942 was just around the corner and, thankfully, as it approached the pace of our flying duties finally cooled down a little. I wanted to give our Staffel colleagues a surprise, so I acquired the necessary ingredients to bake a cake. I made the appropriate arrangements with the cook and satisfied myself that it would be possible to provide an Easter cake for my comrades, with which to celebrate the occasion. I refreshed my baking skills and set to work. Then, on Easter Sunday, I sprung my surprise by producing a sweet course to follow the main meal of the day, sufficient for all the Staffel to enjoy. Everyone was delighted about this and greeted my cake with great enthusiasm. As for myself, I was equally surprised and pleased that my skill as a baker had not deserted me as I had, by now, been in the Luftwaffe for five years – five years away from my former profession.

When the encirclement came to an end our unit was transferred to Kharkov-Rogan, a former Soviet airfield with strong buildings and a reinforced take off strip. Our accommodation here was provided by some of these fortified buildings, not only a somewhat more reassuring prospect than some of our other accommodation, but also reasonably comfortable. Once we had all landed, had settled into our accommodation and our mechanics had caught up, the Geschwader was awarded a day's rest, news that was greeted with joyous enthusiasm. Now, for once, we could lounge around, play sports, go for a walk or take a drive to the town of Kharkov. Alternatively, Rogany was only about 15km east of Kharkov, which, so rumour had it, was well worth a visit. This town had not been badly damaged and there was a soldiers' mess there, which meant that there was beer to drink. There was also a cabaret showing there, provided by some Panzer grenadiers who had been taken from the ranks of a local tank division in order to provide some entertainment for its soldiers. Ohm and I attended a performance and laughed ourselves silly – privates played the girls and danced around the stage to the delight of the audience of watching soldiers. It wasn't really that brilliant, but it was nonetheless a welcome change from a day on operations.

Unfortunately, the day's break passed all too quickly and the next day we were again flying operations in an easterly direction. Our tasks were reconnaissance and disruption of the enemy on the ground. We spent nearly the whole of June in this area, with Rogany as our base airfield. Thankfully this was not an especially difficult month for us and our missions were fairly straightforward.

As a result we got through this phase of the war without suffering any casualties and, for the time being, were therefore spared the pain of mourning lost comrades.

On 15 June I happened to meet 'Poldi' Steinbatz[25], a colleague from the pilots' school at Vienna-Aspern and Neustadt-Glewe. Poldi had recently returned from the Führer's headquarters in East Prussia where he had been decorated with the 'Oakleaves' to the Knight's Cross after achieving ninety-one aerial victories. At that time he held the rank of Oberfeldwebel and was shortly to be promoted to Leutnant. We chatted a little about old times before wishing each other luck and saying our farewells. Only hours later he was back in action, shooting down another three enemy aircraft to bring his total to ninety-nine, just one short of the magic one hundred threshold that usually, at that time, brought the award of the 'Swords'[26] to the 'Oakleaves'[27]. On his way back he was caught by enemy flak, north-west of Schtebelaino, and crashed to his death in a wood, just behind enemy lines. He had flown approximately 300 operational missions. Some time later I learned that Poldi's gallantry had been recognised with the posthumous award of the 'Swords'. His commission to officer rank was also posthumously confirmed. Poldi's death came as a big shock to me, particularly since I had been talking to him only hours before. It proved conclusively, as if proof were needed, that no matter how skilled the pilot, survival was largely a matter of luck. Steinbatz's unfortunate end meant that now only Karl Hammerl and I remained from our original flying Gruppe at Aspern. Hammerl was serving with a fighter unit in the central sector.

On 24 June 1942 our Geschwader was transferred north to a grass airfield at Schatalovka near Kursk. It was a fairly open field with little in the way of covered accommodation. To achieve what cover we could, we parked the aircraft along the edge of a wood, with our mechanics living in tents inside the wood itself. This was not exactly luxury for them, but they would have plenty of time to carry out the maintenance and repair work that had accumulated since, for the time being, we were to be given a break from operations in order to replace lost aircraft and return the Staffel to full strength. We would do this by ferrying replacement Me 109s from the airfield at Uman, well behind the front line. We were to be granted three days' leave for the stopover at Uman and were to be flown there by Ju 52 transport. This was great news since there was mess accommodation in the local town, which would have proper beds, with sheets, and would doubtless have beer to sell since there was actually a brewery located nearby, and a schnapps factory! We would also have the luxury of visiting a proper barber. We knew these things since we had been to Uman before, which also meant that we knew where to go to enjoy ourselves, particularly since we had a number of Russian and German acquaintances whom we could visit. We naturally made the most of this opportunity, but we did not forget our mechanics, who we had left working at the airfield. On such occasions we always took some beer and schnapps back for them. We also got a reasonable supply of provisions, using our contacts from previous visits.

It was now slowly becoming apparent that we were about to enter a new phase in the battle. There were another three grass airfields in close proximity to us that were being occupied by German units. The nearest airfield was only about half an hour away on foot and was now home to JG 3 'Udet'. Otto Dommeratzky's brother was stationed with that Geschwader so they made the effort to see each other as soon as they could. Their reunion was a joyous occasion for them and they were able to get together on several other occasions since all the units had broken off operations at that point and flying activities were reduced to a minimum, with movement on the ground also reduced to virtually nil. Everyone began to talk about the battle that was to come, although nobody knew what form it would take or what our aims would be. The airfield was full of aircraft and the woods full of soldiers. Our mechanics had now been joined by the panzer boys and their tanks.

As we waited to be told what our next move was to be, we whiled away the time as best we could, by walking around, chatting, or playing cards. At around 1100hrs one morning I was sitting near a thorn bush, chatting with a group of pilots, when suddenly we heard the unmistakable sound of the thunder of artillery. After several seconds we could make out the first strikes coming down onto the eastern edge of the airfield. The Russians had the airfield under fire! We wondered anxiously whether it was only a nuisance barrage or whether they intended something more calculated and purposeful. The strikes now moved to the middle of the airfield and the accompanying explosions and showers of earth started to get closer to where we were perched, surveying the scene being played out before us with almost paralysed fascination. But within seconds we had changed our position for a spot below ground level and shielded by a mound of earth. However, this helped our sense of security only momentarily since the subsequent artillery strikes continued to get closer to our position. What were we to do? We hesitated for only a moment more before we leapt back into the woods and jumped into the trenches that had been dug there and were now occupied by our mechanics. As the barrage continued to approach, things gradually became very uncomfortable. One strike came so close that one of the mechanics was injured in the shoulder from a shell fragment, and I wanted to leave the trench at that point, but the strikes were too close to one another and to us for it to be sensible to attempt to leave the relative sanctuary of our somewhat overcrowded trench. But the situation had become critical and we felt that, if we stayed put, we would almost certainly be killed. So we made the decision to move at the first opportunity no matter how risky such an action would be.

As soon as a gap appeared in the fall of shot, we sprang out of the trench and ran as fast as we could in the direction of a nearby railway line. As we sprinted for all we were worth, we repeatedly had to hit the ground and lie waiting for the impact of the shell that was whistling in our ears. Fortunately for us, at that point the Russians switched their fire to the western side of the airfield, which enabled us to complete our dash to the railway line. As we took cover in the shelter of the embankment, we saw a kette (chain) of Stukas that had just taken off from a nearby airfield heading in the direction of the source of the artillery that had us so completely pinned down. As we listened we could soon faintly hear the whine of their airbrakes as they went into their characteristic dive before promptly showering the Russian artillery positions with bombs, bringing a welcome end to that infernal racket as the batteries fell silent.

As we all emerged from our various hiding places, knees still shaking, we mentally gave thanks that we were still alive and had emerged from our ordeal relatively unscathed. We were certainly an experience richer, an experience that had nearly cost us our lives. But now that the dust had settled and the affair was clearly over, everyone was conning themselves that they had been some kind of hero. When we returned to our living area, the first question we were asked was whether we had been under the artillery fire. Relating the whole succession of events to our friends, however, it soon became clear that we had been on the receiving end of the worst of it.

That evening, some more Panzer Grenadiers arrived. Now space was really at a premium with seemingly every area of cover in the woods taken up by ground troops of one form or another, preparing themselves for battle or simply lying in readiness, not knowing whether the forthcoming action would start in the morning or whether they would have to wait for several days before being given the order to move. To help pass the time as we waited, we played cards with them and generally lost; the grenadiers could either play better or cheat better than we could. In any case, by the time we called a halt they had relieved us of large quantities of our cash and many of us were broke.

The whole charade ended at around midnight, when the tankies received an 'alarm' (an immediate order to move) and had to move out. Shortly afterwards our period of extended rest also came to an abrupt end. At 3.00am we were ordered out of our tents and told to report immediately to the command post. As we entered the command post tent, our Kommandeur was already present, awaiting our arrival. It was clear from the activity in there and by the freshly marked maps that he had not been in his bed that evening. Once we were all there, and had got into a position where we could all hear what our Kommandeur had to say, and take notes if necessary, he began to speak. His briefing commenced with a general appraisal of the situation, including the Russian dispositions. The German Army was about to mount a major offensive and it was our task to give the ground troops the maximum amount of support we could. Our initial attacks were to be against Russian artillery positions and were to begin immediately. As we listened we carefully noted down our targets and, satisfied, departed into the darkness, walking in the direction of our aircraft.

In almost pitch blackness our machines were started up and, one by one, we taxied to our start positions, guided by the clearly visible flames from the exhausts of the aircraft in front, which had the effect of lighting up much of the cowling area. At just before 5.00am, as dawn was beginning to break, our entire Gruppe was in the air, heading east towards Voronezh.

Shortly after our departure the offensive began with the roar of artillery fire. Almost immediately afterwards the infantry started leaving their positions and the tanks began to roll out of the hides that had been their home. From our positions in the air we could clearly make out the fire spewing from the mouths of the artillery guns along the whole front. In the half-light below they looked like rows of flickering street lamps merged into an apparently peaceful countryside largely still immersed in the deceptive sanctity of darkness. We took it all in in silence, each of us lost in our thoughts, and flew on to our targets that were now only a couple of minutes away.

We made our final approach to the enemy artillery positions using artificial light and lined ourselves up to drop our bombs. The slaughter was about to begin. One by one we dropped our bombs on our targets, then finished off by flying low-level attacks on any enemy positions we could see, concentrating particularly on breaking up vehicle convoys and destroying as many vehicles as we could. As we pressed home our attacks gradually everything lit up, sometimes, when we hit munitions dumps, in a very spectacular fashion. In the now improving light, and helped by the illuminating effect of the multitude of fires that were now burning on the ground, we could see that we had hit a number of worthwhile targets. We were particularly gratified by this, since the artillery attacks of the previous night had not been entirely ineffective, the JG 3 airfield in particular having suffered extensive damage at the hands of the Russian artillerymen. This was for the JG 3 boys.

With our first task successfully completed and our ammunition largely expended, we turned for home. So far it had all been relatively straightforward, we had encountered no enemy fighters and there really hadn't been much in the way of defensive fire from the ground.

Soviet airfields were prime targets for the Luftwaffe in the early days of the assault on the Crimea. Here the still smoking remains of an Ilyushin DB-3 bomber lie in the revetment that failed to protect it.

Thankfully things remained that way for our flight back and we all returned safely to our airfield some 80 minutes after we had taken off.

As we dismounted from our machines, our mechanics, refuellers and armourers went to work immediately. They had been waiting for our return and had made their well-practised preparations to receive us in order that we could take off for our next sortie as quickly as possible. Everything got under way at once, with our groundcrews working flat out, refuelling, re-arming and loading up fresh bombs. As all this took place, we pilots hastily made our reports and were then informed of our next destination and the targets we were to attack. We then hurried back to our machines and climbed back into the cockpits ready to go again for our second mission before breakfast.

We took off again in loose formation and, once airborne, again headed east. By now the sun had climbed above the horizon and we could clearly see our own troops on the ground. As we surveyed the scene below us, we could see that our infantry was spread perilously thinly far out to the east as they made their advance. Our task was to assist them by breaking up various points of resistance that were obstructing, or likely to obstruct, their advance. This gave us a degree of freedom in selecting our targets and, as we flew along the Russian positions, we selected, for example, clearly visible mortar positions on which to drop our bombs, then flew low-level strafing attacks on our targets. In making our attacks we flew so low that we could make out the Russian infantrymen in their positions, many of whom were attempting to engage us with small arms fire while others concentrated on the direction from which they were expecting to be attacked on the ground.

Our attacks were successful and our ground troops reached the positions they had been ordered to take without a great deal of resistance. We again flew back to our airfield without incident and our aircraft were once again turned around for our third mission of the morning. It was not yet 0930hrs.

We again pressed home our attacks successfully and turned for home. At around 1000hrs we sighted some Ju 88s heading westwards, presumably returning from a bombing mission. As they disappeared from view, heading for their own airfield, we heard that they had come under attack from enemy fighters. The bombers were clearly in trouble and the call was a cry for help. We had no choice but to go to their aid so, low on ammunition, we changed direction to that in which we had just witnessed the bombers disappear.

Evidence of the speed of the German advance can be seen in these Soviet 76.2mm heavy anti-aircraft guns, which show signs of being hastily abandoned. Many guns of this type were captured and re-used against their original owners.

A view along the barrel of a Russian gun that has been smashed by the actions of SchG 1 in August 1942.

Unfortunately we arrived a bit too late. As we approached we watched one of the Ju 88s plunging to the ground in flames, a trail of black smoke indicating the point where it had been shot down. Its crew of four had already taken to their parachutes but, fortunately for them, the wind was blowing in an easterly direction and was therefore taking them towards their own troops. But our appearance did have the effect of forcing the Russians to abandon their attacks and head for home, thereby posing no further threat to the remaining bombers, which could now proceed to their airfield unhindered. Before we departed from the scene we watched over the parachuting crew, who were very lucky; the wind direction was in their favour and they all ended up with their own troops on the ground.

We now headed back to our airfield and, after we had landed, were finally able to eat the food that our mechanics had prepared for us. But we couldn't stop for more than a few minutes since the ground troops urgently needed our support. And so it went on throughout the day, barely stopping for anything. When we had finally completed our last mission late in the evening, we ate our meal in silence, staggered to our tents and fell into bed. It took a long time to comprehend what had happened during what had been a monumental and totally exhausting day. We were thankful at least that we had completed the day without any losses and so had no casualties to mourn. I closed my eyes and was soon asleep, knowing that the following morning we would all be let loose again.

The following days saw more success in the air and on the ground. As we continued to carry out our attacks on the Russian points of resistance, the ground troops swiftly reached their objectives. It was all going like clockwork. The business of dropping bombs and carrying out low-level attacks was becoming second nature, with our routine only occasionally interrupted by aerial battles. It was summer time and the weather stayed perfect for our business, always hot and clear – real holiday weather.

After ten days we again moved east. Our new airfield was another grass strip, this time an enormous field, big enough for a whole Geschwader. Our Gruppe was assigned to the eastern side of it. Without pausing for rest we immediately went back into operations, flying non-stop missions. No one asked the crews whether or how they were coping with the unending strain.

Again and again it was reconnaissance, bomb dropping and low-level attacks. By now the airfields were all overflowing and supplies were mostly flown in by Ju 52 transports. When one had landed, another immediately took off, in between the fighters, the Stukas and us, the 'Schlachter'. It was a real witches' brew in which each man tried to retain his place once he had landed. At that time I was assigned as wingman to the boss and always took off at his side as number two. One day, my Me 109 broke away and raced towards a parked Ju 52. At the last moment I pulled back the stick in an all-or-nothing attempt to clear this aircraft. I prayed that I had enough flying speed to get off the ground since the alternative was almost certain disaster. With only inches to spare I cleared its fuselage with my undercarriage. I breathed a huge sigh of relief that I had escaped that particular threat unscathed. Another piece of luck!

After returning from the operation, I was given a lecture by the boss concerning the near miss between me and the transport. I felt that it was not really my fault but listened politely to what he had to say, expecting that to be the last of it, particularly since our operation had

The weapons and helmets stacked ready for use by the groundcrews show how close to the front lines the 'Schlachters' often were. These fully bombed-up Messerschmitt Bf 109E-7s are from 2./SchG 1, some time in 1942. The nearest aircraft, 'Red O', appears to be finished in the standard day-fighter camouflage scheme of 74/75/76 with yellow noses and tail bands. In the central and northern sectors of the Russian Front these bands were invariably yellow, but on the southern sector, where this picture was taken, they were often white.

The unsung heroine of the Russian Front was 'Auntie Ju', the lumbering Junkers Ju 52/3m, whose ruggedness and reliability made so many of the German military operations possible. Here an unidentified Staffel sweeps low over a typical Russian road and village.

been another total success. I was wrong. When he had finished giving me a lecture on vigilance on the ground and in the air he informed me that I was grounded for eight days. I was stunned by this and initially felt very bitter about the way I had been treated. Later, when I had time to sit down and let what had happened sink in, I was just happy that the near disastrous incident had not turned out worse.

My colleagues continued to fly from early in the morning until late in the evening, making full use of every hour of daylight. As for me, I was on holiday. No one worried about me, so I looked for something to keep me occupied while my comrades were in the air. It wasn't long before I had lined myself up with a really good little job. It involved the young Russian prisoners of war whom we employed to carry out supply replenishment runs for the field kitchen. They made these trips in Panje[28] supply trucks, medium-sized load-carrying vehicles, bringing our cooks whatever rations we had been allocated to keep us fed. But it was a fairly monotonous diet and the meals were never greeted with much enthusiasm. Without too much difficulty I managed to acquire one of these vehicles, along with a Russian to assist me, and drove merrily through the countryside collecting cucumber, tomatoes and any other vegetables I could for the kitchen staff to be able to liven up our meals. After the first couple of meals with my vegetables the boss soon declared that he was pretty happy with my new job, particularly since it meant a more varied diet for the troops. We were often out the whole day, but the yield was worth it. My comrades

Russian prisoners of war at Tazinskaya in 1942, in the typically squalid conditions encountered in the POW compounds. There are at least four women in this group; the Russian Army made much use of female soldiers as nurses and snipers in the front line.

Three pilots from 8./SchG 1 have some fun with one of the Russian Panje horses at Konstantinorovka in July 1942. In winter these sturdy little animals were often the only means of transport for the German forces. Feldwebel Buchner sits on the horse while Unteroffizier Birnbaüer attempts to goad it into movement and Feldwebel Kruger looks on.

were most enthusiastic about the vegetable bus, as they started to call it, and began to look forward to the evening meals in the hope that they would contain something different to eat.

These restful and quite enjoyable days soon came to an end and I was once again assigned to flying duties. I resumed these in a very much refreshed condition and was completely relaxed when I took off for my first mission after my enforced holiday. I was back in my element. In the meantime, the front continued to push slowly eastwards and had nearly reached the town of Voronezh when the direction of the main thrust was turned south-east. The Army's objectives were now the installations at the airfields near Kamensk.

Our orders to transfer to Kamensk arrived immediately, even though the situation was fairly fluid at that time. On the day that we were supposed to move the Army was expected to have already secured the area to our front, thereby rendering our airfield relatively safe for us to occupy. Unfortunately for us, the planned attack had been postponed but the Luftwaffe had not been informed. We flew in as ordered and one by one landed on this totally unsecured airfield, oblivious to the danger we were flying into. As we began to park our machines we caught sight of our troops crouching in their foxholes. Intrigued, I turned off my engine, climbed out and walked towards them to ask what was going on. The man I spoke to explained that the operation had been postponed and that they were now awaiting orders to commence their attack on the Russian positions to their front. He then informed me that I had landed right on the front lines and suggested that I should clear out of there as quickly as possible as we were very exposed and were in great danger of being attacked or caught in the middle of a battle. It was an uneasy situation. Still and quiet, the airfield now had a Gruppe of Me 109s parked on it and already some Ju 52s were starting to arrive with supplies and men to help build our camp. It was a recipe for disaster. As word was quickly passed to let everyone know the seriousness of the situation we were in, the pilots gathered around the boss to see whether there had been any further orders. If there had, he hadn't been informed of any, but a quick decision was required as at that moment the Russian artillery opened up and it was very quickly apparent that they were targeting the airfield. At that point the troops became angry with us and indicated that we should clear cut of there immediately. If we didn't then we would soon give away their positions, to say nothing of the danger that our machines were in.

Any uncertainty over what to do next was soon overtaken by events as the Russians ranged in their artillery. Only two or three plane widths away, a Ju 52 suddenly took a direct hit and burst into flames. As a result mass confusion ensued, with the Jus swiftly lining themselves up to clear out. As for ourselves, we sprinted to our machines and, without the aid of our mechanics, who had not yet arrived, we started our aircraft ourselves using the aircraft cranking handles. It was not the best of times to learn how to carry out the starting procedure normally performed by our mechanics, but, hastened by the situation in which we found ourselves, we turned starters at full speed, removed the winder and leapt into the cockpit to turn on the ignition. It was every man for himself. Luckily for me my engine sprang into life at the first time of asking. I just had time to put on my safety harness before the artillery fire increased in intensity all around me, letting me know that it was time to disappear. I pointed my machine into the wind and was away at full throttle. After that it was a 'breeze'. I lifted off the ground, retracted the undercarriage and pointed the nose westwards to our old airfield. Once I had reached my cruising altitude, it was a simple thing to orientate myself and in a short while I had reached the old airfield. Arriving alone, I made a quick pass and lined myself up for landing, making a perfect three-point touchdown. I then taxied to my old parking place and switched off the engine to wait for the other Staffel pilots to arrive. It was a wonderful feeling to be back, safe and sound, on an orderly airfield.

One after the other, the rest of the machines returned, even the Ju 52. The pilots told us that the Ju had been carrying supplies and men that had been unloaded at the airfield, but not reloaded when the pilot took off. Consequently our field kitchen was still on the airfield at Kamensk, leaving us without cooking facilities. In the rush to take off, a colleague of mine had actually run over one of our own 20mm flak positions, resulting, sadly, in a private soldier having his leg severed above the knee by his propeller. But apart from this unpleasant incident, the temporary loss of our field kitchen and a good number of our clerks, mechanics, cleaners and cooks having several hours of driving with Panje wagons to do, we had got off the whole thing quite lightly. This was a remarkable escape, considering that we had landed a Gruppe of 109s on a grass airfield right on our own front lines. That evening we celebrated and recounted our heroic deeds, trying to make the best of a bad thing.

It turned out that the attack on Kamensk had been postponed for several days because not enough troops and supplies were available to call upon. So, for the time being, our operational duties adopted a more routine nature, which gave us time to relax and regain our energy. It was also good news for the mechanics, who could now take care of the machines in relative peace. Once again the Staffel aircraft were parked up along the edge of a wood, but this time our accommodation was in a village about 3km away. In order to get between the two, we used our POW lads, who we still had with us, to run a sort of taxi service for us, which was arranged around their supply runs. These prisoners, who were quite young, seemed to have had the benefit of a good education and, if not, were certainly endowed with a fair degree of common sense. One day, after having made the same trip a number of times, they asked us for a vehicle pass so that they would not always have to be stopped by our military police at their checkpoints. This didn't seem to be an unreasonable request under the circumstances, so they were issued with their own vehicle pass by the headquarters staff. The pass they were given stated that they were employed by the Staffel as general labourers and were permitted to drive freely within a radius of 5km of the airfield. As they continued with their duties, armed with their new vehicle pass, we didn't give too much thought as to their whereabouts as long as they picked us up when they were supposed to and our provisions continued to arrive on time. Then one day the vehicle didn't turn up and the two helpers were nowhere to be found. It was our own fault for not paying much attention to their movements on an hourly, or even a daily, basis. If they had had any sense at all, and I'm sure they had plenty, they had probably driven away into the countryside in the Panje wagon, making full use of their German vehicle pass, never to be seen again. I'm quite sure that, had we found ourselves in their position, we would have done exactly the same thing.

The front was moving again and remained fluid for several days. It felt like we were playing our part in some absurd play and this was the next act. One night a Heinkel He 111 was returning from a bombing mission to the east of our airfield having received multiple hits to an engine and its undercarriage area. As it came within a few miles of us, it began to struggle to maintain height to the extent that its pilot informed his crew that they were not going to make it back to their own airfield. They therefore began work to find an airfield nearby that would be suitable for them to land on. They came up with ours and radioed to the command post duty crew that they were coming in for an emergency landing. Approaching in darkness, with only a few small lights on the ground to mark the position of the airfield for their arrival, the machine carried out a belly-landing and came to rest in the middle of the airfield. The next morning our Staffel had an early reconnaissance mission to fly. We knew nothing of our unexpected visitor from the night before and therefore taxied to the take off point aided by nothing more elaborate than an electric light, in blissful ignorance of the potentially dangerous obstacle that lay ahead. The boss was leading, myself to his right as number two, with Otto D. as number three and Ohm number four. Leutnant Beutelspacher was the Operations Officer that day and had taken his place at the take off point in order tell us about the hazard to our front, which we could not see in the pre-dawn darkness. As we took up our positions ready for take off, he came forward and climbed up onto the wing of Leutnant Dill's machine to inform him about what lay ahead. Next Beutelspacher came to me and then went to the other pilots in the Schwarm, giving them all the same message, to watch out for the He 111 blocking part of the airfield. When everyone taking part had been informed, we were cleared for take off.

Our Kapitän, Charley Dills, went off first and, following his lead, I gave it full throttle and tucked in behind and to his starboard side. As we gathered speed in the semi-darkness I watched his tail raise in preparation to lift; a second or so later mine would be doing the same. His aircraft then seemed to stop in its tracks as it ploughed into the stricken bomber laying across the airstrip. As I passed him a fireball suddenly erupted immediately to my left, then I was airborne. Everyone else made it into the air without incident but our boss, who had not been so lucky, had been killed in the crash. Realising what had happened, Otto then took command of the Schwarm and we flew our task. When we returned a pall of smoke still hung over the airfield to remind us of the tragic loss of our Staffelkapitän. His death hit us all very hard. He was a popular and fair leader with a quiet personality who always had a good word for everybody. As is often the case, it seemed to be all the harder to accept due to the tragic and wasteful circumstances of his death. Later that morning Hans Stollnberger was appointed as his replacement. It was the start of a new era for our Staffel and we were soon to discover that the relative peace we had enjoyed under the leadership of Leutnant Dills was to become a thing of the past.

In the afternoon we placed our old Kapitän in a bomb crater near the airfield and gave him the best burial we could manage. We marked his grave with a lovely wooden cross that our mechanics had made and the Kommandeur spoke a few moving words. There was then a volley of shots fired by the guard of honour that had been assembled and we all paid our last respects. His resting place was actually near the roadside where we travelled in each morning, so we passed the grave of our former boss every day we flew from that airfield.

The grave of Oberleutnant Karl Dills, Staffelkapitän of 8./SchG 1 from the time of its arrival in Russia until his death in a take off accident near Kamensk on 12 July 1942.

As the front continued to push eastwards we moved to an airfield near the town of Tazinskaya. It was a miserable and exposed place with a complete lack of distinguishing features – no buildings, no trees, no hills, nothing – only wide open and completely flat land. Our area of operations was on the Don, to our east and south. The Russians were in full retreat with our troops in pursuit, and no one was encountering any real opposition. In the town of Tazinskaya was the command post of the VIII Fliegerkorps where our Kommandeur would frequently go to receive his orders for the Gruppe. After his first visit he returned to announce that we were to fly an attack on Astrakhan in the next few days. A quick glance at the map suggested that this was going to be a difficult one since the target we had been given was probably at the extreme limit of our range. We nevertheless applied our brains to the matter, slide rules were brought out and calculations made. It was not long, however, before we knew for sure that this mission was not possible with our 109s. With our range, if we flew to Astrakhan we would only be able to get back as far as Elista in the steppes before being forced to land due to lack of fuel. This made the whole operation unnecessarily dangerous and we made this point absolutely clear to our boss, who seemed reluctant to call off the mission. After a considerable amount of pestering from us, however, he eventually went to see the Kommandeur to explain the situation and to recommend that the mission be called off. Our Kommandeur agreed and went back to HQ VIII Fliegerkorps to try to get the mission aborted. Meanwhile we all nervously waited at the airfield for his return. We feared that, should he not be successful, this could turn out to be a suicide mission for many of us. To our great joy, the authorities saw sense and we all breathed a great sigh of relief.

A few days later part of the Staffel, which thankfully included me, was granted a rest from operations and we made the most of this unexpected break by taking a truck to the Don to go fishing. We had about 30km to drive to the south, which took us about 2 hours. When we arrived at this enormously wide river we found that there was still a battle in progress on its south-eastern bank. Not to be deterred, we were given an assault boat by the Pioneers there. They even gave us a driver who was very helpful, showing us how to catch fish with hand grenades. The Don was very wide there and our catch was correspondingly lucrative. By the time we left we had caught enough fish to feed the whole Staffel. It would be a welcome change from the monotonous menu of the Staffel kitchen.

That same day Helmut Katzerowski, a Viennese, was killed during a low-level attack on Russian artillery positions. His comrades reported that, with his stricken aircraft burning heavily, he had turned around to make an additional attack, at the same time bidding his comrades farewell over the radio. His dramatic announcement finished with the words 'The Führer lives!' before he was seen to crash to his death. Katzerowski was the second of our Staffel pilots to have fallen since the beginning of the offensive at Kursk in July. The other Staffeln had also had their fair share of casualties to mourn. They were all good friends and good pilots, torn from our ranks while still in their prime.

We spent the beginning of August in Tazinskaya. The nights were crystal clear and we often passed the late evenings sitting in front of our tents admiring the numerous shooting stars in the night-time sky. Then the pilots would dream of their homes far away, of Germany or Austria and of their parents and relatives. The nights were mild and the days hot, giving us cockpit temperatures of up to 60°C to endure. To try to fly and fight in such conditions was absolute hell; our clothing very quickly became soaked in sweat and glued itself to our skins. Then, as it soaked through, we became stuck to our seats. Also, the nature of our missions meant that we often did not fly high enough for the air temperature to drop sufficiently for us to feel any cooler. On those occasions when we did, our soaking uniforms clung to us like cold wet towels. To make matters worse, from time to time we would get an electric shock through the throat microphone when we fired our 20mm cannon. Every mission became an ordeal of endurance that steadily sapped our energy and resolve, but we had somehow to work through it.

There was no respite for us as we continued to fly up to eight missions daily. Aided by non-stop Luftwaffe missions, the Army continued its rapid advance and it was soon time for us to move further south-eastwards to a new airfield. So, in mid-August, we moved to the south of Kallatsch, on the Don. This new venue gave us another problem to contend with: mosquitoes, en masse. This made the evenings particularly unpleasant and was disruptive to our normal evening routine. For the first time since the start of the war we dug out our mosquito nets and used them.

I now had more than 100 missions against the enemy behind me and, as a result of the confidence that experience always brings, I had become more calm and thoughtful in the air. Each operation made its mark on us all and slowly we youngsters came to belong to the ranks of the old. But as the war progressed each mission became steadily more dangerous as the Russian resistance got stronger, our missions now being hindered to a much greater extent by anti-aircraft defensive fire. Aerial battles also became increasingly likely as we started to be intercepted by enemy fighters. At the same time the tasks were becoming steadily more difficult, with more complicated routes to follow to the target and greater distances to fly.

Our operations were currently in the region of the Don bridges, near Kallach, and in Stalingrad. As we flew our missions the Russian Rata (Polikarpov I-16), LaGG and Yak fighters became our constant and unwelcome companions. Again and again we had to fight to make the airspace free for us to make our attacks. The flak was more

Russians prisoners were used in the building of a bridge across the Don at
Kallach in 1942. German POWs were also used for the same purpose by their
Russian captors later in the war.

The remains of a Soviet field gun and tractor after the Schlachtflieger had passed,
near Stalingrad in 1942.

concentrated than we had ever seen it before, particularly around Stalingrad, and as we flew over the city something always seemed to be exploding. The constant clouds of smoke above Stalingrad soon made it visible from a great distance, particularly from the air.

In order to reduce the daily distances we were flying, we now transferred to another airfield at Tusow, north of the Tschir railway station. This was a grass airfield in the steppes, a barren place in the extreme with no inhabitants, no houses and no water. For our water supplies we had to rely on what supplies we had with us, supplementing them with what we were able to gather from the occasional rivulet. Our initial supplies soon arrived by Ju 52 and we were accommodated in tents. We stuck out like peas on a plate, without any protection against the constant bombardment. There was another airfield nearby, so the combined Luftwaffe forces in our immediate area consisted of ourselves, SG 1 and a Stuka Gruppe on our airfield, and on the other JG 3 and a Romanian fighter unit of Gruppe strength. For a week we also shared our airfield with an Italian fighter unit. There was another surprise on this airfield that we hadn't seen before – snakes. These were sand vipers, poisonous snakes about 30-40cm in length. At night the warmest place on the airfield was under the floor of our tents, so the snakes soon accumulated there. In the mornings we could sense them hiding; if you lifted up the tent floor you could see them slipping away. One of our pilots, Unteroffizier Lebsanft, from Regensburg, was a passionate snake-catcher. He was so good at it that the boss excused him from flying duties and appointed him official snake remover. He therefore took care that the snakes did not pester us, giving us one less problem to worry about.

An indifferent picture of a Henschel Hs 129B on the steppes near Tusow, some time in 1942. By this time the Schlachtgeschwader were often operating a mixture of aircraft types, as the Bf 109 and Hs 123 began to be replaced by aircraft more specifically tailored to the changing conditions of their work.

A distant view of a Staffel of Henschel Hs 123s taking off from their base near Tusow on the Don in August 1942 for a strike against Soviet targets. The vastness of the Russian steppes is very evident.

Shredded by the ceaseless wind over the steppes, this is the flag of III./SG 1 near Tusow in 1942. All Luftwaffe flags were similar, the only difference being in the background colour, which served to identify the branch. Here it is yellow, signifying a flying unit.

Hermann Buchner plays the accordion outside his palatial dugout near Tusow in August-September 1942 during operations in the Don basin and against Stalingrad. Points of interest include the camouflaged zeltbahn, the waterproof poncho issued to all members of the Wehrmacht, which could be buttoned together to form tents capable of accommodating several men. Socks in the Luftwaffe came in four standard sizes, the difference being indicated by the number of rings around the top. Those drying here have three rings and are therefore 'large'.

Tusow was overrun by poisonous sand vipers. Unteroffizier Lebsanft, seen here near the dugouts occupied by the members of 8./SchG 1, was the unit's champion snake-catcher.

Activity during the months of August and September was intense. We flew bombing missions to Stalingrad from dawn to dusk. The smoke that guided us to this besieged city could now be seen from a tremendous distance, the dark clouds of smoke and dust reaching a height of about 2,000 metres. The Volga city of Stalingrad covered an area measuring roughly 45km by between 4 and 7km. We fought for railway installations, airfields and artillery positions, mostly successfully. On 12 September 1942, at around 1200hrs, I was on one such typical mission over the Volga when I was attacked by an I-16 fighter. My aircraft took hits to the engine and began to smoke. The Russian did not persist with his attack, so I now switched my attention to the temperature gauge, which soon told me that the engine was overheating. As all the coolant drained from my radiator and the engine temperature entered the red zone, it became clear that I was not going to make it back to my airfield. Just as this unpleasant realisation hit me, my engine seized. I now had no choice but to make an emergency landing.

As I descended I looked frantically for somewhere suitable to put down. I was now over the south side of the city and, not exactly spoiled for choice for a landing site, I decided upon an open area provided by a railway freight station. Praying that I had made suitable allowance for the wind direction, I lined my trusty Messerschmitt up for what would probably be its last landing. I then lowered my flaps and pushed the stick forward, keeping a close eye on the air speed indicator to be sure of staying safely above stalling speed, at the same time checking for any drift that may follow from a crosswind I had not allowed for. Praying that there were not any obstacles down there that I had not seen, I went in, raising the nose when about 10 feet above the ground, and put my machine down on its belly. There was an almighty crash as metal impacted with concrete and the Messerschmitt clattered violently across the site. It was a painfully bumpy and nerve-racking roller-coaster ride with chunks flying off the machine as it hit railway tracks, traversed bomb craters and screeched across the uneven concrete surface. It seemed to be an age before the bumping and sliding finally ended and the machine came to a standstill. When it did, I thought of nothing but getting out and away from the wreck as quickly as possible.

Once the fear of being burned alive had subsided, my next concern was to establish where I was. I racked my brains to remember where I had seen our own troops and decided that they were to the south. So I tried to head south, worried and fearful for my safety in these unfamiliar and unwelcoming surroundings. After a while I saw some familiar German vehicles and some men in field grey uniforms walking towards me. They were German soldiers who had been told to head towards the landing site and find me. They began to call out as they drew nearer, intending to reassure me that they were friendly troops and that I was to go to them for assistance.

The German soldiers who welcomed me turned out to be members of the 24th Panzer Division. They took me back to divisional headquarters where I was given some cigarettes and something to eat and was then taken to see their General. He wanted to find out what I knew about the overall situation and in particular about the enemy dispositions to his immediate front. He then gave me the cheery news that the troops I was with were, for the time being, surrounded. I would therefore have to remain in their company for the next few days, performing any duties I was to be given. He told me that he could always use good subordinate commanders.

Once my audience with the General was over, the staff radio operator tried to contact the Luftwaffe to let them know that I had carried out an emergency landing and was safe and well. After a short period of trying he finally got through. It seemed that I had been very lucky in that I had landed directly between the opposing lines. The message came back for me from the Luftwaffe authorities that I would be picked up by a Storch from my Geschwader that night. I was over the moon. It seemed that my apprenticeship as a ground soldier would have to wait for another time.

A small landing strip was prepared for the Storch close to the HQ. All I could do then was wait for my rescuers to arrive. At around 1900hrs the long-awaited aircraft finally arrived, flown by a friend from my Staffel. I was overjoyed to be picked up but the goodbyes between myself and the soldiers of the headquarters staff were hearty and sincere. With all my goodbyes and thanks completed, I climbed aboard the Storch and closed the door behind me. Strapping myself in I suddenly felt a great surge of relief that I was finally safe. To have remained for any length of time with an army unit did not appeal to me at all, especially in such a dangerous situation as those troops were in. As we took off to head back to our airfield I waved my last farewells and we left the men of Stalingrad far behind and below. As we flew back to our airfield I began to think about the ordeal they had in front of them. Would they be relieved from that position of isolation? Would they have to fight to break out? As I relaxed in the Storch and surveyed the scene below me, pondering over the Army's situation, my eyelids became heavy as I gradually felt myself drifting on the edge of sleep, dreaming of what I might have had to face had I not been able to be picked up. But even the worst of my fears never approached the tragedy and horror of what lay ahead over the coming months for those poor souls below me. Had I had any notion of the catastrophe that was to be Stalingrad I would have prayed for them there and then.

After about 45 minutes in the air we landed at the Gruppe airfield at Tusow. After reporting my arrival to the Kapitän, we celebrated my safe return from the ranks of the 'missing in action'.

I was by no means the only one from the Staffel to be forced down and later returned to the Gruppe. In fact, many from our Staffel were shot down a number of times and returned to tell the tale. Some even landed behind enemy lines and got away with it. Leutnant Stollnberger was our king of this particular brand of death-defying heroism. On one occasion he was shot down over the steppes, well behind enemy lines, and remained at large in Russian territory for three days as enemy soldiers scoured the area to find him. On his fourth night on the run he reached the banks of the Don where he waited until dawn before swimming this mighty river to reach our own troops on its western bank. As he climbed out, he was picked up by security troops of the German Army. Several days later he finally completed the tortuous journey to our airfield. As was the normal custom, when he got back there was once again a safe return to celebrate. We were having a good spell and, for the time being, our Staffel was able to go about its duties without having any more casualties to mourn, although emergency landings remained commonplace.

As the operations continued they became progressively more challenging. The tasks of 13 September 1942 were particularly memorable since they came in quick succession and each was more hazardous than the last. We encountered enemy fighter interference from the very first sortie, despite which we nevertheless managed to escape unscathed and complete our mission. On the second mission we again had an aerial battle on our hands. This time, with our bombing already completed, we pursued the LaGGs eastwards to their own airfield, deciding to hit them when they had committed themselves to land. Following them in, I lined myself up behind a LaGG 3 as he in turn lowered his wheels to land. As I scored hits on the enemy machine, I watched chunks fly off it until the pilot lost control and it crashed to the ground, exploding into flames. I now, finally, had my first aerial victory, although the manner in which it was achieved did not give me any particular sense of pleasure or achievement. It had been easy but it had also been achieved in an environment of equal odds. The lease agreement with the USA would soon make a noticeable difference to the Russian strength and the pressure on us would continue to increase for the rest of the war.

At about this time we had our first encounters with the American Curtiss P-40. Now Otto's penchant for attacking and fighting and his general ability in a dogfight came in useful. The increased threat from enemy fighters meant that we could no longer afford to shy away from aerial battle and we started to find ourselves locked in combat on a regular basis. Stollnberger and Dommeratzky did particularly well in this environment and their victory tally climbed steadily. By only the end of October Stollnberger had already chalked up forty-five aerial victories but, as before, the Russians did not prove to be easy opponents for long. The battle in the air, as well as on the ground, was soon to become a great deal more difficult.

At the end of October I went back to Taganrog accompanied by four colleagues to pick up some replacement Me 109s. This time we flew as passengers in a Ju 52 supplied by one of the nearby transport Geschwader. Once there, we moved into accommodation in a former barracks and were given lunch in the soldiers' mess, where we were to eat most of our meals. We didn't think that we were going to be able to take over the aircraft for a few days so we spent much of our time looking around the local area with the primary aim of finding a place where we could have a decent night out. In reality, most of our time was spent sight-seeing around Taganrog although we also spent a day in Rostov.

In Taganrog we struck up a friendship with some of the local fishermen. With these men we discovered that we could exchange bread for good caviar at the seemingly ridiculous exchange rate of one loaf of army bread for half a pail filled to the brim with caviar. We also got to know some Red Cross sisters from the local hospital. After a few days in the town, waiting to be issued with our aircraft; I began to feel unwell, a feeling that steadily worsened. My condition soon became so severe that I could barely muster the energy or the enthusiasm to do anything until eventually, weak with illness, I collapsed. Upon being taken to a doctor I was diagnosed as suffering from a debilitating bout of fever, a serious illness that was clearly going to keep me away from flying for quite some time, or so it seemed.

A view of the German
cemetery at Taganrog in
October 1942. The grave of
Leutnant Fritz Brückmann,
once of SG 1 and who was
apparently killed earlier in
1942, can be seen centre
left. Note the German Red
Cross nurse in the
background.

Having established what was wrong with me, Ohm initially took
it upon himself to take care of me while I fought the fever and made
my recovery. However, as my condition showed no signs of
improvement and was, if anything, worsening, it soon became clear
that I belonged in a hospital and I was promptly taken to the
Luftwaffe hospital in Taganrog. Under different circumstances I
would have found the hospital to be a fairly pleasant place, but in the
now critical state of unconsciousness I was in, I was in no condition
to enjoy its pleasantness. It was, nevertheless, a picturesque spot by
the sea and had formerly been a Russian maternity hospital.

I lay unconscious for several days as doctors and nurses,
seriously concerned about my condition, buzzed around my bed.
When I eventually came round I discovered myself to be in a
comfortable, double-bedded room with a Hauptmann from the
Belgian Legion[29]. Recounting to me the dramas that had taken place
during my unconsciousness, he told me that my condition had been
very serious for a number of days and that I had been the centre of
attention for quite some time. He then went on to tell me how he had
been wounded in the Caucasus and that he desperately wanted to get

back to his unit and to the front line again. I was also visited by my faithful friend Ohm, who brought with him all the latest news from our unit. He subsequently visited every day until, at the beginning of November, he informed me that he would not be able to visit any more, at least for a while. They had finally got the machines we had been waiting for so now he had to return to the Geschwader at the front. We said our goodbyes and wished each other luck before he left me to my hospital bed, and to my thoughts.

As the following days passed, my health improved considerably and I soon felt well enough to travel, if the hospital staff would let me. I decided that it would be a good idea if I could arrange to be transferred to a hospital in Germany. Despite my enthusiasm for this, however, the doctors were not very keen on the idea and it seemed that I was going to have to sit out my convalescence in this nice but dull ex-maternity hospital in occupied Russia. This was not to be, however, since the war soon had a hand in my plan when the front was pulled back from the Caucasus. This meant that the wounded would need to be transferred back, although how far wasn't clear. The move was to be by train, which I was not keen on at all, so I contacted an acquaintance of mine, an engineer at the aircraft transfer airfield, who got me a chance to fly back to Lemberg in a Ju 52. I was lucky to get this and flew back to Germany while my fellow patients took the long, boring and tortuous route back by train. From Lemberg I was finally forced to take a train myself to the Luftwaffe hospital to continue my convalescence. My journey was not a short one since I had to travel via Krakow, Vienna and finally Wels before I reached my destination.

I stayed in hospital care until December 1942, when, my health sufficiently restored to resume my duties, I was transferred to the Frontfliegersammelstelle (Front Line Pilots Assembly Point) at Dortmund-Brackel. This proved to be a pleasant, relaxing stay, which I really enjoyed. The assembly point consisted of three Staffels made up of previously wounded flying personnel who were being prepared to be returned to the front. It seemed that all of the flying branches of the Luftwaffe were represented there. As I got to look around and meet many of the personnel there I spoke to bomber crews, fighter pilots, ground-attack boys like me, transport people, reconnaissance personnel and various other flying representatives. The permanent staff also consisted of former flyers. I was put in the second Staffel, which consisted entirely of fighter and ground-attack pilots who had received either severe burns or amputations as a result of combat – illustrious company. We got on famously and soon a good feeling of camaraderie prevailed. On an almost daily basis we would take the tram to Dortmund to visit the cinema, wander around the shops, or simply have a coffee. For a while the war seemed a long way away; we were determined to make the most of it while it lasted.

I was granted some leave at Christmas and spent several lovely days in Salzburg. Then, in the middle of January, I was finally passed fit for duties. This was welcome news. Now at last I could return to my old unit at the front where I could renew all my old friendships and once again share their experiences in battle.

Unfortunately things did not turn out as I had expected or hoped. Instead of receiving my travel orders to the front, I was ordered to report to the special test Gruppe at Jüterbog. When I arrived I was told that I had been selected as a test pilot at the ERLA factory at Leipzig where the latest variant of the Me 109 was being manufactured. This was a civilian-run unit so I was to be granted sabbatical leave from the military. I would therefore have to give up my uniform and replace it with civilian clothing. After being given my marching orders to ERLA-Leipzig I left my No 2 Staffel in a state of acute disappointment and departed for the railway station, where I took a train to Leipzig. On arrival I was met at the station and was taken to meet my new boss, the chief pilot. I was given a polite reception and the basics of my new job were explained to me. It was all rather straightforward really. ERLA built around 300 of the new Me 109 G-6s a month, from which the factory test pilots were allocated between twenty-five and thirty each to 'fly in' before they could be issued to the front-line units. After all my efforts to get myself out of a training organisation and to the front, this was the bitter end. As I was politely introduced to the other eight test flight pilots I tried hard to conceal my bitter disappointment at this unwelcome turn of events.

There was no accommodation available for me initially so I spent the first few days of my new job accommodated in a local pub. But this arrangement did not last for long and I was soon found private quarters in the centre of Leipzig, with my landlady a widow and singing teacher. It didn't take me too long to settle in and I soon got stuck into my new job in earnest. This was new territory for me and, to my pleasant surprise, I began to find the content of the job to be rather interesting. I had much to learn in the art of test flying and was also pleased to find that my test pilot colleagues were always ready to help, providing me with the wealth of information I required to become truly effective in this new and challenging role.

The factory was a very interesting place, employing many French immigrant workers with whom I felt I was soon getting on rather well. The test flying began to progress nicely too, and I soon felt thoroughly comfortable in my new employment away from the Luftwaffe, effectively as a civilian pilot. However, my by now established routine was soon to be shattered by an incident for which I had not bargained. It came completely unexpectedly on a relatively straightforward flight in an Me 109 G6, flying at full throttle at an altitude of about 6,000 metres. This was all routine stuff and, with no indications that anything was amiss, I casually glanced at my instruments to check that the machine was behaving properly; there was nothing to suggest that it wasn't, so I enjoyed the flight. Then suddenly, and without any warning, my aircraft was violently rocked by a loud explosion in the engine compartment. Almost immediately afterwards, and before I had a chance to survey my instruments to establish the extent of the damage, my machine was engulfed in flames and began to buffet violently.

My initial reaction was to try to hold my machine under control, but as the flames soon made it all but impossible for me to see forward it was clear that I had no choice but to eject the canopy and bale out. With this realisation I reached for the emergency release handle but was horrified to find that, as hard as I pulled, the canopy refused to budge. It was stuck fast! By now the aircraft had become uncontrollable due to a complete loss of visibility through the canopy Perspex and, with waves of panic threatening to overcome me, I placed two hands firmly on the canopy fastening handle and wrenched at it for all I was worth but still did not meet with success. As I persevered with the only course of action open to me, I eventually ended up with the opening handle detached in my hand, but still the roof just would not open. Frantically racking my brains for what to do next I then undid my seat harness and tried with both hands to push the roof off – still nothing. Again waves of panic racked my body as the prospect of death seemed to be getting ever nearer.

However, through a supreme effort of will, I managed to convince myself of the need to stay calm, brought myself under control and collected my strength for one last effort to save my life, which was now hanging on a thread. Adopting a crouched standing position, I placed both hands against the roof and, with both feet flat on the floor, I pushed upwards with every ounce of strength I could muster. My life depended on it. Initially there was no movement, but I was not to be defeated and, finally, it happened. With enormous relief I finally felt the cockpit roof fly away into the sky, upon which

I was hit by a blast of hot air as the oncoming rush of air brought with it the flames from the engine that were engulfing my aircraft. With the machine plunging vertically towards the ground my hands and face were now being singed by the ferocity of the heat. But at that moment I had more important matters on my mind – if I wanted to survive, I had to get out of the machine and, with my altitude rapidly decreasing, I didn't have much time.

Looking downwards I seemed to be over an industrial installation of some sort, hardly the ideal ground to parachute down onto but I was in no position to choose where I fell and to remain in the aircraft meant almost certain death. So, with all my remaining strength, I climbed out of the cockpit and pushed against the fuselage with both legs, falling safely away from my stricken machine. At that point I believe I must have lapsed into unconsciousness since I have no recollection of the initial part of my fall. The first image I recall was one of clouds, blue sky, the ground, railway tracks and a large industrial site. I then pulled my ripcord and my parachute sprung open with an unfamiliar popping sound. As I dangled from the rigging I looked up to check that everything was all right and, to my horror, saw that part of the parachute was torn, with gaping holes preventing it from doing its job properly and arresting my descent to a degree that would give me a reasonable chance of a safe landing. I quickly looked downwards in an effort to see where I was likely to land and perhaps get a better idea of my speed of descent. As I did so I found myself looking at an equally shocking sight, the soles of my feet. When I had baled out I must have fallen onto the fuselage and twisted my feet. This would explain my apparent loss of consciousness. But there was no time to worry about this now as I was nearing the ground and things were starting to happen very quickly.

Directly beneath me lay the industrial site, with a battery of cooling towers in its centre surrounded by large buildings. As I surveyed the rapidly approaching scene below me my machine plunged past me, crashing into one of the buildings, which immediately began to burn. I frantically considered how best to land since landing on my upturned feet was clearly going to be very painful. But there was no longer any time as the cooling towers came racing towards me and I prepared myself for the worst. However, to my good fortune my parachute caught on a platform on the edge of one of the towers, arresting my fall. I swung violently and, as I did so, my head struck the outer covering of the tower, injuring my forehead.

This movement had been sudden and painful but I had at least stopped falling, which, for the time being, had prevented my feet from incurring any further injury. I now hung like a jumping jack, dangling in my harness waiting for whatever was going to happen next but grateful that things had turned out reasonably well for me in the end.

I was hanging about 30 metres up the tower and, as I dangled helplessly, I watched people on the ground frantically dashing around in an effort to do something about the building, which seemed to be burning out of control. Firemen had already arrived and were trying to extinguish the flames, but as yet no one had seen me hanging on the tower wall so I began to call down for help.

Finally, after what seemed like an age of shouting and arm waving, a fireman spotted me and gathered some of his colleagues together, presumably to initiate a rescue. After a quick chat, during which I could clearly see their faces as they looked up at me, they disappeared in a number of directions. They were not away for long, however, and before long they had reappeared with their fire engine, which they parked at the base of the chimney. They then began to extend the ladder until it reached high up onto the wall, eventually reaching the point where I was hanging so helplessly. As it contacted me it did not stop its ascent but continued to rise, in turn raising me to the height of the walking platform that surrounded the chimney at approximately three-quarters of its height. When I got there, there were several pairs of hands waiting to drag me onto the platform and I was soon lying on it being questioned by my curious rescuers.

As several more people quickly arrived on the platform the first question I was asked was whether I was English or German. I quickly explained that I was a test pilot for the ERLA-Leipzig firm, whereupon I was promptly given emergency aid. Meanwhile, a group of onlookers had gathered on the ground below, eager to see who this mysterious pilot actually was who had just dropped out of the sky; I was suddenly very glad that I was a Luftwaffe pilot, and not an enemy who doubtless would otherwise have incurred their wrath due to a particularly destructive series of air raids they had recently experienced.

Initially my rescuers wanted to lower me using a mountain rescue sack, but this did not seem to be the brightest of ideas to me and I declined to go along with their plan. I was then given a body harness, to which I was duly fastened and told that I was to abseil down the chimney, using the ladder to steady me. I hadn't done this sort of thing before so I was a little nervous at the prospect, but, deciding that I didn't want to spend the rest of the day up that chimney, I promptly followed their instructions and began to lower myself downwards. Despite my initial consternation, this method of descent did not in the event prove to be too difficult at all, although my descent was somewhat faster than I had imagined. Just before I reached the ground, the medics took over and gently lifted me onto a stretcher. Then, just as I was expecting to be taken away to somewhere where I would receive some proper medical attention, the director of the company into which I had fallen arrived, together with his wife, and introduced themselves to me. The director then explained that he had an excellent set of medics and that they would take care of me until I could be taken to a hospital. They all seemed very friendly and, as the medics did what they could to make my feet more comfortable, the director's wife handed me a glass of schnapps and, raising our glasses, we made a toast and downed our drinks. There was of course also a policeman present and he now busied himself taking a series of statements. As this went on, I was given a light anaesthetic, which unfortunately meant that I was not able to continue drinking the schnapps I was being offered, which was a pity since I was by now starting to feel a lot better.

After all the formalities had been taken care of, I was taken by ambulance to a hospital in Leipzig. Throughout the journey, which lasted about 50 minutes, a medic sat at my side, keeping an eye on my condition. When we eventually reached the hospital it seemed that they were not expecting us and that the hospital was full; in any event, no one there was prepared to take me in.

Quickly departing for an alternative hospital, we drove around for a while longer until we arrived at the Leipzig First Reserve Hospital, which, it turned out, was run by a religious order of some sort. Thankfully they were not full and declared themselves ready to take me in.

Once it was clear that I was going in, I was carried out of the ambulance and my stretcher was set down in the hospital reception area. Then, after what seemed a considerable time, a doctor finally appeared and, without further delay, examined my injuries. When he had seen enough he embarked on a discussion with the nurse, calmly telling her, among other things, that my right lower leg would have to be amputated!

On hearing this, shock waves pulsated through me and I was suddenly wide awake, my defence mechanism in action. I hurriedly explained to the doctor that this was simply out of the question for me as I was a pilot and would not be able to remain so without any feet – they simply had to find another way! This outburst seemed to have some effect since there then ensued a lengthy discussion during which I continued to speak out vehemently against an operation. Another doctor was called for and, after a while, an older staff doctor appeared and made his own examination. Satisfied with what he had found, he then set about calming me down, explaining that it would after all be possible to repair the bone without amputation. On hearing this I breathed a huge sigh of relief – my stubbornness had won the day.

I was then taken to a small empty room where the nurses set about removing my clothes, giving me instead a hospital gown and a sedative injection. By now it was quite late, but the hospital staff went to work on my feet immediately, continuing their work well into the night as I slept comfortably, under the influence of the anaesthetic they had given me. They had little difficulty in sorting out my left ankle, but my right ankle was much more badly damaged and needed major surgery.

I awoke from the anaesthetic at 6.00am and opened my eyes to my first hospital visitors of the day. However, I felt no elation at this particular show of concern after my welfare since, as my eyes struggled to focus, I soon recognised the uniforms of the men sitting beside my bed as those of the SS/SD, the Security Service of the SS. These men did not smile and did not waste time on polite formalities but began to question me immediately. They wanted to know all about the crash and, in particular, why I had crashed my aircraft into the Brawag installation when there had been no reports of any enemy air activity in the area at that time. My head spun at the implications of what they were saying, but I was too groggy either to think clearly or to give them any sort of coherent reply. As I struggled to respond I was suddenly, and very fortunately, rescued by a doctor on duty who forbade any further questioning until I had had chance to sleep off the medication. I was left to sleep in peace.

At around midday I was transferred to a five-bed room, my right foot in a splint, the leg in plaster and my head bandaged. As I lay awake in my new surroundings, with time to deliberate over the events that had led to my confinement, the tension I had felt since my visit from the SS began to ease and my thoughts were now consumed by my last flight, which had so nearly ended in complete disaster for me. Above all else, one thought consumed me – had I made some kind of mistake? As my thoughts raced back and forth over each and every aspect of the flight, from take off to baling out, I became more and more convinced that I had not been at fault and that I had done everything possible to try to save the machine and prevent the crash that had followed. Under the circumstances in which I had found myself, there was little if anything that I could have done to have prevented my aircraft from crashing into the factory below. What I did not know, but which, if I had, would have set my mind at rest regarding any thoughts of my own negligence, was that, on the same day as my crash, other test pilots from the factory had also mysteriously crashed during similar test flights.

In the afternoon the uniformed men of the SS/SD reappeared and continued to question me about the crash, although their manner had by now become noticeably less hostile towards me. They told me that my machine had crashed into a hall at the Brawag factory in Böhlen, near Leipzig, causing a considerable amount of damage. Brawag was a hydrogenation plant that produced automotive fuel from coal and was therefore important to the war effort. Once they had completed their questioning, however, they did not reappear, so it was soon clear to me that I was not in trouble with the authorities in the way I had feared, and settled down to recover from my injuries. I was later to learn that the subsequent board of inquiry had concluded that my crash, in common with the other similar incidents that day involving other test pilots, had been caused by sabotage, more than likely at the hands of the approximately forty percent of French workers employed in the factory. The enquiry conclusively showed that an explosive device had been placed in the engine of my aircraft.

My first days in the hospital were not at all pleasant, as I was in constant pain. My roommates were soldiers who had been wounded in Russia and their injuries were also bad. The Reserve Hospital that we were in had formerly been a Catholic Hospital but had now been requisitioned by the military. The doctors were now mainly military although it retained nuns as nurses. The inmates of my room all had the same surgeon, which was fortunate for all of us since he was outstanding and we therefore received the best possible care.

Despite the seriousness of my own injuries, my roommates were all more badly injured than myself; I was the only one, for example, who could use my hands. In the bed next to me was an SS man who had already been in hospital for six months. He was in a very bad way with two badly shot-up legs and having been blinded in both eyes. He had been riding a motor cycle during the attack on Kaluga when he had driven over a mine. I felt particularly sorry for him. But our convalescence was made bearable by our nurse, Amadea, who took a great deal of trouble over us, working exceptionally hard to look after us. I was also visited by the directors of the ERLA factory. They told me that they were very much looking forward to me returning to the factory after my convalescence. But my thoughts were with my old Staffel in Russia; I desperately wanted to go back to 8 Staffel, back to my old comrades.

Time passed slowly but after several weeks I made my first attempts at walking with crutches. Once I could move around the hospital I would be allowed to go into town, so I worked hard to master the technique with my two injured feet. Then one day the monotony of hospital life was broken by a miracle in our midst. After more than six months the man in the bed next to me had finally regained his sight. It was a wonderful moment and we were all thrilled for him.

I received regular visits from my colleagues at the ERLA factory who kept me amused with all their latest flying stories, and also kept me up to date regarding the new Me 109 series that the factory was now producing. By now I was becoming much more mobile, and therefore more independent, and with this the healing process seemed to accelerate. I began to feel that I would soon be fit for active duty again.

In July I was ordered to report to the Pilots' Examination Centre at Halle/Dallan in order to assess whether I was fit for service. I spent fourteen days in Halle and had a great time there. More importantly, I got the result I wanted – fit for flying duties.

My use of my connections with my old Staffel worked beautifully for me this time and, to my enormous relief, I was informed that I was to return to the front for operational duties. However, there were a number of stages I would have to go through before I would be able to rejoin my old comrades. First I had to 'rejoin' the military, after which I would have to be converted to the Focke-Wulf FW 190. My initial move was to Jüterbog, to a special operational training unit where I was given back my uniform, prior to my first conversion flight on the FW 190. A mechanic drove me to where the aircraft were parked and uncovered the nearest machine for my first close-up view of the 190. I stared at it for a moment, taking in the differences between it and the trusty old Me 109. It seemed to be bigger, more rugged yet less sleek than the 109, but the comparison would be made in the air and I was keen to get airborne to see how she performed.

Having looked over this somewhat sturdy-looking bird, I climbed into the cockpit, whereupon the mechanic explained the intricacies of

A line-up of Focke-Wulf FW 190s of II./SchG 1 at Deblin-Irena early in 1943.
The aircraft are all very clean, and most seem to have had the sides of their
engine cowlings recently resprayed with RLM 65 paint. At least three carry the
unit emblem, but on a red disc to match the spinner fronts.

the machine to me, the instruments in the cockpit, the start-up procedure
and the peculiarities of take off and landing. The weather was beautiful
and the air was clear, with no low-lying mist or cross-winds to trouble
me, so I could make my first conversion flight there and then.

I strapped myself in and adjusted the rudder pedals, all the time
casting my eyes over the instruments, familiarising myself with

Unteroffizier Wiezorck,
Hermann Buchner's crew chief,
in front of 'his' aircraft,
probably in the Ukraine in
autumn 1943.

Otto Dommeratzky of 8./SchG 1 and his crew chief. The FW 190, Blue or Black
'T', is extremely weathered and the white of the fuselage cross appears to have
been darkened. Again, the photograph was probably taken in the Ukraine near
Kiev in the autumn of 1943.

their layout. Once satisfied, I went through the engine priming procedure, yelled to the mechanic to 'clear prop' and hit the starter. The engine fired first time and the BMW air-cooled radial roared into life. I then waved to the mechanic to remove the wheel chocks and taxied the aircraft to the take off point, taking care to line it up properly, and once again checked over the instruments. Once I was satisfied that I was ready to go, I radioed to the tower, requesting permission to lift; the reply came back, 'Cleared to take off.' I then opened the throttle to its maximum and the machine began to move forward, quickly gathering pace. After what seemed like a very short time the Focke-Wulf began to lift, at which point I gently pulled back the stick and we were airborne. Almost without thinking I now raised the landing gear and flaps and the machine quickly picked up speed. It was a great feeling to be in the saddle again after so many months.

Once I had reached a safe altitude, I tried my first manoeuvres, gently banking the aircraft to left and right, gradually increasing the steepness and tightness of the turns as my confidence in this new and unfamiliar machine grew. The aircraft contained no unpleasant surprises and seemed to be remarkably easy to fly. Pretty soon I was thoroughly enjoying myself, revelling in the experience of flying after such a long absence. However, I did not allow myself to be carried away by my excitement and restricted myself to just doing enough to get the feel of the machine without being too adventurous on my first flight. Once I was happy that I had done enough, I flew back to the airfield and began the landing process. Having announced my intentions over the radio, I lowered the undercarriage and landing flaps and held my position for landing. As the runway drew up I raised the nose into the stall position and eased the aircraft down for a perfect three-point landing, final proof to myself that I had not forgotten how to fly. I subsequently made a few more circuits, gaining in confidence with each flight, until I was completely at ease with this wonderful aircraft. My appetite for returning to the front was now greater than ever; my posting to a front-line unit must have no further delays.

After a week's stand-down in Jüterbog I was posted to Erganzungsgruppe Deblin-Irena, south of Warsaw. I already had some acquaintances among the many pilots there, who also wanted to get to the front. I did not spend long there, however, no more than ten days, and in any event I did not feel that I belonged in such an organisation after all my previous experience at the front. All I wanted was to get back there, to my old comrades in my own 8 Staffel. Finally, after what seemed like an inordinate amount of wasted time, my transfer came through and I was finally able to pack my bags and get moving. I took the good old train, the surest way of reaching one's destination at that time, and travelled to Lemberg where I was able to catch a transport plane to Kharkov. That part of the journey went relatively quickly. The 'bus drivers' who flew the Jus always gladly took the Schlachter pilots along with them. At Kharkov I had a further two-day wait before again taking a Ju 52 to Varvarovka, the airfield from which my Geschwader was operating. It was early July 1943 and, after a prolonged and eventful absence, I was about to rejoin my old Staffel where I would be back with my old comrades at last. I began to feel a sense of apprehensive excitement – excited by the prospect of resuming operations with my old comrades, apprehensive about what I would find and how many of my old friends would no longer be there.

When I arrived my first move was to report to the Gruppenkommandeur. Once the formalities were over he told me that, during my long absence, Stollnberger had become Staffelkapitän and, of the old pilots, only Dommeratzky and Ohm were still there. I struggled to hide my disappointment that so many of my old comrades were either dead or had been transferred to other units, thanked him for his time, and moved into my tent, my place of abode for the foreseeable future.

Fortunately for me, I did not have to fly on my first day back at the Staffel, so I settled down to enjoy the warm summer sunshine and catch up on all the news. It was glorious weather and rumours were rife that we were about to embark on another summer offensive, making the most of the fine flying weather and firm going for tanks and wheeled vehicles. I made the most of my day off; I knew that it would probably be quite a while before I got another.

The following day Ohm and I were tasked to carry out an early-morning mission over the front. In common with the many previous dawn sorties I had flown, we took off in near total darkness, guided only by electric lights and the glow of the exhausts from the machine in front. There were four of us taking part in this mission and, as soon as we were airborne, we formed up into a loose Schwarm formation and I settled into position

Feldwebel Hermann Buchner seen in a formal portrait taken during home leave in Salzburg in 1943. He wears the Iron Cross in both 1st and 2nd Class grades, the Schlachtflieger Operational Flying Clasp, what appears to be the Combined Pilot and Observer badge, and the civilian Glider Pilot's 'C' Certificate Badge. On his pocket flap is the ribbon of the medal commemorating the entry into Czechoslovakia with the 'Prague Castle' bar. In his lapel is a small enamel badge featuring the infantry assault badge emblem.

Groundcrew parade in front of their new charges at Deblin-Irena in Poland in March 1943, as SG 1 converts to the Focke-Wulf FW 190. 'Mickey Mouse' is now on a red disc, the same colour as the spinner tip, but whether this was in use as a Staffel or Gruppe marking is not clear.

behind and to one side of Ohm, the Schwarm leader, as I had been tasked to fly as his wingman, the number two of the Schwarm. As the colours of dawn began to break through, the clearness of the early morning air made it possible to see for miles around. We took in the beauty of the morning, scanning the sky for signs of enemy aircraft, but all was quiet and peaceful, no sign of anyone else being airborne at that moment in time. The calm atmosphere and the exhilaration of being airborne made it possible, just for the moment, to forget the war and any thought of danger, and simply enjoy the peace and solitude of the morning. However, I did not let such thoughts consume me for long since the somewhat surreal feeling of wellbeing in such a potentially hostile sky gradually made me feel uncomfortable; it all seemed a little too quiet, enticing us to lower our guard. However, I didn't let it worry me too much since I was flying with four seasoned professionals in whom I had complete faith. In particular, our Schwarm leader was enormously experienced and I reassured myself that he knew exactly what he was doing and settled down to concentrate on making my first mission since my return to operations a good one.

After 40 minutes flying time we turned west at an altitude of about 4,000 metres at which point Ohm's voice suddenly crackled in my ears, to ask me where we were! Unfortunately, I wasn't too sure myself, so I was unable to give him a satisfactory answer. It was an uncomfortable moment. Continuing in a generally westward direction, we then flew back and forth over the area, trying to find something on the ground with which to orientate ourselves. After a while, I started to get the distinctly uncomfortable feeling that this flight could turn out very badly for us and redoubled my efforts in searching for a landmark that I could recognise on the map. Suddenly my thoughts were interrupted by the excited voice of our number four over the radio, who began shouting into his throat mike, 'An airfield under us!'

I banked my aircraft to see where he was indicating, puzzled as to why I had not seen it first, and soon realised that he was mistaken. What he had seen was a row of former artillery settlements, lined up in a row, giving the impression from altitude of a hastily constructed grass airstrip. As we went down for a closer look, we could soon make out scars on the landscape, indicating to us that at some time a battle had taken place in this area. However, with a significant proportion of our fuel consumed, and still with no idea of where we were, we were going to have to abandon our mission and concentrate on finding our way back to our own airfield. Without putting too fine a point on it, we were lost. As we flew on, searching for anything that may give us a clue as to our whereabouts, a railway line suddenly appeared under us. We were really too high to gain any real clues from this, so I radioed to Ohm to stay where he was to cover me, while I went a bit lower to get a better look. There is such an expression as airman's luck, and at that point in time we desperately needed some. As if by divine providence, a goods train suddenly appeared on the horizon, steaming towards us from the south-west. I turned my aircraft to fly towards it, straining to see anything that would give away the nationality of the train. Either way, we would soon know which side of the front we were on, at least. I passed over the train at high speed and, as I did so, I could clearly make out the familiar shapes of German vehicles loaded on the railway trucks. I was momentarily overjoyed at the relief of the train being one of ours, although I still did not know where we were. But our exact location was no longer my primary concern since, now that I had established that we were safely behind our own lines, we could look for a place to land. This had become our most important consideration as we had by now been airborne for almost 12 hours and were getting precariously short of fuel.

As I flew on ahead of the train, in a north-westerly direction, I pulled up again and looked around for a place suitable for us to land, radioing to Ohm to explain my intentions. Before long I had found what looked like a field suitable for our purposes, which was conveniently located close to a level-crossing attendant's house. I banked my aircraft and began to circle, carefully surveying the field for any obstacles that would be likely to present a hazard to us, and went down for a closer look. It didn't seem at all bad, so I concluded that this would suit our purposes and lined myself up in a direction parallel to the railway line to make my approach to land.

As I touched down the machine rolled along remarkably smoothly; the ground was actually smoother than I had expected, and I rolled to a halt without difficulty. I then radioed to Ohm to remain airborne until I had had chance to check that we would be safe here, screwed the throttle tight shut and dismounted from my machine, my PPK pistol in my hand, ready to fire. As I walked across the field towards the railwayman's house, some Russian women appeared and began walking towards me. They seemed friendly enough and told me that there were German soldiers nearby, some of whom were accommodated in the railwayman's house. Happy that it was now safe for the others to land, I jogged back to my aircraft and, leaning over the side of the cockpit, turned the power on and reached for the throat mike. Ohm answered my call immediately, whereupon I explained to him that it was safe for the rest of the Schwarm to land and that, once down, we would be able to use the soldiers' radio to get some fuel brought to us.

Within only a couple of minutes of my call, the other three machines were safely on the ground and we all thanked our lucky stars that, after having flown to near the limit of our endurance in a condition of total disorientation, we had still managed to land safely behind German lines. We then made our way to the railwayman's house to speak to the soldiers in there who, as luck would have it, turned out to be from a signals unit. After consultation with them and a careful study of the map, we soon knew where we were and made a radio call to Division to inform them of our location and, at the same time, ask that some fuel be delivered.

We were actually mid-way between Kharkov and Poltava, around 300km away from our own airfield. It was fortunate, therefore, that the signals soldiers had a good relationship with the Russian women since we were all provided with a hearty breakfast. We were in no

When the German forces occupied Russian villages it was usual to find that the population consisted almost entirely of women and young children. The men were almost all either in the army or had left to join a partisan band. These typical Russian peasant women are seen in a village near Tazinskaya in July 1942.

The primitive conditions in which most Russian peasants lived can be gauged from the state of the house behind these women, who appear to be sorting grapes at Kallatsch, somewhere on the steppes in the Don basin, in August 1942.

doubt that we would be stuck there for some time since, in the first instance, we had to wait for further orders from our division. Until we heard from them, we simply had to sit tight, and wait.

The soldiers did their bit to make us feel at home, supplying us with generous quantities of bread and vodka. As we chatted merrily about our exploits during the day, we each knew that our biggest problem was yet to come; how on earth were we going to explain getting lost to the boss? The weather was fine and we had had no enemy contact so there were no obvious excuses readily at hand, nor were any of us really sure what the explanation was. Why had we become disorientated?

At around midday we received the radio message from Division that we had been waiting for, informing us that a Ju 52 carrying enough fuel to get us back would be arriving in the next few hours. Happy with the good news, we sat back and waited for the familiar drone of the three engines of the good old Junkers. At around 1500hrs we began to make out the faint sound of an aircraft engine and, rushing outside, we strained our eyes to make out where the sound was coming from. When we eventually spotted the machine we were looking for, its silhouette was unmistakably that of a Ju 52, obviously the one that had been sent out to bring us the fuel that we needed. Without wasting any time, we sent up a distress flare and set alight one of our location marking roman candles. As we watched, anxious that the pilot had seen our markers, the Ju banked towards us and flew past, positioning itself for an into-wind landing. Landing had not been a problem for our FWs so the big transport would not be troubled by the terrain and I was quite convinced from the couple of times that I had had the opportunity to pilot one of these big birds that there was ample room for him to land. Sure enough, the landing was no problem at all for the Ju 52, which pulled up in front of our machines that we had parked in a row at the edge of the field. It was going to be a different proposition, however, to figure out how to transfer the fuel from the Junkers to our own machines. Nevertheless, with the help of the signals boys and a large number of fuel cans, we managed to solve that particular problem and eventually got our aircraft fuelled up for the trip back to our airfield. Having thanked the Ju crew, the signals boys and the Russian women, we climbed into our machines and started the engines. A short while later we were back in the air, formed up into Schwarm formation ready for a low-level and direct trip back to our airfield.

After approximately 40 minutes in the air we reached our airfield, landed and taxied to our parking spots. We turned off the engines and, one by one, climbed out, mentally preparing ourselves for the onslaught that we would soon have to face. The mechanics didn't help matters by telling us that we could expect a real rocket from the boss. We laughed nonchalantly at their remarks but we knew that they were right – there was going to be hell to pay. Rather sheepishly, we reported to the command post where the boss met, or perhaps even exceeded, all our expectations and really bawled us out. Unfortunately, we didn't really have any excuses to hand so we kept quiet and took it. When it was all over and we had time to reflect on our experience, we knew that we were all one lesson wiser and were each determined never to let such a fundamental and potentially catastrophic thing happen again.

The battle for Orel and Kursk raged to a ferocious climax and, faced with a Russian advance of overwhelming force, our ground troops were forced to retreat. In order to maintain our distance from the front line, we correspondingly moved our operating base to Kharkov-Rogan. I remembered the airfield from the summer of 1942 when we had been on the advance. I had happy memories of the place but much had changed in the intervening period and the magnitude of our task now seemed to be much more daunting. Our Russian opponents were now not only greater in number, but were also using much better equipment and were tactically more aware. On my previous visit I was flying as a wingman to more experienced operational pilots than myself. Now I was one of the old hands, this time leading a Schwarm. As always, I was on the go from early morning until late evening when, with daylight almost gone, I would grab a late-night meal and collapse onto my bed, totally exhausted. The weather was glorious almost every day so there was no respite to the intensity of operations, which, in addition to taking its toll on the exhausted pilots, put enormous pressure on the mechanics and armourers who were on hand before and after every sortie and worked virtually round the clock to keep us operationally effective.

As the daily grind of mission after mission continued, our reminiscences of any particular trip tended to blur with others and it was only the exceptional trips that we remembered. One such mission was when we caught a Russian fuel supply column in the open as it tried to make its way to re-supply the tank units in the south. There were between ten and fourteen vehicles in the convoy and, electing to attack, my Rotte leader took the lead vehicle and I set about the rearmost vehicle, immediately setting it afire with my guns. The column was thus brought to an immediate standstill. We were then in a position to pick off our targets until they were all destroyed. The target shooting began in earnest with us attacking entirely at will, as though we were practicing on some spectacular shooting range that had been laid on especially for us. The game lasted a quarter of an hour until all the vehicles were burning brightly, with the dense smoke climbing to some 500 or 600 metres into the air and visible for miles around. As we paused to survey the destruction we had wrought, it was perfectly clear that these vehicles wouldn't be fuelling up any more Russian tanks and, pleased with our work, we turned for home. This was one of many spectacular attacks on a multitude of ground targets that sticks in my memory, but there were many, many more as there never seemed to be an end to the targets on the ground that presented themselves to us.

In spite of all our efforts, and a superhuman effort by the Army, the ground troops could not halt the onslaught, which was relentless. Under the overwhelming pressure that the Russians were able to apply, the front often moved so quickly that our commanders were

Leutnant Fröhlich and the unit transport NCO of SchG 1 somewhere in the Kuban bridgehead in March 1943. Fröhlich wears the white sheepskin jerkin of the two-piece winter-weight flying suit, which was being introduced into service at about this time.

A group of cold-looking pilots of the 6th Staffel of SG 2 somewhere in Russia in the autumn of 1943.

Berer haggling in the market in Kiev, late in 1943. Note on the table the stove with its large chimney.

unable to keep up with the fluidity of the situation. On the edge of our airfield was a main road that was a principal supply route to the front and, as such, was in regular use by Army units, including the infantry. One day, as one of many infantry units to pass by marched past us, our mechanics, ever eager to glean whatever information they could, asked the soldiers where they were marching to. The soldiers replied that they were withdrawing westwards and added that they were the last of the Divisional Regiments to withdraw and, if we waited around any longer, the next unit to arrive would be Russian. This cheerful news really sparked us into action. We immediately reported the news to our boss who went straight to the Gruppenkommandeur to make him aware of the urgency of the situation. Geschwader and Divisional Headquarters were immediately informed of our predicament and we nervously awaited orders to move.

Within no more than an hour our Gruppe had transferred westward, to Pol-Rudka, an airfield north of Poltava. Although we were now safely out of the mire, we took little comfort in it since we were all somewhat disturbed that, in the confusion of the rapidly moving situation, no one had informed our Gruppe of what was going on. We were soon to discover how close we had come to disaster since, that same evening, Rogan was taken by the Russians. We had, nevertheless, managed to transfer all our ground element, our equipment and our machines back without any casualties. We were like a travelling circus; each of us knew his duty and, at the blowing of a whistle, the whole outfit simply pulled out. We did not leave one machine behind. In their customary manner, the trusty Ju 52 crews were right on the spot to help us. Without them we in the East would long since have gone under. Those brave crews who flew continuously, often incurring horrific losses, were the unsung heroes of the Luftwaffe.

Pol-Rudka was an airfield that had been converted from an ordinary farmer's field. To the south of the field was the local village and, when we were able to get across there and have a look, we found the villagers to be very friendly. Our operations from here were to the north and the north-west. Our first task was a reconnaissance mission to ascertain the locations of our own troop units, the position of the forward lines, and to get a feel of the general situation so that it could be reported back up to Division. As we arrived at what appeared to be the front line, we were actually able to see areas that were still being overrun by the Russians. The spearhead of the drive by the

Russian tanks was rapidly pushing south and south-west. The implications of what we were witnessing were obvious to all of us; the Russians had broken through our front lines in several places and were in the process of a massive push forward.

As always, our mechanics had their hands full as we were on the go from very early morning until late evening. Our main task was to engage known formations of enemy tanks and their supply units. As we returned from mission after mission we reported huge numbers of tanks and supply vehicles destroyed, but we did so with no particular elation since we knew that the sheer quantity of equipment that the Russians had at their disposal meant that, despite our Herculean efforts, we were really only scratching the surface. We could inflict considerable damage on them, but the flood had become a tidal wave and we Schlachtflieger were too few in number to halt it.

A montage of two pictures showing a German aircraft graveyard somewhere in Russia. The carcases of two SchG 1 Bf 109Es can be seen, the nearest clearly marked with the Schlacht triangle. Other machines visible are from JG 53 and JG 2.

Another montage showing abandoned Bf 109Es, two of which were once with II./SchG 1. Of interest is the wing carrying the yellow Romanian cross insignia.

The situation was so confused that, at one stage, we were able to see a long column of Wehrmacht vehicles heading south with, ahead of them and a few kilometres further to the west, a Russian tank unit speedily advancing. It was a motley column, a mix of tanks, heavy vehicles and self-propelled artillery, secured on its flanks by infantry. On seeing this and realising the potential for disaster if they were not warned of the situation they found themselves in, I decided that someone would have to land near the column in order to speak to them. First I wanted to make absolutely sure that we were not mistaken and that they were definitely our own soldiers down there.

We flew in closer to take a better look and, as we did so, they laid a number of cloths out over the tops of their vehicles, obviously having already decided that we were friendly and wishing to avoid any chance of being attacked by their own side. I then told the Rotte leader of my intention to land, and ordered him to circle over the area while I made absolutely sure that it was safe for me to do so. As soon as I was happy, I put my machine down without difficulty near some vehicles. I then throttled my engine back to idle and secured the throttle. I was still occupied in the cockpit when a motorcyclist and officer pulled up beside my aircraft. After climbing out and introducing myself I explained why I had landed, whereupon the officer informed me which units were in the column and explained that they were unaware of the situation in their area, except in very general terms, and that they desperately needed orders to tell them where to head for. I promised him that I would be back in no more than 2 hours with orders for him, then climbed back into my cockpit, opened the throttle and took off.

Once back in the air I was picked up by my comrades and we flew straight back to Pol-Rudka. As soon as I landed I went straight to the command post to report the results of my reconnaissance mission. The fact that there were German units still intact in the depths of the Russian breakthrough, and thus, given the right orders, in a position to surprise the Russians from their rear, was greeted as welcome news. Our Kommandeur got in touch with the Corps Headquarters immediately and, after a short while, I was given the task of returning to the column that I had discovered and once again landing there to give them their orders from Corps. In addition, I was to seek out any other German units that were in a similar position and to let them know what the situation was. I was given maps to take, which had been marked with the known enemy positions and the withdrawal routes that the German units were to take. This time I was to turn off the engine, hand over the orders directly to the commander, clarify the situation and bring back any messages or requirements.

My Schwarm was soon airborne again heading in the direction of the missing German troop column. As soon as we found them I landed, putting my machine down close to a smoke dispenser, which had been put out to indicate to me where I was to land. When I got down I realised that they had prepared a deliberate spot for me that was within easy reach of the commanding General. I radioed to my Rotte leader to keep the remainder of the Schwarm circling above the column and wait for me to return to my aircraft. I expected to be no more than 30 to 40 minutes, by which time I should have finished my job on the ground and be ready to take off again.

Once I had brought my machine to a halt, I switched off the engine and climbed out of the cockpit. I then jumped into the vehicle that had pulled up beside me, ready to take me to the waiting General. The driver held the door open for me and, once inside, we headed for the Command Vehicle at full speed. The vehicle then ground to a rapid halt whereupon the door was once again opened for me and I was taken to the General. With the introductions quickly over, I made my report and handed over the prepared maps. At the same time, I asked if there were any urgent requirements for the troops. The General had a number of requests to make but it was not long before I was once again ready to return to my aircraft. I promised to ensure that all of the General's requests were passed on and added that I would return once again with any answers. The escorting officer then took me back to my machine in his vehicle.

Back at my aircraft I took leave of the infantrymen who had been left to guard it and climbed back into the cockpit. Once back in my seat, I strapped myself in and hit the starting button. The engine fired into life immediately and I prepared myself for take off. Shortly afterwards, I gave the waiting soldiers a short nod, indicating that I was ready to go and, with the engine howling, I began my take off run, quickly gathering speed. As the rapidly growing cloud of dust behind me began to obscure my rearward vision, I was suddenly airborne, having been away for little more than 20 minutes. My Schwarm then rejoined me and we flew back to Pol-Rudka, grateful that the whole episode had passed off without an enemy encounter.

Once we had landed back at our own airfield, events began to gather pace. Corps Headquarters was immediately informed of my report and the necessary arrangements to evacuate the missing troops went into action. As for myself, I had to return once again to the column as soon as my machine had been refuelled. This time my trip was deemed to be a little less dangerous since my task was now simply to drop a message container to the troops below. I was therefore told that I was to take a wingman only and we took off almost immediately for the final leg of my unusual liaison mission.

My last trip to the column went off without a hitch and, that same evening, the isolated troops were supplied with the fuel and ammunition that the General had asked for, their supplies being delivered by a Ju 52 transport unit that flew in with accompanying fighter escort. They landed close to where I had put down my FW 190 earlier in the day and, once they had handed over their supplies, they took the columns' Red Cross nurses and wounded on board and took off for the German lines.

A few days later the Gross Deutschland Division made a counter-attack north of Pol-Rudka and picked up the incoming troops that had been making their way to that part of the front, as per the orders that I had delivered to their commanding General. The detached troops managed to get back to the Corps with only minor casualties and a disastrous situation involving large numbers of our own troops had been averted.

The intensity of our missions from Pol-Rudka continued, during which time I flew my 300th mission against the enemy. But the intensity of the operations meant that there was no time to have a big celebration and we flew on. However, I got my reward a few days later when we were told that, due in no small part to our success in destroying so much armour from the air, the situation along the Dneiper had finally stabilised. Suitably pleased with our work, we allowed ourselves a brief period of respite from the relentless flying, before things hotted up again, as we knew they soon would.

A shirtless Hermann Buchner greets an old schoolfriend who had been wounded and was being evacuated from the Kuban bridgehead on one of the ubiquitous Junkers 52s. Many thousands of German servicemen owe their lives to the rugged dependability of this ponderous aircraft.

Although strong and reliable, the Junkers 52 was not invulnerable. Hundreds of aircraft, with their crews, were lost trying to bring supplies in and wounded out. The one seen blazing furiously here crashed during the advance at Kamensk in 1942. Another Ju 52 can be seen low down in the distance, while what appears to be the wreck of a Russian R-5 lies in the background.

Two unidentified NCO pilots from 6./SG 2 share a joke at Bakau, Romania. The blurred figure on the right wearing the breast badge of the German Cross may be the author.

Even before the author can leave the cockpit at Pol-Rudka on 27 August 1943, his faithful groundcrew are ready with a placard to congratulate him on reaching 300 operational sorties.

The author celebrates his safe return from his 300th operational mission to his base at Pol-Rudka in the Ukraine.

On the same day Hermann Buchner receives the congratulations of his squadron mates after completing his 300th operational mission. On his left is Otto Dommeratzky.

Chapter Nine

From now on, fire-fighting
Autumn 1943-May 1944

A ll hell had broken loose on the Mius. The Russians had broken through and we moved to the area south of Stalino. From early until late we flew against the tanks that had broken through and the mounted infantry, but also against the cavalry regiments who rode in masses westwards over the steppes. Our troops were overtaxed, they were inundated, a flood rolled away over them. One day an enemy tank column succeeded in breaking through to our airfield. Everyone who was available was pulled in to help load bombs and ammunition. Everybody – the cooks, the clerks, the cleaners, the sergeants – buckled to and carried bombs to the machines. We hardly had time to eat a piece of bread. Towards the end the operations lasted only 20 minutes or less.

We brought the last enemy tank to a standstill just before the eastern boundary of the airfield. It was terrible. With 20mm cannon we shot up the cavalry and the mounted infantry. The tanks were successfully fought with 50kg armour-piercing bombs. In any case, there was no mercy: either the attackers were destroyed or our airfield would be overrun. That evening on the eastern side of the airfield smoke still rose from the destroyed tank; the breakthrough had been brought to a standstill, and the sun was heading towards the horizon. Now our cooks had time to prepare a meal for the Staffel. It had been a hard day and the comradeship and the team spirit had paid off. Through our determination we had allowed the troops an easier and more orderly retreat and we had held our airfield.

The next day was peace itself. The enemy had suffered a large number of casualties, and we used the quiet to overhaul the machines. But the battle raged elsewhere and the Schlachtflieger were needed, as unfortunately there was only a single Geschwader. We transferred to northern Stalino in the Donets Basin, and remained there in 1942 during the encirclement of Kharkov. From Stalino we again flew against tanks and accompanying infantry that had broken through the lines. The tanks were our primary targets. We Schlachtflieger, with our robust FW 190s, were needed everywhere, and with our on-board weapons and bombs we achieved good success. However, there were too few of us and the enemy's superior strength was too great. Against the enemy fighters in the air we had no problems, nor did the ground defences (flak) give us any special difficulties, and our losses were few. It was worse, much worse, for the ground troops, the infantry, the tanks – they all had their hands full. Hardly had they put up their lines of resistance when the Soviet T-34 tanks would appear again. Through our non-stop low-level attacks we succeeded in relieving the strain for our own troops.

Aircraft of the Schlachter units were never very colourful, most being almost anonymous. These Focke-Wulf FW 190Gs over Romania, returning from a mission with empty bomb racks, have been variously identified as being from II./SG 2, SG 4 or SKG 10, but they serve to illustrate the unacknowledged ground-attack heroes.

Two Rotte of Messerschmitt Bf 110s sweep low over a Focke-Wulf FW 190 'White I' of an unidentified ground-attack unit somewhere on the steppes in Russia. The date is probably some time in 1943. The pole in the foreground carries an electrical cable, probably a field telephone line to the dispersal.

We had only been in Stalino for a few days (29 August-4 September 1943) when the orders arrived for the Gruppe to transfer. Our new airfield would be Kiev-Postvollinsk. The Gruppe moved, and my Schwarm again stayed behind for the final removals as airfield protection and tank-killers. Alone on the airfield, with only a few mechanics, we flew our operations, fought successfully against groups of tanks breaking through and waited for the order for the Schwarm to transfer. The Pioneers had rigged the airfield to explode and the control point was set up where we parked the aircraft. Our orders were that when the Russian tanks reached the eastern boundary the timing device would be set off (with a timed delay of 30 minutes) and the Schwarm would immediately take off. Our next airfield would be Dneiper-Petrovsk. Ohm was still in the process of polishing off a cutlet when the order came to blow the airfield. Sure enough, the T34s were carefully rolling onto the eastern side of the airfield. The Pioneers urged us to hurry. Now things were serious, the timing switch was set, into the machines, start the engines – and do nothing but get away! Again we bombed the tanks and shot at the visible accompanying infantry. We were away and the blast could do its job. As always, the Pioneers had done their job well, as so often happened during our withdrawal.

After a flight of 35 minutes we landed at Dneiper-Petrovsk South II. After we had switched off our machines we enquired of flight control the whereabouts of our Gruppe, but no one knew a thing. For the time being we set about finding ourselves some accommodation and some food. It was a real peacetime operation here – they had no idea that in a few days the Russians could be here, and probably *would* be here. After two days we still had no information about where we should be flying. No one could tell us. So we left flight control our addresses and disappeared into the lovely city of Dneiper-Petrovsk, where there still prevailed the aura of a resting place. The soldiers lived here like God in France. The people here, I think, although I don't know, had no idea that the front would soon be here, that the huge flood would soon begin.

In the coffee bars the Russians danced to the music, but so did the soldiers. The people were very friendly and nothing, absolutely nothing, stank of war. We, Ohm and I, got to know a pharmacist who took us along to the park and threw a big feast for us, a roaring party – with women and lots to drink. On the fourth day (8 September) it happened – they were already looking for us and we were to fly immediately to Kiev. After moving out of our accommodation, we signed off with flight control and began the flight to Kiev. The flight followed without incident along the Dneiper, the weather was perfect and the enemy air force was not to be seen. In such a short time we had toured the south like a wandering circus and given our performances. The Kommandeur greeted us, pleased that we were back again with the Gruppe. The first few days at Kiev-South were scheduled for the pilots to recuperate and for the aircraft to be overhauled. We visited the bazaar – Kiev was also a peaceful garrison, but for how much longer? Meanwhile, we visited a swimming baths, which we shared with the Russians and where we could have a shower. It was as if we were in the depths of peacetime. Unfortunately, appearances are deceptive – we knew the reality. Naturally we took a car to central Kiev, a really beautiful city with hills on the Dneiper. On one main street in the city we saw sailors in blue kit, members of a punishment battalion, who were digging out air raid protection shelters. We noticed them because of their blue uniforms. We also visited the banks of the Dneiper and other places in the city. Just before dark we drove back to our airfield. We still had some more peaceful days.

That evening an Army front line theatre troupe was our guest. They had a very good programme and it was a brilliant evening, with partying until the early hours. Dawn was just breaking when operational orders came through. It was all happening again – the lovely days were past for us pilots. We wistfully bade the artists goodbye and went to the operational briefing. As was often the case, it was, 'Buchner, you're flying the initial reconnaissance!' The west bank of the Dneiper was the new area to bring under control. In places the Russians were already near the river, and the situation was very confused. After our return the Army was informed of the actual situation and we subsequently received the new job of providing support for our own units. Our Gruppe was a proper fire brigade, but there were too few of us. Low-level attacks were made against airfields in Konotop, around 200km behind the lines, with attacks against tanks and other armoured vehicles.

Here we had our first encounter with Spitfires (flown by Russians). It was a short air battle, but our opponent was looking for some opportunity to resolve the fight. We didn't really want to pursue them – after all, we were Schlachtflieger, not fighters. We flew operations in nearly all weather conditions regardless, as our own troops needed our support. Day after day we managed to provide our troops in difficulties with a breathing space. In the south the Russians had broken through at Zaporozhe, and within a few hours we were transferred to Kirovograd. The airfield already contained a Geschwader of fighters (JG 52), Stuka 77, a bomber Geschwader with He 111s, and in the meantime a Ju 52 transporter landed with fuel and bombs and to take injured soldiers out on his return flight. There was mass confusion on the airfield. We, the Schlachter, were accommodated in a former barracks. Relations with the locals in the city were still friendly and there were still theatres, in one of which we saw a great performance.

Fighting alongside the FW 190-equipped ground-attack units of Luftflotte IV were the sturdy Junkers 87 Stukas. S2+NM is a late D-model from 4./StG 77, ploughing its way through the quagmire of a Russian landing ground.

There was no front line, the Russians having broken through in many places, laying into the larger cities with masses of tanks. Everything repeated itself: the rear areas a muddle, with many civil servants and their relations. The weather had become worse, but we nevertheless flew our operations in all conditions, from early until late. We often had difficulties in landing when we returned from our missions. The fighters were returning, the bombers were flying off for their night operations, the transports were bringing fuel, and we would be returning from battle with our last drops of fuel. I shot in front of the cockpit of a Ju 52 with my 2cm cannon and forced him away so that I could continue my landing. While taxiing, another Ju 52 stood immediately in front of me. This time I had no choice – either shear away the undercarriage or roll into the Ju 52. I gave it full right rudder and, sure enough, my undercarriage was sheared off. Afterwards, as I lay on the ground with my machine, the pilot of the Ju 52 simply gave it a bit of throttle and headed towards the parking place. My 190 lay on the ground and I had the trouble of going to my superiors to explain what had really happened. The Ju 52 that had allegedly stood in the way was no longer there, so lent no credence to my statement.

The 29th of September 1943 was another great day! That evening, near Krivoi Rog, a tank counter-attack began and we were to fly support. I was assigned as Schwarmflieger and Hans Wilmerdinger as Rottenflieger. From far away one could already see the clouds of smoke, interspersed with the blast clouds from the flak. We were to drop our bombs, but the Yaks and LaGGs appeared, so we jettisoned them. We were ready and looking for a fight. A furious turning battle began.

My Rotte was alone in a group of Russians, but I got into a good shooting position and shot down a Yak in flames. Another Yak was still in front of me and I was in a good position to shoot. My wingman called over the radio that the coast was clear. It was an old habit of mine that, before opening fire, I glanced behind me. To my horror I saw gunfire coming from a Yak with a red engine cover at close range – how had it got there? Already the rounds were hitting my cockpit; he'd hit the armour plating near my head and the splinters injured my head and neck. Instinctively I pulled the stick hard against my chest, my 190 climbed steeply upwards and I lost consciousness. I was unconscious only momentarily, there was a frightful roar and a gust of wind blew my maps out of the cockpit. My eyes opened and I regained my senses. My machine was in a spin and plummeting towards the ground. On the ground everything was burning and smoking, but I had enough altitude to stabilise my machine and bring it under control, initially towards the sun, to the west. My gauges were wrecked and the wind had blown my maps away. Anything that was not well anchored down had been blown out of the cabin. I had to stay calm and keep my nerve. I could hear or see nothing of my wingman, I was alone in the area and my course for the time being was westwards towards the sun. The motor howled, but the tachometer was broken. I throttled back, the engine revs went down and I flew the machine by ear. All instruments were destroyed – only the engine reacted when the throttle was applied. My luck was that I was alone, without enemy aircraft nearby. But I had no idea where I was. At about 500m altitude, I continued to fly westwards. I calmed down a bit and thought about what I should do next. But then came my next unpleasant discovery: my back was warm and my neck damp. I reached up to examine my neck and to my horror I confirmed that I was bleeding. My hand was sticky with blood – the back of my head had been wounded. I had to keep my nerve and try to find an airfield. It was my luck, as mentioned, that no enemy fighters were in the area, so I had to be over our own territory.

After flying for 25-30 minutes I flew over a small brook running from right to left, so deduced it was flowing from north to south. I turned right and flew along the bed of the stream – somewhere along it there had to be a settlement or airfield. I reckoned I was flying at about 1,000 metres, my wounds had stopped bleeding, everything was sticky, and the engine just ran and ran. I was slowly becoming uneasy: no settlements, no airfields in sight – where on earth was I? There, in the distance I could make out a town. Just stay calm, for the closer I came, the more I would have to concentrate. On the north-east side of the town – it was definitely a town – I found an airfield that had German aircraft on it; He 111s, fighters and Stukas were parked there. I was relieved, after so much uncertainty, to be back with my own people. I lined up to land from the east, throttled back – everything by feel with the instruments out of order – lowered the undercarriage and gently came down onto the ground. My 190 landed quietly on the ground and taxied. I had done that with my last ounce of strength. I fell headlong over the controls and lost consciousness. How long I was there and how long my 190 stood on the edge of the airfield I cannot say. Our mechanics were not concerned when they saw a 190 standing on the edge of the airfield; they simply took a motorbike to the standing machine and discovered me unconscious. Then everything moved quickly. A doctor gave me emergency first aid and I came to again. I was sent to the hospital in Kirovograd for medical treatment. When the first machines from the Staffel returned from the mission, the pilots said that Buchner had fallen in an aerial battle over Krivoi Rog. Our mechanics enlightened them with the fact that Buchner had been back for some time and now found himself in hospital.

Hans Wilmerdinger related the details of the aerial battle to our colleagues, my aerial victory and my departure. Anyhow, he was convinced that I had been injured and that I would not get out of the spinning 190 alive. For everyone it had been a ferocious battle. Our radio listening service had listened in on the Russians' radio traffic and found out that the Russians had reported me shot down. That evening we were all together again back at Kirovograd and I was able to celebrate my 24th birthday, albeit spoiled a bit by a dressing around my head.

The Russians had broken through at Kiev and we, the 'fire brigade', transferred on 30 October 1943 to Byala-Zerkov, a railway junction south-west of Kiev. I made the transfer in a Ju 52. I was temporarily relieved from flying duties, so was able to look around the area a bit. The Staffel flew operations against tanks and infantry that had broken through – Kiev had already fallen. Near Cherkassy parts of some divisions had been surrounded, and again our front lines were unknown. My comrades flew reconnaissance missions to ascertain the location of our own troops. It was a dirty job for the pilots; the weather was very bad and parts of the Dneiper Heights

These two FW 190G-3s are almost certainly of II./SchG 1, probably during 'Operation Citadel', the huge tank battle of Kursk in July 1943. Hermann Buchner flew an aircraft marked 'L' on 22 August 1943 from Pol-Rudka and later in October from Kirovograd while with 8. Staffel. It was in such an aircraft that he scored his fifth victory, over a Polikarpov R-5, to become an 'experte' on 24 October, by which time he was with 6./SG 2. Apart from carrying a blue or black number and bar, his aircraft would probably have looked much like those here.

Poised ready for the next mission, this Focke-Wulf FW 190 appears to be an F-1 variant. Probably belonging to II./SchG 1 on an airfield in Russia some time in 1943, it is carrying an SC 250 bomb.

A look at the lethal contents of an AB 250 weapons container holding seventeen SD 10A anti-personnel bombs – a favourite for use against troops in open ground. The FW 190 could carry these just as easily as conventional demolition bombs.

were in clouds, forcing the 190s to fly at low altitude over the Russian positions. I lost my number four on one of these operations, shot down by our own artillery fire. The situation was unclear during this time; hardly had a gap been filled, restoring the front to a semblance of order, when all hell would break loose again.

For days we had not flown, the fog lay right down to the ground and flying was out of the question. The reports from the front were unsettling. The Kommandeur called all the pilots together and the situation was discussed: march back and blow up the 190s or fly back in the existing weather conditions to airfields in the west. The alternative airfields were about 300km away and the only railway was the Zhitomir-Berdichev-Vinnitsa line, which ran north-south. We were all of the same opinion: the mechanics would go in the tail of the machines and we would fly back at low level. Blowing up the aircraft was out of the question. At any rate, the parts of the unit on wheels were sent back in a vehicle convoy.

We waited one more day, hoping that perhaps the weather would improve, but unfortunately to no avail. We flew back in Rotte formations, each taking off at 5-minute intervals. The weather was bloody awful: it was already snowing on the ground and it was foggy as well, with visibility on the ground hardly 300-500 metres. The flight itself was pretty adventurous, sometimes flying with flaps out. We were trying to cover the longest distance westwards with the shortest journey possible. Even for an old hand like me it was a struggle. After flying about 45 minutes we reached a place on a railway line and after some circuits at about 30-40 metres altitude in Berdichev, we recognised an airfield and lined up to land. Some of our Staffel were already there, and they had had enough as well. Even the Kommandeur declared that he was fed up to the back teeth – this had been the most difficult flight he had ever made. Anyhow, we managed to get all the machines back without any casualties, even though some of our Gruppe landed in Zhitomir and Vinnitsa. The most important thing was that we had got away from the destruction.

After a couple of days rest, on 10 November 1943 we transferred to Zhitomir to support the Army. There our Gruppe was complete – even our ground element had reappeared. Again II. Gruppe 'Immelmann' had succeeded in escaping encirclement or being overrun. But the weather was very bad – it rained and was already bitterly cold. Additionally, my condition, after having been injured, was still not perfect and the doctor had decreed that I was not to fly any operations. The Kommandeur tersely sent me to Germany for four weeks' convalescence. I got my papers and things ready and looked for transport to Germany. I quickly discovered a pilot who was going across and who was willing to take me to Lemberg. With my leave certificate in my pocket, I said my goodbyes to my friends. On the airfield all hell had broken loose; the Russians had broken through, their tanks stood just near the airfield and I was flying to Lemberg on a Junkers W34. An Unteroffizier was the pilot and the second pilot was an Obergefreiter. On board with me was an Oberstleutnant from the infantry. We were lucky and managed to take off from the ground with no problems, in spite of the turmoil on the airfield. The pilot wanted to get to Lemberg, about a 3-hour flight.

Initially the flight went without any special incidents, except that it slowly became dark and Lemberg was still not in sight. The weather deteriorated considerably and the ground below us was cut across by the foothills of the Carpathian Mountains. We had already been flying for about 2 hours at an altitude between 100 and 200 metres. To the right and left of us were mountain slopes and, in addition, it was one snow shower after another. I found this situation a bit disturbing. The pilot had obviously lost his bearings. A decision was now long overdue – we had to get away from the bad weather. I pushed through the hatch and asked that the second pilot leave his seat and go to the back. I spoke to the pilot and, as he was unable to say where we were, I took over the controls and turned the machine round 180° out of the valley, heading eastwards again.

The decision was right – we got out of the awkward situation. Meanwhile it was already dark, we had been flying for 3 hours and had no idea where we were. After we left the valley I went to a higher altitude and tried to spot any lights in the darkness. In addition we had no radio man on board, so the situation was slowly becoming uncomfortable. We had left the mountains behind us and we had a safe altitude – but where on earth were we? Our course was eastwards and, in my opinion, we would come upon a fairly large town or we would have to do an emergency landing in the next hour because we'd have run out of fuel. Finally, in the distance, some lights – or were they stars? Just keep calm. The nearer we came, the clearer one could tell that they were lights. They were not stars at all, but aircraft position lights; somewhere out there, there must be an airfield. We were lucky, for here was an airfield that was active at night. After reducing altitude we queued to land and made a proper night landing, after 4 hours of flying finding ourselves again on the ground. With the help of flashlights, we were assigned a parking place. I shut off the engine and was happy to be on the ground. First of all, I gave the Unteroffizier a lecture on bad weather flying and explained to him that I was on holiday and didn't particularly want to bite the dust. He was definitely not a bad pilot, simply lacking in experience. As we left the machine we asked the mechanics where we had landed. We were lucky – we had landed in Tarnopol, where there was an active night-flying operation in the process of evacuating Vinnitsa using Ju 52s. What a piece of luck for us to have found an airfield! For the moment all I wanted to do was to find a place where I could sleep and have a bit of peace.

After a good night's sleep and some breakfast, the pilot expressed his intentions to fly onwards to Lemberg. I told him that I would be giving up my place on the aircraft. My trust in him had been lost during the flight from Zhitomir to Tarnopol and I did not want to come a cropper, at least not so cheaply. As an old hand wanting to reach Germany by plane, I went to the aircraft hangars and asked an Oberwerkmeister (crew chief) if it would be possible to get hold of a place in a transport machine flying to Breslau. The Oberwerkmeister offered me a Fieseler Storch to fly back to Germany – it needed to be flown to Dresden for a major overhaul – so I took him up on his offer and made the necessary flight preparations After a short time flying control had even allotted somebody to fly along with me – another person who would rather take an old aircraft than the train to Germany. After getting a weather report and loading the machine, we flew to Breslau in good weather conditions, the mountainous country now behind us. We fuelled up in Breslau and went on to Dresden. After landing I handed over the Storch to the hangar there and was now officially on leave from the front. My passenger was as happy as I to have got to Germany in such a relatively short time. We said goodbye and I went off to the railway station and took the train back to my home town of Salzburg.

So, at the end of November 1943, I was back in Salzburg. My parents were overjoyed at my arrival. They were also filled with consternation over my injury, but the first thing I had to do was go to hospital to have the stitches removed from my head. The doctor was pleased that the wound had healed well and took out the stitches. Now I was free again. I got all my mountain climbing gear together and took off into the mountains. My parents were not enthusiastic, but I loved my mountains above all else. I had fourteen days all to myself, tramping in the mountains: Wimmerhütte (in the Tennen mountains), Hochkönig and the Pinzgauer grass mountains. The days flew by. The weather wasn't exactly good, but I was on my own and took what routes I wanted to. I then returned home and celebrated Christmas there. I celebrated New Year's Eve with some friends who, by chance, were on leave, and also by going to see *The Flying Dutchman* at the Festival Playhouse, an excellent performance. After drinking all night, it was back to business in the morning. I gathered together my uniform and other kit and at about 1700hrs again took the train eastwards. My father took me to the station for the third time.

For me it had almost become a routine, my father taking me to the station, always at 1700hrs, taking the tram to the Eastern Railway Station and leaving there at 2200hrs with others returning from leave destined for Lemberg. In Vienna the military police were busily occupied with organising and counting the soldiers returning from leave. If you were on the ball you arrived late and would have to leave and appear again the next day to be transported, allowing you an extra day in Vienna. Because of this, I tried hard to get a place in the train since I wasn't keen on staying overnight in Vienna, preferring to get back to my comrades at the front. Towards morning we reached Lemberg and I left the train there.

Again I was at the airfield at Lemberg, and again I went to flight control and tried to get hold of a place as a passenger. I again wrote a letter to my parents, already the third one. After a while I was lucky when the pilot of an He 111 took me and some other colleagues to Uman in the Ukraine (my Gruppe was now in this area). After flying for 2½ hours, most of it at low level to impress the nurses who were with us, we reached Uman. After the goodbyes and a thanks to the pilot, I inquired at the Front Regional Headquarters as to the exact whereabouts of my Gruppe. The new airfield was about 80km eastwards. Again, I found a Ju 52 transport aircraft, which took me along to Malaya Whiski. By evening I was back again with my friends, back with my Staffel. After two days and a night I was once again with my unit.

The joy of seeing each other again was great. I had to tell them all about my holidays, but I was also confronted with the events that had occurred in the Staffel during my absence. Here it was deepest winter, the countryside was covered in snow and we were accommodated in a school. The airfield was on the southern edge of town. On the airfield itself, a Gruppe of JG 52 was quartered.

The enemy situation wasn't exactly rosy. The Russians had broken through at Kirovograd and all the main roads were choked with tank columns of divisional strength heading south-west, as well as their supply vehicles. The weather for Schlachter operations was reasonably fair, and we again had our hands full. On 12 January 1944 I flew my first enemy mission again, and it was again a real drama. Our attacks were supported by a Stuka Gruppe under Rudel[30] and fighter protection was flown by the pilots of the JG 52 Gruppe. Apart from the Luftwaffe, there was no strength available for defence. We flew from early until late. The Russians were very unpleasant and revenge followed on foot as well. During the night of 13 January an enemy tank unit succeeded in breaking through to our airfield. Around midnight the battle alarm was sounded and our Adjutant woke the pilots. At the same time we were ordered to individually get to the airfield dispersal and to gather near the Staffel dispersals. The Russians had some of their infantry in parts of the area, and they held the eastern part of the airfield, JG 52's dispersal, having overrun it with T-34 tanks; they had taken away eight of the Jagdgeschwader's machines. One of their T-34s rolled over the earth wall protecting the flight control barracks and crashed into the trenches behind. Our airfield flak and the sets of quadruple 20mm cannon (20mm Vierling) were put into position to fight the infantry accompanying the tanks.

We found ourselves on the western side of the airfield, with orders to blow the 190s on a signal from the command post. The teams gathered on the western side and afterwards marched westwards. Together with the mechanics, we prepared to destroy the machines; the night was very dark and also crisply cold. At around 3.00am a figure came towards us. It was an officer who explained that most of the Me 109s from his group had been overrun by tanks. Forty years later, I related this tale to former pilots and one of the officers present (General Haiböck) said, 'That was me.' Our own flak went with the motorised quad 2cm cannon to the eastern side of the airfield and took up the fight against the enemy troops. Also, the 88mm weapons on the airfield shot at the tanks at short range with a good degree of success. We froze, standing around our machines and hearing the noise of the battle in expectation of the forthcoming orders.

Towards dawn, the noise of the battle diminished somewhat and in the airfield lights we could see three He 111s coming at low level from the south with the intention of dropping bombs on the airfield; the crews were probably of the opinion that the airfield had been taken over by the

Russians. We sent up a signal to stop them. After the bombers came Stukas, looking for targets for the bombs that they were carrying. We were close-range observers of this action and saw a Ju 87 hit by tank flak, forcing the crew to take to their parachutes and arrive safely on the ground. We had a turbulent night behind us and still the matter was not over. Around 1000hrs our flak, together with some remaining infantry units still stationed in the town, succeeded in clearing up the breakthrough of the tanks. All the tanks that had broken through had been knocked out, and the accompanying infantry had been destroyed or taken prisoner. Everyone breathed a sigh of relief, for our 190s had remained undamaged. On the eastern side of the airfield smoke still billowed from the wreckage of a tank and its accompanying vehicles. The Gruppe from JG 52 had simply lost 109s and in the flight control bunker a clerk had been crushed to death by the tank that had broken in. Our Gruppe carried on with its daily duties as normal and the Kommandeur informed us of our new tasks. We had survived this mess well and the patter again fell easily from the pilots' lips. My new task was to bring our Gruppe four 190s from the aircraft park at Uman.

We flew off in a Ju 52, and were happy to be away from this hell. But we were going from the frying-pan into the fire, for in Uman the situation was even more dismal. No one could say what was going to happen. For the moment we were accommodated in a building on the edge of the airfield. Luftflotte 4 headquarters staff who were accommodated on the airfield were hastily evacuating their accommodation. For us Schlachter pilots, it was a reassuring picture to see general staff officers fleeing on the loading platforms of overloaded Henschel three-axle trucks. There were around eight to ten of us pilots (Me 109 and FW 190) who were there to take over machines. Because of the situation we were held back and used to form an 'Uman Kommando'. I was assigned as Kommandant, and our aircraft consisted of 190s, 109s and a single Henschel Hs 123. We got our orders from the Uman battle group commander. The Russians had broken through a large area of the front and nobody had a clear picture of the situation. A Rotte from our Kommando flew a reconnaissance mission, so we got a reasonable idea of the current position.

The Hs 123 again made the headlines. On 15 January 1944 Unteroffizier Müller was given the task of flying to a base in the north and landing there. He was to deliver orders to the Kommandant of a reserve infantry unit, asking him to immediately

There are at least eleven Focke-Wulf FW 190s visible in this picture. The nearest machine is an F-3/R-1/Trop with an SC 250 bomb hanging on the centreline rack. The aircraft carries a command chevron, while other aircraft in the background carry the horizontal bar identifying II. Gruppe. Just discernable in the background of the original print are two Henschel Hs 123s. In January 1944 the author led an ad hoc 'Uman Kommando', which still had at least one Hs 123 on strength, but whether this is the date and place is not known.

Armourers wrestle to load an AB 250 weapons container under an FW 190 somewhere on the Russian Front. All that can be guessed from this picture is that the aircraft is probably an early F-model, possibly an F-3 as it has underwing ETC 50 bomb racks, and tropical intakes can just be made out on it.

move his unit south and assemble in the Uman Heights. Erich Müller flew away in his 123 and, after 2 hours, was still not back in Uman. We began to worry as to his whereabouts. Due to a lack of fuel he should have been back for a good while. Fundamentally, the situation was very tense and a real muddle. The last Luftwaffe soldiers were leaving the airfield – only those of us from the Uman Kommando and the Luftwaffe construction engineers were still there. Then, towards evening, the 123 carrying Erich Müller appeared on the horizon, landed and he climbed out unhurt. Surely he couldn't have been in the air the whole time.

Müller related the events of his flight. After flying for about 40 minutes, he had reached the village of the aforementioned reserve unit. He also found a snowy field and landed smoothly near some peasants' cottages. He shut off the engine, climbed out of his 123 and looked for the commander of the unit. The commander was surprised at the visit and asked the reason for it. This Kompanie still lived as it had in the steppes and had no idea that the Russians had broken through. He immediately gave the alarm and got his Kompanie ready to march out. Naturally Müller was entertained and questioned about the latest happenings and the particular situation. A Hauptmann in the Reserve asked Müller to do him one favour, to notify the Kommandant of a neighbouring Kompanie. The telephone lines were down and they had no means of communicating by radio. The Hauptmann was afraid that this Kompanie also had no idea of the situation.

So Müller flew to three further villages, landed on snow-covered fields and notified the remaining reserve units of the alarming situation. After he had informed them all, he flew back to Uman, thereby having surely spared many German soldiers the hard lot of imprisonment. Anyway, we, his friends, were happy that he was back in our company again, healthy and unhurt.

On 16 January 1944 we flew to Novo-Ukraina to our Gruppe. Uman was evacuated and I was, as was so often the case, one of the last pilots allowed to leave the airfield. Uman, the lovely town, where we had passed so many pleasant hours, we had to vacate. The situation was becoming increasingly dangerous. The Russians broke through our positions at Nikopol and our ground troops were not in a position to stabilise the front. The Crimean Peninsula had been surrounded since November and could only be reached by aeroplanes flying over the sea from the mainland.

From Novo-Ukraina we flew operations in the Krivoi Rog region. The weather was very bad with a great deal of fog and a countryside white with snow. The flight there was very long, so we attempted to get an airfield closer to the front and transferred to an airfield about 80km eastwards, from where we could support the defensive battles of the infantry. My Schwarm was the first to land there and we got a nasty surprise. The airfield was like a skating rink, the brakes were useless and the 190s slid across the area. After we had come to a standstill with churning stomachs, the pilots were of a single opinion – back to Novo-Ukraina. It would be impossible to fly operations from here. Taking off again was extremely difficult and everyone was happy to be in the air again. We radioed our other colleagues concerning our return, and our decision was approved by the Kommandeur. In the meantime, the operational situation for our Gruppe had changed. We were to transfer in the next three or four days to the Crimea. In the opinion of the Kommandeur, we only needed to take a face cloth, soap and toothbrush, for we would be back on the mainland in a few days.

On 23 January we were ready, and the Gruppe transferred thirty FW 190s via Nikolayev to the Crimea. We landed in Nikolayev to fuel up the machines and to discuss the next leg of the journey. The weather was good, so we could fly over the Russian territory at an altitude of 4,000-5,000 metres. All of the Schwarme made it to Sarabuz (Ukromnoi) without encountering the enemy. After two years the older pilots were again in Sarabuz, again in the Crimea. It was already afternoon by the time we landed. Now we considered whether we ought to fly on to Bagarovo-Kerch or not. The mechanics checked over the machines and we pilots talked with the crew of a nearby Ju 52. They had the task of flying the Kuban Army Front Line Theatre Group, which included a cargo of lots of ladies, to Bagarovo. Some of the pilots chatted up the leader of the troop and arranged a meeting with the group in Bagarovo.

The decision had been made; we were to fly onwards to Bagarovo and I was assigned to the last Schwarm. I arrived in Bagarovo just as it began to get dark. Part of the airfield was already prepared for demolition and there were 1,000kg bombs distributed around the airfield. Bagarovo was an airfield west of Kerch; it was actually three airfields, although we didn't know it at the time. We were extremely lucky and landed between the bombs. The people on the ground were really agitated and signalled to us that we should stay there, stop the engines and get out of the aircraft. Meanwhile, it had become dark and the 190 was towed by tractor to the dispersal.

Note on the colour plates

Readers will have noticed that few photos exist showing the aircraft that Hermann Buchner actually flew. The majority of these colour illustrations are therefore reconstructions based on the few pictures available, details in the logbooks, the author's memory and what is generally known of aircraft in use at the times stated. The publishers (and the author) would welcome any further information.

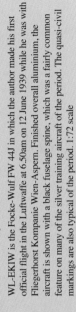

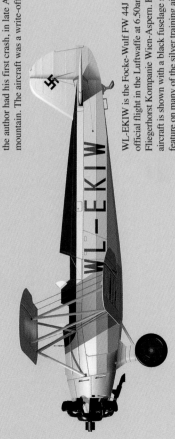

OE-TCI, DNr 4015, is an Austrian-built Focke-Wulf FW 44J, based at Aigen and in service with Bombenstaffel 1 of the Österreichischen Luftstreitkräfte. Finished overall aluminium, it carried 220mm-wide red/white/red rudder stripes with a black registration on both sides of the fuselage and above and below the wings. This was the aircraft in which the author had his first crash, in late April 1938, on the Planner Alm mountain. The aircraft was a write-off . 1:72 scale

WL-EKIW is the Focke-Wulf FW 44J in which the author made his first official flight in the Luftwaffe at 6.50am on 12 June 1939 while he was with Fliegerhorst Kompanie Wien-Aspern. Finished overall aluminium, the aircraft is shown with a black fuselage spine, which was a fairly common feature on many of the silver training aircraft of the period. The quasi-civil markings are also typical of the period. 1:72 scale

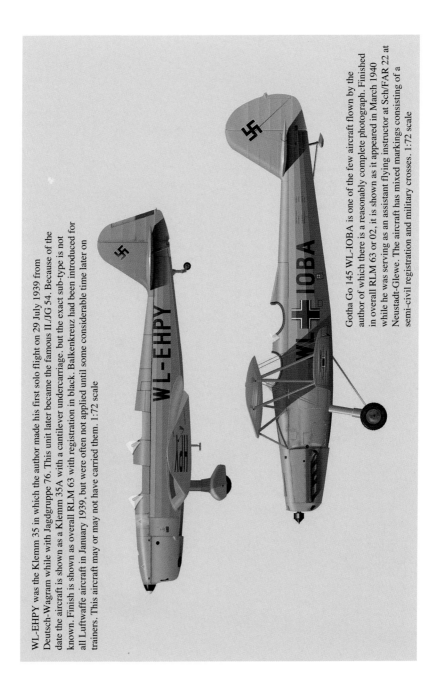

WL-EHPY was the Klemm 35 in which the author made his first solo flight on 29 July 1939 from Deutsch-Wagram while with Jagdgruppe 76. This unit later became the famous II./JG 54. Because of the date the aircraft is shown as a Klemm 35A with a cantilever undercarriage, but the exact sub-type is not known. Finish is shown as overall RLM 63 with registration in black. Balkenkreuz had been introduced for all Luftwaffe aircraft in January 1939, but were often not applied until some considerable time later on trainers. This aircraft may or may not have carried them. 1:72 scale

Gotha Go 145 WL-IOBA is one of the few aircraft flown by the author of which there is a reasonably complete photograph. Finished in overall RLM 63 or 02, it is shown as it appeared in March 1940 while he was serving as an assistant flying instructor at Sch/FAR 22 at Neustadt-Gleve. The aircraft has mixed markings consisting of a semi-civil registration and military crosses. 1:72 scale

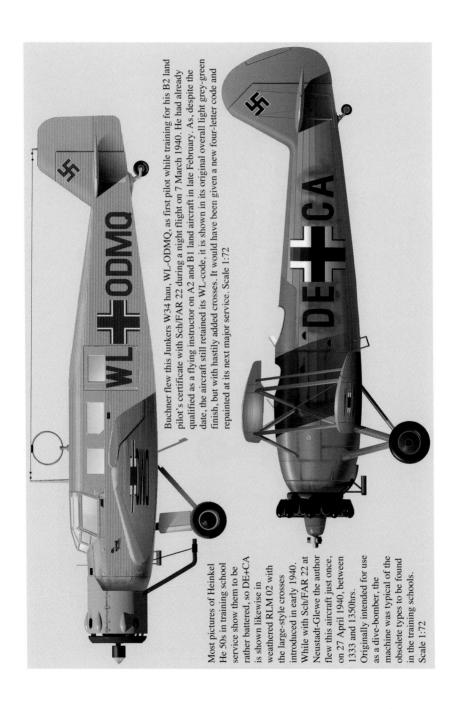

Buchner flew this Junkers W34 hau, WL-ODMQ, as first pilot while training for his B2 land pilot's certificate with Sch/FAR 22 during a night flight on 7 March 1940. He had already qualified as a flying instructor on A2 and B1 land aircraft in late February. As, despite the date, the aircraft still retained its WL-code, it is shown in its original overall light grey-green finish, but with hastily added crosses. It would have been given a new four-letter code and repainted at its next major service. Scale 1:72

Most pictures of Heinkel He 50s in training school service show them to be rather battered, so DE+CA is shown likewise in weathered RLM 02 with the large-style crosses introduced in early 1940. While with Sch/FAR 22 at Neustadt-Glewe the author flew this aircraft just once, on 27 April 1940, between 1333 and 1350hrs. Originally intended for use as a dive-bomber, the machine was typical of the obsolete types to be found in the training schools. Scale 1:72

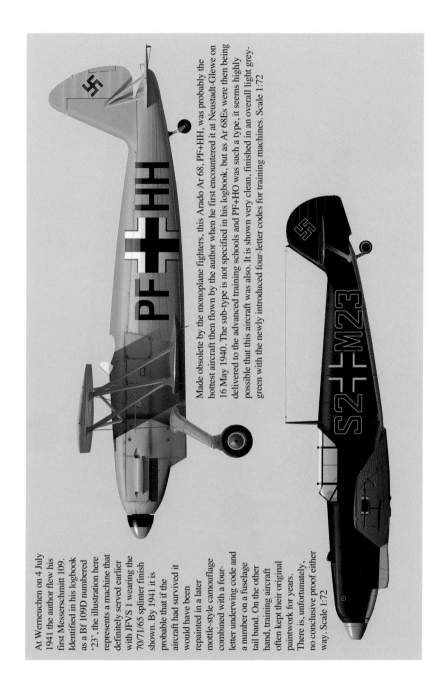

At Werneuchen on 4 July 1941 the author flew his first Messerschmitt 109. Identified in his logbook as a Bf 109D numbered '23', the illustration here represents a machine that definitely served earlier with JFVS 1 wearing the 70/71/65 splinter finish shown. By 1941 it is probable that if the aircraft had survived it would have been repainted in a later mottle-style camouflage combined with a four-letter underwing code and a number on a fuselage tail band. On the other hand, training aircraft often kept their original paintwork for years. There is, unfortunately, no conclusive proof either way. Scale 1:72

Made obsolete by the monoplane fighters, this Arado Ar 68, PF+HH, was probably the hottest aircraft then flown by the author when he first encountered it at Neustadt-Glewe on 16 May 1940. The sub-type is not specified in his logbook, but as Ar 68Es were then being delivered to the advanced training schools and PF+HO was such a type, it seems highly possible that this aircraft was also. It is shown very clean, finished in an overall light grey-green with the newly introduced four-letter codes for training machines. Scale 1:72

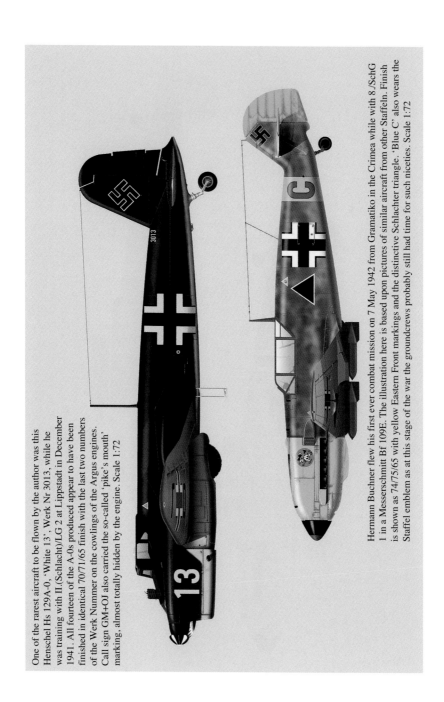

One of the rarest aircraft to be flown by the author was this Henschel Hs 129A-0, 'White 13', Werk Nr 3013, while he was training with II.(Schlacht)/LG 2 at Lippstadt in December 1941. All fourteen of the A-0s produced appear to have been finished in identical 70/71/65 finish with the last two numbers of the Werk Nummer on the cowlings of the Argus engines. Call sign GM+OI also carried the so-called 'pike's mouth' marking, almost totally hidden by the engine. Scale 1:72

Hermann Buchner flew his first ever combat mission on 7 May 1942 from Gramatiko in the Crimea while with 8./SchG 1 in a Messerschmitt Bf 109E. The illustration here is based upon pictures of similar aircraft from other Staffeln. Finish is shown as 74/75/65 with yellow Eastern Front markings and the distinctive Schlachter triangle. 'Blue C' also wears the Staffel emblem as at this stage of the war the groundcrews probably still had time for such niceties. Scale 1:72

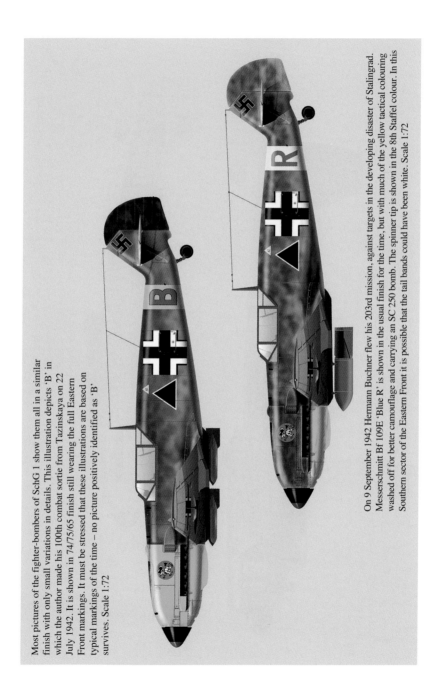

Most pictures of the fighter-bombers of SchG 1 show them all in a similar finish with only small variations in details. This illustration depicts 'B' in which the author made his 100th combat sortie from Tazinskaya on 22 July 1942. It is shown in 74/75/65 finish still wearing the full Eastern Front markings. It must be stressed that these illustrations are based on typical markings of the time – no picture positively identified as 'B' survives. Scale 1:72

On 9 September 1942 Hermann Buchner flew his 203rd mission, against targets in the developing disaster of Stalingrad. Messerschmitt Bf 109E 'Blue R' is shown in the usual finish for the time, but with much of the yellow tactical colouring washed off for better camouflage and carrying an SC 250 bomb. The spinner tip is shown in the 8th Staffel colour. In this Southern sector of the Eastern Front it is possible that the tail bands could have been white. Scale 1:72

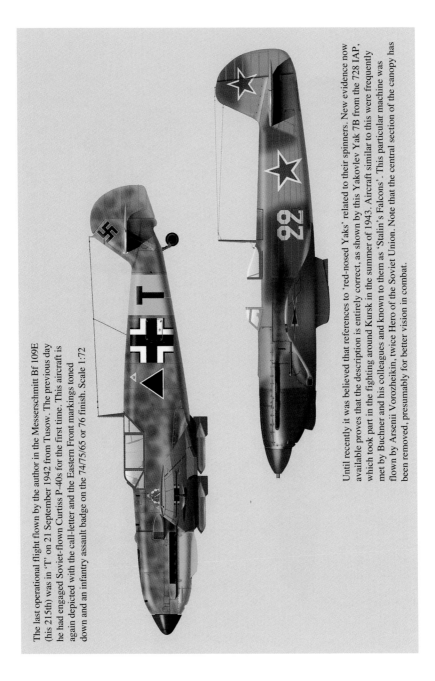

The last operational flight flown by the author in the Messerschmitt Bf 109E (his 215th) was in 'T' on 21 September 1942 from Tusow. The previous day he had engaged Soviet-flown Curtiss P-40s for the first time. This aircraft is again depicted with the call-letter and the Eastern Front markings toned down and an infantry assault badge on the 74/75/65 or 76 finish. Scale 1:72

Until recently it was believed that references to 'red-nosed Yaks' related to their spinners. New evidence now available proves that the description is entirely correct, as shown by this Yakovlev Yak 7B from the 728 IAP, which took part in the fighting around Kursk in the summer of 1943. Aircraft similar to this were frequently met by Buchner and his colleagues and known to them as 'Stalin's Falcons'. This particular machine was flown by Arsenii Vorozheikin, twice Hero of the Soviet Union. Note that the central section of the canopy has been removed, presumably for better vision in combat.

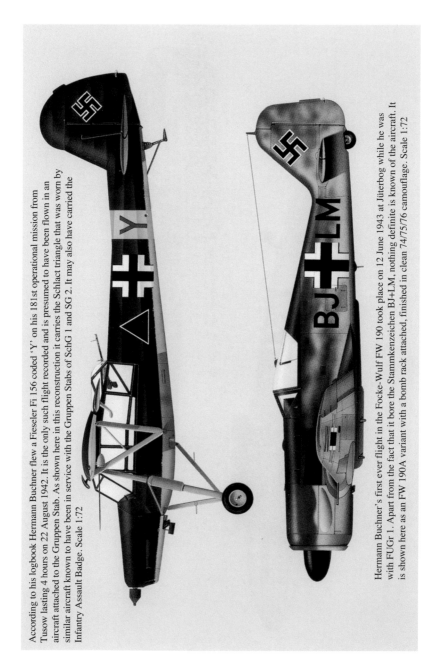

According to his logbook Hermann Buchner flew a Fieseler Fi 156 coded 'Y' on his 181st operational mission from Tusow lasting 4 hours on 22 August 1942. It is the only such flight recorded and is presumed to have been flown in an aircraft attached to the Gruppen Stab. As shown here in this reconstruction it carries the Schlact triangle that was worn by similar aircraft known to have been in service with the Gruppen Stabs of SchG 1 and SG 2. It may also have carried the Infantry Assault Badge. Scale 1:72

Hermann Buchner's first ever flight in the Focke-Wulf FW 190 took place on 12 June 1943 at Jüterbog while he was with FUGr 1. Apart from the fact that it bore the Stammkenzeichen BJ+LM, nothing definite is known of the aircraft. It is shown here as an FW 190A variant with a bomb rack attached, finished in clean 74/75/76 camouflage. Scale 1:72

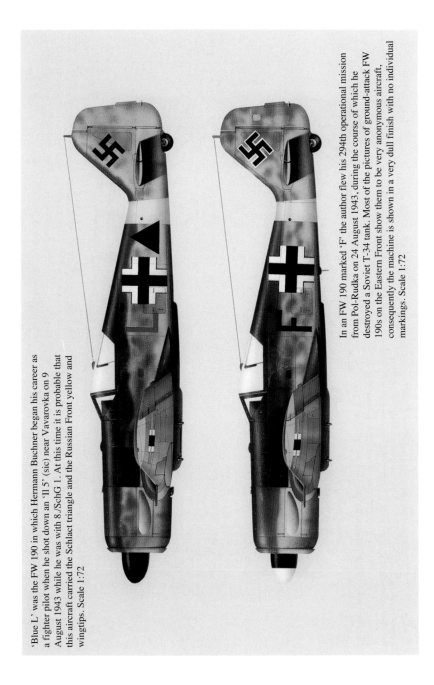

'Blue L' was the FW 190 in which Hermann Buchner began his career as a fighter pilot when he shot down an 'Il 5' (sic) near Vavarovka on 9 August 1943 while he was with 8./SchG 1. At this time it is probable that this aircraft carried the Schlact triangle and the Russian Front yellow and wingtips. Scale 1:72

In an FW 190 marked 'F' the author flew his 294th operational mission from Pol-Rudka on 24 August 1943, during the course of which he destroyed a Soviet T-34 tank. Most of the pictures of ground-attack FW 190s on the Eastern Front show them to be very anonymous aircraft, consequently the machine is shown in a very dull finish with no individual markings. Scale 1:72

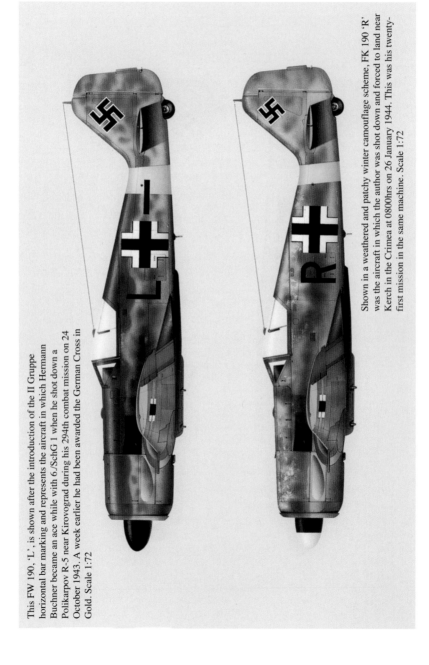

This FW 190, 'L', is shown after the introduction of the II Gruppe horizontal bar marking and represents the aircraft in which Hermann Buchner became an ace while with 6./SchG 1 when he shot down a Polikarpov R-5 near Kirovograd during his 294th combat mission on 24 October 1943. A week earlier he had been awarded the German Cross in Gold. Scale 1:72

Shown in a weathered and patchy winter camouflage scheme, FK 190 'R' was the aircraft in which the author was shot down and forced to land near Kerch in the Crimea at 0800hrs on 26 January 1944. This was his twenty-first mission in the same machine. Scale 1:72

FW 190A 'L' was the machine in which Hermann Buchner completed his 500th operational sortie on 4 March 1944. Finished in the nondescript camouflage typical of the aircraft of his unit, the illustration shows the undercarriage with the wheel covers removed, a common practice during the winter months in Russia when mud on the airfields was a major problem. This may or may not have been the same aircraft in which he became an ace. Scale 1:72

Probably the most colourful of all the FW 190s flown by Hermann Buchner, this illustration represents the aircraft in which he flew from Bakau and Zilistea in Romania during early June 1944. There was a lull of three days during which he did not fly a combat mission and his groundcrew took the opportunity to decorate his aircraft as shown. According to the author's memory it also still carried the Schlact triangle. Scale 1:72

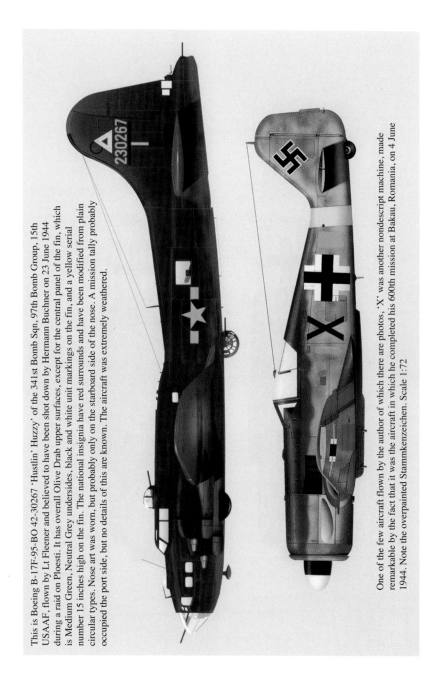

This is Boeing B-17F-95-BO 42-30267 'Hustlin' Huzzy' of the 341st Bomb Sqn, 97th Bomb Group, 15th USAAF, flown by Lt Fleener and believed to have been shot down by Hermann Buchner on 23 June 1944 during a raid on Ploesti. It has overall Olive Drab upper surfaces, except for the central panel of the fin, which is Medium Green, Neutral Grey undersides, black and white unit markings on the fin, and a yellow serial number 15 inches high on the fin. The national insignia have red surrounds and have been modified from plain circular types. Nose art was worn, but probably only on the starboard side of the nose. A mission tally probably occupied the port side, but no details of this are known. The aircraft was extremely weathered.

One of the few aircraft flown by the author of which there are photos, 'X' was another nondescript machine, made remarkable by the fact that it was the aircraft in which he completed his 600th mission at Bakau, Romania, on 4 June 1944. Note the overpainted Stammkenzeichen. Scale 1:72

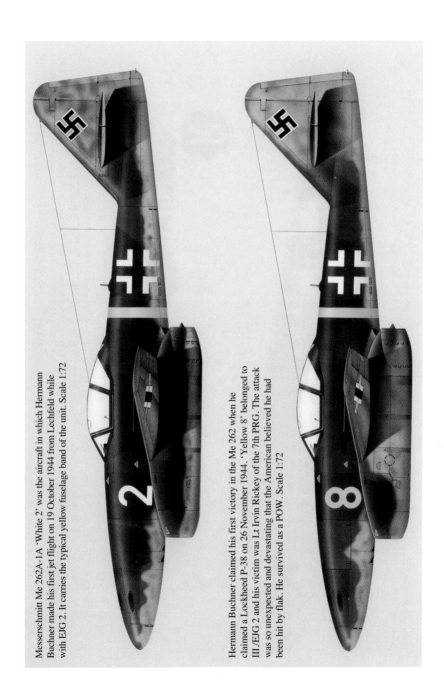

Messerschmitt Me 262A-1A 'White 2' was the aircraft in which Hermann Buchner made his first jet flight on 19 October 1944 from Lechfeld while with EJG 2. It carries the typical yellow fuselage band of the unit. Scale 1:72

Hermann Buchner claimed his first victory in the Me 262 when he claimed a Lockheed P-38 on 26 November 1944. 'Yellow 8' belonged to III./EJG 2 and his victim was Lt Irvin Rickey of the 7th PRG. The attack was so unexpected and devastating that the American believed he had been hit by flak. He survived as a POW. Scale 1:72

This is Lockheed F-5E Lightning 43-28619 flown by Lt Irvin J. Rickey of the 27th Photo Recon Sqn, 7th Photo Recon Group, 8th USAAF, when he was shot down by Buchner on 26 November 1944. No pictures exist of the aircraft so it is depicted as was the practice in the unit at the time: overall PRU Blue with black and white invasion stripes on the wing undersides and lower half of the tail booms, dark blue spinners and intake scoop panels, and '619' in 12-inch-high white numerals on the engine cowling. It carried no serial on the tail. It was named 'Ruth', but the exact style is unknown. Scale 1:72

North American P-51D-5-NA, serial number 44-13994, flown by Lt Francis Radley of the 383rd Fighter Sqn, 364th Fighter Group, 8th USAAF, was shot down by Buchner on 22 February 1945. The aircraft is in the standard finish for the period. Note how the white fuselage stars are overpainted pale grey. The squadron code 'N2' was in black, aft of the star and bar. On the fin and rudder, overlapping the serial, was a black disc with a white aircraft letter. The exact letter is unknown, but is either C, F, G, K, L, M, P, Q, R, S or U. Around the nose were alternate 6-inch medium blue and white stripes. Nose art within the Group was very restrained, so it is quite possible that the aircraft had none. Scale 1:72

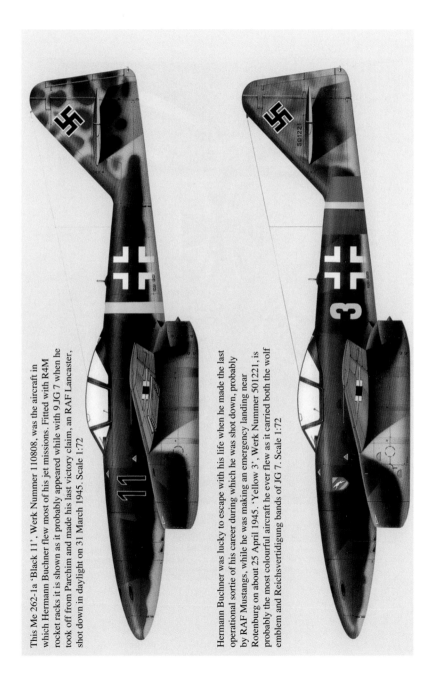

This Me 262-1a 'Black 11', Werk Nummer 110808, was the aircraft in which Hermann Buchner flew most of his jet missions. Fitted with R4M rocket racks it is shown as it probably appeared while with 9.JG 7 when he took off from Parchim and made his last victory claim, an RAF Lancaster, shot down in daylight on 31 March 1945. Scale 1:72

Hermann Buchner was lucky to escape with his life when he made the last operational sortie of his career during which he was shot down, probably by RAF Mustangs, while he was making an emergency landing near Rotenburg on about 25 April 1945. 'Yellow 3', Werk Nummer 501221, is probably the most colourful aircraft he ever flew as it carried both the wolf emblem and Reichsvertidigung bands of JG 7. Scale 1:72

To the victor the spoils? A selection of Herman Buchner's medals and awards.
At the top is the Ritterkreuz – the Knight's Cross of the Iron Cross. Centre left is
the Deutsche Kreuz in Gold, and to the right the Verleihungserkunde, the
ground-attack pilot's Combat Clasp in Gold with a pendant for 600 missions. At
the bottom is a very fine example of the Pilot's Badge.

Near the runway there was a barracks where there was an Officers' Club of a Gruppe of the fighter unit JG 52. The fighter boys were pleased to see our Gruppe arrive as reinforcements. We were generously entertained and the stories made the rounds. The fighters told us that in the next few days a theatre group would be arriving and would be performing in Bagarovo. We Schlachter went one better, and told them that we had already made contact with the girls in Sarabuz. In any case, we had staked our claims! The fighter pilots also told us that their Kommandeur would have his 250th aerial victory in the next few days. They were expecting a huge celebration and we were invited.

Things began badly. On 26 January I was shot at during a low-level attack on Russian positions and only managed to make it to our own lines with a great deal of effort after my engine quit and I made an emergency landing behind the lines. I set my machine down in a field north-west of Kerch and it creaked and threw up dust, the tail finally turning through 180° before stopping. However, it was down and I crawled out of the wreckage – uninjured!

Far and wide there wasn't a house or tree to be seen; the landscape lay around me, dreary and desolate, with only some Panje horses moving nearby. The area was not cultivated and I didn't know exactly where I was. For the moment I tried to catch a horse. After about an hour two soldiers arrived on a motorbike with a sidecar and asked whether I had been wounded, who had shot me down and where I had taken off from. They were Pioneers from a transport unit who had seen me shot down and taken a look out of curiosity. They could only tell me that the front lay about 2km to the east and a main road must be south. They probably took off because they couldn't make anything from me and my problems. I was alone again and considered what I should do next. I relieved the machine, or at least its remains, of its flight book and maps and headed south-west. I would have to reach the road at some stage. After a while I made a second attempt to catch a Panje horse and, succeeding, I tried to climb on to its back and thus make the journey as a rider. It was not easy for me, not being a rider and without a saddle, but it was definitely better than stumbling across this landscape. Anyway, it was better and faster and the little horse was very well-behaved for me.

Around midday I stopped for a rest, but there were no soldiers, houses or trees to be seen, and one could only hear the thunder of distant shooting as background music. I was thirsty, but there was no water in the area and no question of finding something edible. I was in a barren waste, alone and deserted. Towards evening I reached the longed-for road, or rather I should describe it as the longed-for street or, better, dirt track. I could now let my trusty horse go; he got nothing more than a pat on the mane, not even a bit of sugar, for I was so poor I had nothing at all myself. The trusty nag stayed with me and I sat at the edge of the road in expectation of an Army vehicle passing. It was slowly getting dark and there was still no sign of a vehicle.

Then, just in the nick of time a Kfz 17 (wireless truck) came from the east, which would probably be able to help me. I got up and made signs for the vehicle to halt. I was lucky, for it stopped and an officer, who was acting as co-driver, asked me where I came from and where I wanted to go. After a short explanation as to how I'd got there, he congratulated me, introduced himself and offered me a lift back to Bagarovo. The officer, a major, was the Kommandeur of some artillery in this sector and had his command post in Bagarovo. We drove together westwards over the atrocious road. We talked about the bad roads, the rumbles and jerks of the vehicle interrupting the conversation. After driving for about an hour there was a crack and the wagon leaned over on its left side. The driver got out and examined his vehicle. The left axle was broken and our journey was again at an end. By now it was well into the night, but the Kommandeur decided to carry on on foot. I had the choice of staying with the driver or going along on the hike. The driver was told to stay with the truck and wait until a repair vehicle appeared.

It was difficult, but nevertheless I decided to accompany the major on foot to Bagarovo, so away we went into the dark night. The road was sodden and muddy and the major had good footwear on, but I, with my flying boots, was at a terrible disadvantage. With every step I stuck in the mud. Anyway, I had to work really hard to keep up with the officer. We went swiftly onwards, speaking little. Towards midnight we reached the Kommandeur's command post in Bagarovo. He and I got something to eat and, of course, a vodka; here I was again, rescued. In a short while the major had made contact with my Gruppe, informing them that he had fished me off the road and brought me here. Now everything happened quite quickly. About an hour later our transport sergeant appeared with a truck and picked me up. I thanked the major for the lift and for his soldiers looking after me and feeding me and said my goodbyes.

After midnight I was once again, as was so often the case, back with 6 Staffel. Naturally, another bottle was cracked open and tales were told. The next day I was forbidden to fly, so could wander around the area a bit, with success. At hangar 4/40 on the airfield I found a school friend from Salzburg, Feldwebel Rudolf Zuschki; we had gone to the same school together. He was Werkmeister at the hangar and the joy at the chance meeting was very great. Naturally, I sacrificed a bottle of vodka from my stock and drank a few glasses with Rudi. The day of rest soon past and I was again back with the troops. We flew missions in the Kerch area, on the Taman Road (which connected the Black Sea and the Sea of Asov) and attacked the fighter base in Taman.

The next day it happened again. I was shot down during an aerial battle and once again had to do an emergency landing behind our lines, the second within a week. Again, I tramped to the nearest road and hitch-hiked back to my airfield. For the second time I was shot down with an 'R' as my Kennzeichen (aircraft identity letter), and because of that the Kommandeur forbade any further use of the letter 'R' in the Staffel.

Barkhorn[31], the Kommandeur of JG 52, was about to make his 250th aerial victory, the *Deutsche Wochenschau* newspaper was present, but the Russians hadn't appeared in the skies. So our Kommandant made an agreement with the fighter pilots; we would take a Schwarm and fly a low-level attack on the airfield at Taman, which should bring up the Russian fighters. This was the plan and this was also how it was carried out. I was assigned as Schwarm leader and went off with my Schwarm. It was a lovely day, not a cloud in the sky, but also not a single fighter or Il 2[32]. We had radio contact with our fighters. As usual we led with our low-level attack on the Taman Russian fighter base and tried to destroy LaGGs stationed there. The Russians took to the air and were embroiled in an aerial battle with the fighters following behind us. Now Barkhorn could make his 250th kill.

During the operation some of the Russians were taken out of the sky, but we had no casualties. After landing Barkhorn was given the red carpet treatment, and was filmed and courted by reporters. That evening there was a big party and the Kommandeurs were trying to outdo each other with tales of the quality of their pilots. As usual, it all boiled down to 'pumping' (press-ups), and the fighters started with thirty. Our Kommandeur said that his men could do fifty at the same time, and so the number climbed. We pilots, poor devils, had to do the press-ups. We went to bed long after midnight.

Hauptmann Gerhard Barkhorn, still seated in the cockpit of his Messerschmitt
Bf 109G, celebrates his 250th aerial victory with his crew chief on 13 February
1944. Only three weeks earlier he had become the first German airman to
complete 1,000 operational missions. He was also one of only two men ever to
be credited with more than 300 confirmed kills, with 301. The other man was his
long-time friend Erich Hartmann, with 352.

The numerical superiority of the Russian pilots was always
noticeable, for we encountered them during nearly every mission. The
enemy artillery also made itself felt. The Russian guns could reach to
the eastern side of the airfield, and in their attempts to hit it a round hit
our accommodation, which went up in flames. They couldn't reach
our airfield, however, so our flying operations were maintained.

By the end of February the pressure became increasingly strong
and we transferred to Karankut on the western side of the island. From
here we now flew our operations eastwards and northwards on the
Siwasch and the Sea of Azov. Our promise, or that of our
Kommandeur, that our stay on the Crimea would only be three or four
days, had long since been broken. We were already into our sixth week.

The Russians tried to erect a bridgehead in the north. German
POWs were pulled in to build the bridge, and in a new stratagem the
top of the bridge was 10cm under the surface of the water and was
only being built at night. Because of this our reconnaissance did not
discover the Russian plans for some time. After the bridge was
finished the Russians intended to push a division towards us and by
Easter 1944 would have pushed or even broken through as far as
Tschangoi. After our reconnaissance confirmed that the bridge was
continually being repaired by German POWs after we had damaged it,

we did not attack it anymore. In spite of the numerical superiority of the enemy fighters, we were still in a position to take air superiority at any time or in any place. It turned out that the same Staffeln were always deployed against us. We recognised them from the winter of '43 at Kirovograd, for their machines had red engine covers and gold Soviet stars, the 'Red Falcons'. We would arrive at a given sector and our friends would turn up again. Even when fighting was at its most severe, our Gruppen were always superior to the Russians, for we were more experienced and better trained. We were on the Crimea for two months and were entangled daily in aerial battles, with some success, but we did not lose any pilots. Machines could be replaced.

It was a typical day – grey clouds, mist and the ground sodden. It was only possible to fly from the Russian-built concrete runways, on either side of which the Staffel's machines were set up. The operational briefing over, the pilots climbed into their machines, turned them on and the mechanics started the engines. Across from me stood 7 Staffel aircraft, which were preparing, as I was, to take off. Suddenly something ignited in their machines – they were being shot at by Russian pilots. My mechanic made a leap and disappeared from the wing. Across from me the machines were already in flames, but my engine was running. I closed my canopy and tried to take off. In my haste I took off, not on the runway, but straight across the muddy wasteland heading north. I was past the point of no return and raced through the mud directly towards the hangar.

The Russians consisted of a group of around nine Yaks, diving out of the clouds from an altitude of about 1,000 metres and flying as a group towards the FW 190s parked on the runway. To my luck, most of the Yaks shot at the machines on the left side; they made only a single attack then disappeared as they had come. As it later turned out, one remained and made a second attack on my FW 190. With a great deal of effort I had managed to leave the ground and just managed to clear the hangar with difficulty, my undercarriage still down, when the Yak shot at me. I was lucky in that the Russian was far too fast and was himself surprised at his opportunity. He missed me entirely, shooting away past me with his machine. I had been warned and was now aware of what the Russians would do in this situation. With the undercarriage and flaps in, the 190 was making up ground, the weapons ready, my 250kg bombs jettisoned in preparation to take up the aerial battle. Unfortunately, I didn't have much time – the Yak 9 was already behind me and shooting, but the pilot must have been a beginner, for again his aim wasn't very good. At this stage I still did not know whether he was alone or whether there were still other Yaks in the area. Meanwhile I had reached sufficient speed to do battle.

I could observe my opponent, now the chances were even and it boiled down to flying ability. I was given an advantage; ground control informed me on the radio that this was the only Yak around, at least in this area. Subsequently I succeeded in getting behind him, but my shots were also unsuccessful – I was a bit nervous. The furious turning battle was played out about 300-400 metres over the airfield. In addition my colleagues on the ground were on the radio playing along. I told them to shut their mouths and turn off the radio. A savage battle now began; the pilot was better than I had reckoned him to be at the beginning. Each of us tried to get behind the other and get into a good position. While turning, each of us managed to fire, but neither of us made any successful hits. We had been circling now for more than 5 minutes when the Russian made the decisive error by trying to break out of the turning circle and leave the area, heading off to the right. He set his machine on the horizontal and, at this moment, I sat about 50-80 metres behind him and had him full in my sights. I pressed the trigger on the cannon and something flared up in his cockpit. The Yak tipped over on its right wing and fell to the ground.

My friends were shouting into the radio, 'You've shot him down! You can land – there are no more Russians over the airfield.' I could hardly believe that the battle had been so quickly decided; the flight only lasted 15 minutes and the fight with the Yak about 9-10 minutes. After landing I taxied to my parking place and shut off the engine, happy to be on the ground again. So many times over the last few weeks I had not escaped unscathed and had had to land after being attacked. My mechanics greeted me joyfully; they had been up there with me in spirit, and told me that nine or ten Yaks had come out of the clouds and attacked the airfield. One had turned back and attacked my 190, the other Yak pilots leaving their colleague in the lurch and flying back to their base.

The Staffelkapitän congratulated me on my success and drove me to the crash site of the Yak. The pilot was a Kapitän with about 350 enemy flights. He had papers and a letter from his parents on him. His name was Kapitän Ivanov, 24 years old and an old hand flying at the front, with blue eyes and blond hair and medals as well. He even wore Czarist shoulder epaulettes, the first we had ever seen.

We then drove to the Gruppe command post and I reported to the Kommandeur. He said briefly, 'Buchner, at 1400hrs there's a Ju 52 going to Breslau and there's a place for you on it.'

He congratulated me on the success, but was of the opinion that I had had a bit of luck at the beginning of the aerial battle, but subsequently showed, as we fought, what the 190 could achieve. One didn't always have so much luck. Because I had been shot down twice in the last few weeks, I was being sent to the Fighter Pilots' Home at Bad-Wiessee in Germany. Following that, I got another three weeks' home leave. I quickly got my things together, sorted out my papers and said goodbye to my friends. I hurried to get to the Ju 52 accompanied by my friends.

We were encircled. The Crimean Peninsula had been surrounded since November 1943 and the safest way to the mainland was still by air. A crowd of solders were standing in front of the Ju and a Feldwebel from the crew was informing the passengers that a place was reserved for me. I got hold of a place beside the radio-man. After a short time we were in the air and heading westwards towards the Black Sea. The Junkers was full of soldiers from all arms of the service whose thoughts were already in Germany, not knowing that we first had to make it over the Black Sea. For me, as a pilot, the question was, what were our friends from the other side doing? Were they in the air – would they see the Ju? After flying for about 14 hours we reached Odessa, the Ju flying over the sea at an altitude of about 50-100 metres. After Odessa a blanket of cloud came towards us from the north-west, and the Ju coachman had to go to a higher altitude, flying above the clouds in the direction of home. After hours of flying we could still not see the ground. The radio-man now began to handle his instrument and strip it down. I had a premonition that something unpleasant was going to happen.

After a short time he asked me if I had a fuse in my pocket. Because I was wearing a Luftwaffe shirt with the German Cross in Gold, but no pilot insignia, he must have thought that I might have been a radio-man myself. Unfortunately, I couldn't help him, but the pilot still wanted a bearing. Anyway, the crew didn't know where we were exactly and we still weren't through the clouds. We were out of the area that had been surrounded, so hopefully we would soon reach an airfield in a short while. After flying for 4 hours the pilot finally pushed through the clouds at about 200 metres altitude, we could see the ground and after another 20 minutes we were in Lemberg. The pilot had done a superb job of flying by the seat of his pants and could happily do without his radio-man. The soldiers and I were all happy to have reached Lemberg after so long a flight. I thanked the pilot, an Oberfeldwebel, and said goodbye. Now to the railway station and via Breslau, Dresden and Munich to Bad-Wiessee. After a day spent catching and changing trains I finally reached the Fighter Pilots' Home, making the last leg of the journey over the Wiessee on a steamer.

Just near the mooring there was a lovely pension – this would be my home for the next four weeks. Many fighter pilots approached me and each wanted to know where I had come from and what Geschwader I was with. There were also familiar faces here from JG 3 and JG 52 who had been with our Gruppe on the same airfields in Russia. There were lots of questions and lots to tell and just as much to celebrate. Once a week, every Friday, we had to appear at lunch in uniform, which was the closest we came to strict military protocol. The rest of the time we were given a free rein to go our own way. I, at any rate, spent some marvellous days there; one could go skiing (the equipment was provided), or take a boat trip, and there was plenty to drink.

With a suitcase full of drink (a 0.7 litre bottle cost DM 2), I took the train to Salzburg. There I put the suitcase in a locker at the station and made my way home on foot. My parents were surprised and very happy at my arrival. I had been home at Christmas and now, three months later, I was again at home on leave. First, I convinced my father to take the handcart and go to the railway station with me to pick up the suitcase and its contents. My father was very pleased to get these very drinkable items – in our home town you could only get such things with coupons.

Well, as usual I went off into the mountains. Unfortunately there were hardly any of my friends left at home; most were at the front and many had fallen. Naturally I told my parents the reason why I had again got leave to go home after such a short period. They implored me to be more careful in the future and to have some regard for my life. The three weeks at home passed quickly, too quickly, then it was the usual: things packed and off to the railway station. My father gave me a good piece of advice. My mother was, as usual, sad and very worried – she felt that I should be careful and not too much of a daredevil – so I went to the railway station alone. To say goodbye at the railway station was too sad for me, and the many women and children saying goodbye to their husbands and fathers made me very pensive. How many of them would never come back?

For the fourth time I went eastwards on the train via Vienna and Krakow. On earlier occasions my father had always taken me to the station to say goodbye, but the scenes that were played out there ... well, I couldn't do that to my old father. In Vienna, at the Eastern Railway Station, it was the same old nonsense: step up, be counted and climb into the holiday train to the front. The people who came last couldn't come, but got a stamp from the Station Headquarters and had to appear again the next day for the same procedure.

With this dodge one could pad out the holiday for a day or two in Vienna. However, this ruse was no incentive for me – I wanted to get back to the front to my Staffel. From Vienna the train went as far as Reichshof in Poland. There was a pool of Schlacht pilots who had been kept back, and also an aircraft park. The pilots who were on their way to units in Russia got FW 190s to fly over to their units, which saved using transfer pilots who were reputed to be really bad, and lost a lot of aircraft on the transfer flights. This method also meant that the pilots from the front did not have to take the troop train and the machines, as well as taking them less time to arrive at their units.

At Reichshof there were already a number of pilots present who were going to the front to join my Gruppe. The unit commander at Reichshof appointed me group leader, so I had to lead fourteen FW 190s to Romania and further on to the Crimea. Among these young pilots was Oberleutnant Biermann, a former signals officer from our Gruppe. He wanted to do pilots' training and was now returning to the unit as a pilot. After a few days in Reichshof I gathered my pilots together and gave a flying lecture, assigned three Schwarme and announced the flight plan and the next airfield we were landing at. On 6 April 1944 we flew out of Jaslonka, via Prossnitz, Vienna, Aspern, Budapest, Belgrade and Semlin. In Semlin we had to wait because of bad weather. The 'Iron Gate' and the Carpathians were closed and a pilots' information service had been set up close by. An old Lufthansa captain in a Ju 88 was flying ahead as group leader, pushing through the cloud cover and taking groups as far as Bucharest. I called him and explained my mission; he was experienced at flying blind and said that we should wait another two days in Semlin, then see what happened. I was to come back again in two days, but my crew should be ready for departure. After a pilots' conference we knocked around Belgrade and partied, as far as it was possible to get anything to do so. The quiet period was not unpleasant for me, but the young pilots wanted to get to the front – they were in a hurry. They were pushing to get there and were driving the pilots' guide service people crazy.

Then we were ready. The weather was definitely not better, but the flight captain had had enough of the youngsters' eternal questions. He explained to the assembled pilots that take off would be at 1200hrs and we would fly in formation, seven machines hanging on to his left wing and seven hanging on to the right one. He would fly into the barrier at 400kmph and pull through the clouds. Above the clouds he would lead us as far as Bucharest, where he would shoot off a signal. He would then leave and fly back to Semlin. We were then to push down through the cloud. I instructed my pilots and assigned the take off and flight sequence, as well as that for the breakthrough over Bucharest. The young pilots rolled their eyes, but they had annoyed the guide and now he was serious. On the 13th we took off, with myself taking position on the left wing of the Ju 88. At about 500 metres we went into cloud and headed upwards. The radio was quiet; I stayed calmly on his wing so that the others could also keep their positions. The guide held the promised speed constant and after flying for about 20 minutes we were in the sun above the clouds. The guide turned eastwards and held his 400kmph. Suddenly he was ready and fired off his signal flare, turned around and was away.

We were over Bucharest. I assembled my flock and reduced speed. Doing 350kmph we dived into the clouds, heading east-south-east. Slowly we lost altitude and I waited for the landscape to appear. The weather was merciful to us, for at 800 metres above ground we came out of the clouds in an orderly fashion, the young pilots were all right and the formation had held in the clouds. After correcting the course southwards, I tried to get my bearings and asked my colleagues over the radio whether any of them knew our position. We were lucky: after flying for about 10 minutes we reached the city limits of Bucharest. Our guide, with his good sense of position, had left us near there. The Bucharest-Baniasa airfield was in the south-east part of the city, it was easy for us to find it and, after a total flight of 90 minutes, we landed there smoothly. While I went off to flight control to take care of the formalities, our machines were refuelled and taken care of. The Command there informed me that I was to fly to Mamaia and report there to the Fliegerführer Krim (Commander, Flying, Crimea). After a short flight conference we continued, the three Schwarme again pushing eastwards. After flying for about 35 minutes we reached the coast of the Black Sea and Mamaia, an airfield on the edge of the Black Sea, north of Konstanza. Here there was only an old wooden hangar, nothing else – no accommodation and no other buildings. The nearest good-sized building was in the direction of Konstanza, the villa of the Romanian King Michael.

After landing our machines we were directed to a parking place, where we shut off the engines. We had successfully taken our fourteen machines, without major incident, to the front. On the airfield itself lively activity reigned, with a number of transport machines, Ju 52s, Messerschmitt Me 323 Gigants and Savoia-Marchetti SM 82s[33] ferrying wounded soldiers from, and ammunition to, the Crimea. The airfield was totally overtaxed; the wounded lay on the ground around the perimeter of the airfield, without protection from the sun and without nursing care.

So, what was going to happen now? I took myself off to the command post and reported to Fliegerführer Krim. I was generally received heartily, for, after all, I had brought fourteen operationally ready 190s to Mamaia. Then came the first surprise: there would be no more machines flown to Sevastopol. The Crimea was being evacuated and we were to wait for further orders. The position was frantic and unclear. No one knew what the actual situation was from the battlefield. The transports flew non-stop, picking up the wounded from Sevastopol. The weather was really bad, the clouds were hardly higher than 200 metres and visibility was only 300-500 metres. The flight distance from Mamaia to Seva was exactly 400km. For the moment I was to look and see if I could get hold of a place in a tent, then report to the command post again in 2 hours.

Large, slow and fairly vulnerable, the Messerschmitt Me 323 still made a highly significant contribution to Luftwaffe airlift operations throughout the Mediterranean and Russian theatres. The enormous size of the beast is immediately apparent by comparison with the truck.

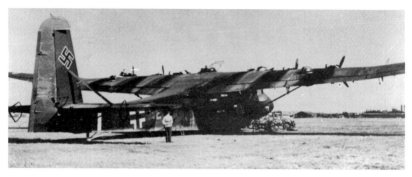

In this rear view of a Messerschmitt Me 323 the tailfin and rudder tower some 10 metres high. Without power-assisted controls the type demanded strong pilots to fly it. Usually grossly overloaded, and despite the risks of interception, slow-flying machines of I./TG 5 similar to this performed near-miracles in ferrying out hundreds of wounded soldiers from the shrinking German holdings in the Crimea.

After speaking to my pilots, who were getting to know what life in the field was like for the first time, we made plans to occupy the next few hours. One took care of the refuelling of the machines, another looked for places to sleep, a third organised some food and the rest kept watch over the machines and our belongings.

Thus nearly everybody had something to do and our idleness was at an end. During my whole time on the front in Russia I had never seen such a state of affairs. There was a total feeling of doom. Everyone was overtaxed, no one had any idea of what was going on and there was no Kommandant on the airfield responsible for accommodation and rations.

After each pilot had been given his duty, I went back to the command post and asked if there were any new orders. Here, because of my request, I was promised a guide, an Me 110 from a night-fighter Gruppe[34] in Zilistea. He should be here in Mamaia on the following day. Up to that time the weather conditions had been so bad that a crossing would have been irresponsible. In Khersones (Sevastopol West), there remained only a strip 5km wide in German hands. In the poor visibility in the south, if we were to fly past this strip we would reach land in Tuapse and land on Russian territory. It was fundamentally a ticklish situation, but the young pilots wanted to get to the front. They believed that they had arrived too late.

It was dark and my men had not found any accommodation. So we did what we then so often had to do in the East: we took a tarpaulin and set up a place under the machines. At first they looked at it with consternation, but in the end they all had a good night's sleep. In the morning we again had problems finding breakfast, but sorted it out in the end. Around midday I was ordered to the command post and now it was all systems go. The flying ban was lifted, the guide machine had arrived and we were to fly out at 1400hrs. At the same time the pilot of the 110 was introduced, an old Oberfeldwebel, who explained the proposed flight to me. I asked him to come along to my pilots and give a talk on his plan for flying across to Seva: we would start heading eastwards with seven machines on each side in tight formation, no radio traffic (except in emergencies), 400kmph speed, 100 metres altitude, and over Khersones he would give three green light signals. Without speaking over the radio, the 110 would then turn back to the mainland. Apart from that, he wished us luck. Actually, he wasn't very pleased about this task, and was happy that he would soon be back in Zilistea again.

On 14 April 1944 at 1600hrs we took off in very bad weather, heading for the Crimea. We positioned ourselves at the take off point and off we went. The guide doggedly held his course, altitude and speed and there was nothing to be heard on the radio. At times one could not see the sea. I was very pleased then that I had asked the command for a guide. After flying for an hour we flew over the lighthouse at Khersones, the green signals blazed and the 110 turned away south.

We were on our own and put ourselves into our landing order. The guide said nothing over the radio; he certainly didn't want to be pestered by the Russians. We landed the machines uneventfully. After nine days we had finally reached our Gruppe together. After landing I reported to the Kommandeur and, at the same time, introduced the pilots who had been posted to the Geschwader. My friends were overjoyed that I was back with the Staffel. That evening we exchanged news and I was told of the situation at the front. In a word – sickening. The next day, because of the weather, no operations were flown. I went to visit friends in the other Staffels. The star of our Gruppe was August Lambert from 4 Staffel; he had first arrived in the Crimea in March, but shot down Russians like flies. He had been forbidden to fly for some time because he had had difficulties with the adjutant; at that time the practice was still so strict that they could punish a very good pilot with a flying ban. Thus they prevented Leutnant Lambert from being in line for a Knight's Cross. In the months of March and April he shot down ninety-nine aircraft. At the beginning of May, because he was not allowed to fly, he was withdrawn from operations and flown out by Ju 52 to Mamaia.

Oberfeldwebel Hermann Buchner on a fine spring day near Zilistea in Romania.

The strain is beginning to tell: the author has just landed at Karankut after his 500th mission on 4 March 1944. His aircraft, 'Black L', is in the background.

We were up nearly every day and had contact with the Russians on every operation. I was in good form and shot down many Russian aircraft during these missions – Il 2s, Yak 9s and Boston bombers were rich booty for my 190. Sadly, we lost a very good friend in Sevastopol, Feldwebel Hans Schwertfeger from 6 Staffel. He crashed to his death near the English Cemetery (from the Crimean War).

The front came ever closer to the airfield and the situation for our Gruppe was ever more threatening. Daily the Russians attacked the airfield from the air with bombs and cannon. The artillery was active, shooting out to sea, and at night the ships' gunfire was uncomfortably easy to see. When we were not in the air we pilots were nearby in a naval coastal artillery shelter. This bunker had been built by the OG Todt after the conquest of the Crimea in 1942; it had a 2-metre-thick concrete roof and another 2 metres of gravel on top of that.

One night we were hit midships by a 500kg bomb in one of the incessant attacks. It thundered frighteningly, the wooden beds shook and dust was everywhere. The lights went out and no one knew what was actually happening. Some tried to reach the open, up more than twenty stairs in the dark, with only the starry night sky visible. There was a crater down to the concrete roof and our vehicle was a wreck, but the roof had held.

On 26 April Oberfeldwebel Fred Lagois was awarded the Knight's Cross, and that night the other parts of the Gruppe assembled to see the Kommandeur hang it around him. We celebrated with Fred for half the night, and our music was the sound of Russian bombs on the airfield. In the morning Fred was to fly a reconnaissance mission. We told him that one of us would fly the mission instead. Fred disagreed with the suggestion – he wanted to fly his reconnaissance mission himself. On his return he was shot down by his own 4cm flak over the airfield. He and his wingman came into the airfield from the north-west, the flak began to shoot, set up a barrage and all the flak on the airfield opened fire. Of all things, a gun just near our bunker, a 4cm naval gun, hit the 190 as it was pulling up over the sea. He didn't have a chance and the 190 plunged vertically into the sea. Another of the old ones had fallen. Fred had been with me and the Gruppe since Werl. He was buried in the depths of the Black Sea, together with many soldiers of the Wehrmacht.

Only meagre supplies were now coming through from the home base in Mamaia, Romania. The Staffels had only three or four operational aircraft available. The fighter Gruppe on the airfield was also just barely operational. Our airfield, Khersones, was the last in use in the Crimea. Day and night it came under bombardment from the artillery, the ships and, not least, the Russian aircraft. It was overflowing with wounded soldiers waiting to be shipped out by the Kriegsmarine or the Luftwaffe transport aircraft; they lay on the ground in the open air in the hot sun and were rained on by bombs. No one could help the poor soldiers; the unfortunate men could not be protected as there were only a few shelters still available.

The last days and nights were terrible. At the beaches the embarkation officers were armed with machine guns to bring some kind of order to the crush of soldiers. Yes, in the end, even Generals were assigned as marshals or embarkation officers. The landing positions on the west bank and on the cliffs were besieged by scattered soldiers, for each wanted to get back to the mainland. The ferries and the various landing boats that were still bringing supplies were stormed by soldiers, who simply threw the ships' supplies overboard. The embarkation officers had no chance of bringing order to the unloading and reloading process. The ferries

At Khersones, near Sevastopol, in the Crimea, in April 1944, Russian artillery fire can be seen in the background, with the dugouts in which the author and his comrades lived for four months in the foreground.

Oblt Ernst Beutelspacher (left) and Lt Boole of 6./SG 2 stand outside their bunker at Khersones in May 1944. Beutelspacher was a long-serving member of SchG 1/SG 2, and won the Knight's Cross in May 1944 after 500 missions. He was killed in action against US fighters over Romania in July with five victories to his credit.

Pilots of 6./SG 2 relax in the company of two attractive young Russian women at Khersones in March 1944. The author may be the man lying down at the rear of the group.

No mistaking who lives here! The Schlacht triangle and field direction sign
point the way to the command post of II./SG 2 in the Crimea, March 1944.

A bleak scene on the steppes in winter: probably taken during the winter of
1943-44, this is a typical front-line landing ground with the FW 190s of this
unidentified Schlachter unit left in the open and only the minimum of shelter for
the crews. The nearest aircraft is already bombed up ready for the next strike.

The nearest of these two Focke-Wulf FW 190s is an unusual variant to find in a winter scene such as this, as it is an F-2/Trop with tropical filters to the oil cooler intakes. Possibly the opposite effect was hoped for. The aircraft to the rear carries wing bomb racks and is an A-5/U17 or F-3/R1. It also carries the horizontal bar of an unidentified II Gruppe and a yellow Eastern Front band on the fuselage. The cowl ring also appears to be yellow while the spinner seems to be white. Note how the nearest aircraft has had its wheel covers removed to avoid them being fouled with mud.

This is a closer view of the rear aircraft in the previous photograph. An opening in the leading edge of the port wing for a gun camera can be made out, and the slight bump over the MG 17 guns in the upper fuselage can just be seen.

Most aircraft servicing on the Eastern Front had to be done entirely in the open air, so the groundcrew of FW 190 'N' were extremely fortunate. Apart from the II Gruppe bar there are no other clues as to which ground-attack unit the machine belongs to.

were overloaded: instead of 400 men there were 800-900 men on board. The sailors in the Navy accomplished the impossible; the soldiers baled out water with their steel helmets. Luckily, the swell during the days of evacuation was not high.

The front was now only 2-3km from the eastern edge of the airfield, and all operations were carried out under mortar fire. Our mechanics achieved the impossible – they were the silent heroes. Near each aircraft bay they had dug one-man holes, which provided some protection during bomb attacks or artillery bombardment. In haste we pilots also looked out for these holes. After a low-level attack from Il 2 pilots, one of the shot-up aircraft had to make an emergency landing. With lowered landing gear it came diagonally across to the landing area. Just before setting down the pilot opened fire. Again he found himself on the receiving end of a burst of fire from the flak, whereupon he pulled up his landing gear again and did a belly-landing near our bunker. After he came to a standstill in his Il 2, he climbed out and opened fire with his pistol at German soldiers running towards him. In a short while he was taken prisoner.

In accordance with an order from the XVII Army, the troops had to hand over all horses from the horse-drawn units to a special unit near our airfield – they were not to fall into Russian hands. They were all unbridled and shot dead with machine guns on the south side of the island. The bridles were taken back to the mainland on marine ships. The members of the Kommando had their hands full. Around 30,000 horses found their graves in the Black Sea; in a gentle easterly breeze one could smell the stench from the corpses that had been driven into the sea, and flying over the south coast one could make out the carcases, looking a bit like vegetables in a clear soup. For us it was obvious that the island, and Khersones, could no longer be held. The transports, Ju 52s, Gigants and the He 111s, could only carry out supply flights at night.

Because of the hopeless situation and the few machines left to us, on 9 May 1944 a joint Schwarm of Me 109s and FW 190s was formed. The Staffels had no operationally ready machines available. Schwarm leaders were to be pilots of JG 52. Around 1000hrs my wingman and I taxied to the start. Unfortunately my number two rolled into a bomb crater and thus ended his mission. I arrived somewhat late at the starting point. An Me 109 was already in position and waited for us. Unfortunately another Me 109, probably the first pilot's wingman, had also encountered difficulties while taxiing. The fact was that only one 109 and one 190 reached the start. The 109 had Kommandeur pennants on the side of the tail; the pilot indicated with a single gesture that he would be leading the Rotte.

We lined up and took off. The take off was westwards, and after a short spell of climbing I could tell that my 190 wasn't bad. I could keep up well. Over the sea, at about 1,000 metres altitude, we received our first information from the Ground Control Station 'Christian': 'Indians in the Sevastopol harbour area, altitude 3,000-4,000 metres.' My Schwarm leader climbed steadily and soon we had reached 4,000 metres. Coming from the west, we flew towards Seva and already could discern our enemy brothers. Now the game began – my Schwarm leader came through on the radio: 'Attack!'

He flew straight into the middle of the pile of twenty-five or thirty Yaks and scattered our friends in all directions. We circled with the Russian fighters for about 10 minutes without being able to make a single shot, but we succeeded in driving them out of the airspace. I had the opportunity here of meeting a Schwarm leader 'par excellence'. 'Christian' came over the radio again and gave us the task of flying in the Balaclava area. The 109 slowed its speed and the pilot made hand signals indicating that I should lead the Rotte. With my 190 I was now in front of the 109 in the battle lines. After flying for a short while, we found ourselves in the area we had been ordered to and could make out the blast clouds from the flak. We had only been there a few minutes when the dance began up front – a wild curving battle with Yak 9s, who were there in large numbers. I was lucky and shot down a Yak 9. It was a good shot and the aircraft crashed to the ground, burning. The 'Indians' took off eastwards and we let our friends go. Far beneath us, Il 2s were passing, flying attacks against our artillery positions in the Balaclava area. We dived down and attacked them from behind. They were just in the process of dropping their bombs and definitely did not notice our approach. After a few bursts of fire I succeeded in sending an Il 2 to the happy hunting grounds. The left flaps on the Ilyushin burned brightly, he lost height rapidly and crashed to the ground. After a total flying time of about 45 minutes, my Schwarm leader took over the Rotte and flew back to Khersones. After landing smoothly, we split up and taxied to our parking places. Shortly the Schwarm leader, a Hauptmann, came over to our parking area and asked, 'Where is the pilot of the 190 who just flew a mission?' I came forward and the Hauptmann congratulated me.

Nobody, neither the fighter pilot nor myself, as a Schlachter pilot, had had difficulties in flying an operation together. Together we drove to our command post of II. SG 2 'Immelmann'. Our Kommandeur was very happy with our report of the joint operation. He poured out a round of vodka and toasted the good 'Jäger-Schlachter' battle partnership during the defence of the Crimea, which had lasted from 23 January until 9 May 1944. Our Kommandeur made it clear to us that, during the evacuation, we would have to take all the airfield personnel (clerks, mechanics and medics) back to the mainland in the rear fuselage of our aircraft. In addition, it was stipulated that my Schwarm and I would fly protection over the airfield when the Gruppe took off, then land again and refuel. At midday on 9 May the order to evacuate came through. As previously arranged everything was ready. Unfortunately, the refuelling vehicles had already rashly been blown up and, when we landed, we were forced to refuel using buckets. The situation was very dismal, for everywhere there were soldiers who wanted to get back to the mainland. There was no more transport by air – my Schwarm was the last flying unit. My Gruppe, or more accurately, the rest of my Gruppe, was already on its way to Mamaia.

Around 1800hrs we were ready and we taxied to the start. The pilot of the fourth machine had a bit of bad luck when he rolled over a bomb crater and did a headstand. We remaining three pilots shut off our engines. Around us there burned vehicles, aircraft and piles of stores. Each of us took a person from the damaged 190. It was slowly becoming high time that we got into the air so that we could reach Mamaia.

Again we turned on the engines and taxied to the start positions. While we were trying to make up for lost time, the Russians bombarded the airfield as our goodbye from Khersones. On the west side of the airfield, near the lighthouse, we had to fly through thick clouds from the detonations. We also managed to get through this darkness and reach the open sea, where, at about 500 metres, we had to play with a few Yak 9s who wanted to spoil our trip home to Mamaia. In spite of the people in the back of the aircraft, the Yaks still had no chance with us. We weren't looking for a fight, with our trusty mechanics in the back – all we wanted to do was to reach the mainland.

In any event the Russians couldn't chalk up another success with us. After a few attempts at attacking, our 'Red Friends' broke away and flew back towards Seva. After I was convinced that the Yaks were gone, we throttled down and flew in bad visibility at about 1,500 metres altitude westwards towards Mamaia. Slowly the sun began to set and we flew into the night. After flying for about 40 minutes, one could just discern light signals in the distance – our comrades on the Romanian coast were already waiting for us. We were still 30-40km away from the coast, but nothing could happen to us now, for we had escaped from hell. Around 1900hrs, after flying for an hour, we reached the mainland. Makeshift lights had been set up on the landing strip using lanterns. My Schwarm (only three aircraft) had been the last Jäger or Schlachter unit to leave the Khersones/Sevastopol airfield. During that night (9-10 May) and the following (10-11), only the occasional He 111 and Ju 52 landed, bringing over wounded and the remainder of the Army Staff. For our Gruppe, the short posting that had taken place in January 1944 (supposedly for two or three days) had finally come to an end after four months.

After taking off as the last one in Seva, I was the last to land my 190 in Mamaia. The night was dark, the landing strip lighting makeshift. On taxiing my 190 I noticed that my friend's 190 still stood in front of me on the runway. I was forced to brake to try and bring my aircraft to a standstill, unfortunately without success. To

An aerial view of the lighthouse at Khersones, which was such a landmark for navigators on both sea and air. It was the last part of the Crimea to be given up by the Germans and the last sight of the Crimea that the author and his comrades saw as they finally evacuated the peninsula.

avoid a collision I trod on the right pedal and turned so that the undercarriage would shear away. No sooner said than done – there was a terrific crash and my 190 lay on the ground.

It was just in time, for right in front of me lay one of the Jäger's Me 109s on the ground. Having other worries, I leapt out of the machine: I had to free my mechanics from the tail, so I opened the cover with a screwdriver and freed them from the dark. The machine was actually badly damaged, but my friends and I were back on the mainland, safely on the ground with the rest of our friends and our Gruppe. We, the Gruppe, had kept our promise and brought our

The Junkers Ju 52 floatplane shown here is actually in the Aegean, but the usefulness of such types was recognised in the Black Sea area. In early 1943 twenty aircraft were locally converted to floatplanes and used to supply the Kuban bridgehead. Flights to and from the besieged German 17th Army in the Crimea continued until the final evacuation on 11 May 1944.

Across the Black Sea from the Crimea was the Romanian maritime aircraft base of Mamaia. Reconnaissance and ASR aircraft from both the Luftwaffe and the Romanian Air Force were based there. This is Heinkel He 114C-1 No 2 in service with either the Romanian 101 or 102 Coastal Reconnaissance Squadron.

ground personnel back to the mainland with us. I reported back to
the Kommandeur. He was very happy that his last soldiers had
reached the mainland as well. My mechanics had also stowed a
demi-john of vodka in the tail, which was fetched and opened. The
landing, the crash and the rescue were now suitably celebrated. The
party came to an end very late – we were very tired. We slept in the
open air, the same place we had just been celebrating in.

Chapter Ten

Romania
10 May 1944-July 1944

The 10th of May 1944 – a new day. In the morning we could review the situation, and saw that the fighters had had to accept several crashes on landing. But I had also damaged my 190. One of the fighter pilots had taxied a 109 over the border of the airfield and turned over. He had mechanics sitting in his tail, as did we, but they survived the ground loop well.

My colleagues moved further towards Zilistea, near Buzau, a distance of about 150km, where our ground element had landed from the Ukraine. The remaining parts of the Crimean Command waited for a Ju 52 transport flight to Zilistea. Around midday the transporter arrived, we were loaded on and off we went to Zilistea. We were the last of the Gruppe to have survived that operation and come back. After four months' hard fighting we had lost some good pilots and good friends, but we had also achieved a great deal of success. After four months' absence, we came back to our Staffels, to our personal belongings. We could shower again and bath again, for there was plenty of hot water available. Finally, we could change our underwear and carry out various other little jobs. The disadvantage, naturally, was that we again had a Spiess, who was intent on making soldiers out of our mechanics and out of us pilots as well. These people from the part of the Command that had been left behind had still not twigged that we now found ourselves on the retreat. The Herr Hauptfeldwebel simply could not believe that the mechanics from the Crimean Commando had been awarded the Iron Cross Class II by the Kommandeur that last day at Khersones. He couldn't understand how this decoration ceremony could have taken place without his knowledge. He was definitely too far away from the front.

In the following days our Gruppe had a rest from operations while we were re-supplied with materiel and a few new pilots came to the Staffels. I got another new 190, and my mechanics and I polished it. On the front left side of the fuselage was put an Indian smoking a peace pipe and the fin was painted with the number of aerial victories. Now I had a 190 I was again ready for duty. We were accommodated with Romanian farmers in a village near the airfield. I shared a room in a farmer's mud cottage with Gefreiter Wolfgang Richthofen (son of General Richthofen). The farm people

The author celebrates his safe return from his 600th operational mission on 4 June 1944. Seen here at Bakau in Romania, he is flanked by his comrades who made up the Rotte formation. On the left is Dieter Voigt, with Theo Winter on the right. Buchner's groundcrew have made their own contribution to the celebrations by giving him another crate to fly – literally!

were very friendly to us and often entertained us with food and drink. The farmer supplied us with schnapps and we also often took a vehicle to the neighbouring town of Buzau. Here, total peace still prevailed. We could hardly believe that only a few days previously we had been on the Crimea, not knowing whether we would die, get out or be captured. In any case, neither the local population nor the Germans had any idea of the real war situation. We were flying in our Staffels and practising attacks on Ju 88s, which were simulating US

An ecstatic Hermann Buchner receives congratulations from Ernst Beutelspacher immediately after landing at the end of his 600th combat mission.

A few moments later the reaction is setting in. With the mandatory placard around his neck, a more pensive Buchner is in conversation with his crew chief at the conclusion of his 600th mission. Six weeks later he was awarded the Knight's Cross. On the left is Gefreiter Wolfgang Richthofen, Buchner's wingman and the son of General Wolfram von Richthofen, who disappeared somewhere over Romania after an air combat with Soviet fighters.

bombers. Every day we flew twenty-three practice missions with built-in cameras, which was useful training for us Schlachter pilots. Around this time the Americans were flying missions from Italy (Bari) against the oilfields in Ploesti-Mezil in Romania.

In the middle of June I was tasked with leading the 4th Staffel. I left 6 Staffel with a feeling of melancholy, for I had been with them for nearly two years and was one of the oldest there, along with Beutelspacher. The 4th was composed of all young pilots who had only come from Germany a few weeks previously. August Lambert had gone to Germany to regain his health, having achieved ninety-nine aerial victories in a very short time on the Crimea. Only some of the pilots in 4 Staffel had even flown enemy missions, the rest were beginners. My days were filled with instruction in tactics and combat flying. For me the task was fascinating and the pilots were enthusiastic students. After several days of regeneration we were ready; the Gruppe was considered operationally ready again and transferred to Bakau, north of Foçsani. It was basically a grass airfield near a town; we were accommodated in tents and the parking places were close to

The author undertakes last-minute checks with his crew chief. His FW 190 in the background carries the code letter 'Z'; he flew such an aircraft in late April-early May from Khersones in the Crimea, and at the end of May from Bakau in Romania. As he was then still with 6./SG 2, the letter is presumably yellow.

the Staffel accommodation. Bakau was an old former monarchy town and more then half of its inhabitants were Jews, proper eastern Jews with caftans. Here also reigned total peace. In the evenings and on Sundays the people went into town in their best clothing and walked in the park. During these days the majority of my pilots flew their first operations. Like us the enemy had not yet deployed their best Staffels on the front. The German Army was attempting to build a new line of defence in the north and the east. This was actually very useful for

Oberleutnant Beutelspacher (left) and Leutnant Lambert were photographed some time between 4 May 1944, when Ernst Beutelspacher received his Knight's Cross, and 22 July, when he was killed in action against US fighters over Foçsani, Romania. At the time he was Staffelkapitän of 6./SG 2.

breaking in my young pilots gently. The work of the last few weeks paid off and the men enjoyed the daily flying. Our Kommandeur provided a bit of variety for us, and between operations we were able to take a vehicle into town and drink coffee. For us old ones it wasn't a war any more. Life in the town passed by peacefully, the people having no idea that the front would shortly overrun the town.

Slowly things at the front took on their familiar degree of harshness. The Yak 9s with their red engine covers were again in the skies, loud heroes of the Soviet Union. For months our enemies, good pilots, had not shied away from battle. In June we lost the boss of 6 Staffel, who had been with me in the old 8 Staffel of SG 1. Bleckmann was already on his return flight when his 190 exploded and he had no chance to take to his parachute. I also lost my wingman, Wolfgang Richthofen, in an aerial battle over Jassy at 3,000 metres. We were fighting against about fifteen Yak 9s – our familiar 'Stalin Falcons' were there again. We circled a bit and both got an aerial victory. I congratulated Richthofen over the radio, but got no answer. The curving battle was wild and I attempted to get out of the mêlée, which I succeeded in doing. I could see nothing or find nothing of my wingman, and I couldn't make radio contact with him. I was alone over Jassy. The Russians had disappeared as well, so I decided to return to Bakau. After landing I asked the mechanics if Richthofen had already got back. The answer came back negative. I reported to the Kommandeur and noted the loss of my wingman Wolfgang Richthofen after an aerial battle over Jassy. Enquiries with army units in the area revealed that some ground troops had seen such an aerial battle between Yak 9s and two FW 190s and that two Yak 9s had been shot down. At the end of the aerial battle one of the 190s had flown away to the north. We never heard another thing as to the whereabouts of Richthofen. It was a real shame – he was a very nice young pilot in the Staffel. His father, General Oberst von Richthofen, was shattered by his son's disappearance.

Now things were really serious. We made our first acquaintance with the US fighters over Romania. My Rotte and I, with Unteroffizier Ertl flying as my wingman, were employed against Russian bombers. After taking off we were instructed to head southeast at an altitude of 2,000 metres. After a flying time of about 30 minutes we were in the Focsani area, but we didn't spy a single aircraft. We received instructions to climb higher and take a westward course. Still no Russian bombers, but then they never flew at those altitudes and certainly not so far into the enemy hinterland. We had reached 4,000 metres and ground control ordered us to climb even higher, but our machines didn't carry oxygen – we Schlachter never flew at such altitudes and we had never needed oxygen. We climbed further, but it was clear to me that either we had been mistakenly directed or that we were being set up against US units. Over the radio I said as much to Ertl, and he wanted to watch the skies and stay in the area nonetheless. In any case, it was an uncomfortable situation.

We found ourselves on a westwards course and climbing when suddenly some fighters came diving towards us out of the sun! I brought them to the attention of my wingman and turned towards the approaching group. Shining like silver they came, from a great height, around thirty of them. They weren't 109s, they were American Mustangs. It was the first enemy encounter with US fighters for Ertl, and my first over Romania. The Americans still had a great distance to cover, so it took them a few seconds to start circling. Nevertheless, almost immediately a wild turning battle begun. 'Edi, be careful!' were my last instructions to my wingman. One thing was clear to me: just don't stop circling; he who stayed in the inner circle had a better chance of surviving. Unfortunately, Ertl was hit and subsequently had to take to his parachute. Their superior strength was too great and I couldn't help him. I circled and shot at the enemy. Luckily, the majority of the US fighters had quit the turning battle and continued on their course. Only two or three fighters remained and I was ready for those.

My enemy also received hits, but these appeared to have no effect. I succeeded in detaching myself from the battle and taking off eastwards. In any case, I got away from the Americans and now had to orientate myself so that I could find Bakau. There was nothing but silence over the radio – there had been no more orders or instructions for more than a quarter of an hour. How had my wingman fared? Hopefully, he had arrived safely on the ground and hopefully on our own side.

When I reached Foçsani it was only another hop, skip and a jump before I could land safely back at my airfield, another experience richer. The mechanics were already waiting patiently for our return and I related the events of the battle with the US fighters, the loss of Ertl and my return to the airfield. After reporting to the command post, I again reported the course of events of the first US encounter. Up to that time I still had no idea that my wingman had been able to take to his parachute and had landed safely south of Foçsani. From that time on the situation in the air over Romania changed. Of the Schlachtgeschwadern, I had the honour of being the first 190 pilot to come through an aerial battle against US fighters. It was clear to everybody that we now had a formidable new enemy in the sky. The intelligence officers now had a lot of overtime to do – the documents on the US Air Force had to be obtained. The first-hand reports of our own units in the west were studied. We were very happy about this, for we learned a great many interesting things. To me, one thing was clear: the Americans might shit just like us but their superior strength, the numbers of bombers and escort fighters, was a real surprise to those of us who had fought in Russia.

From now on, because of the influx of American units, the fighter and Schlacht Gruppen (equipped with 109s and 190s) were pulled from the Eastern Front and ordered to Zilistea. Under the codeword 'Sternflug' (starflight), the Gruppen assembled before 0900hrs at Zilistea airfield and took off from there against the incoming American units. All airfields around Bucharest were prepared to receive and care for the Jäger and Schlachter that had arrived. In the briefing assembly for Operation 'Sternflug', we met with pilots from other Gruppen whom we knew from Russia. We exchanged old experiences and news of people, and found out that so many old mates were no longer with us. The best part of the whole thing was how we were looked after by the ground staff, a fabulous piece of entertaining. While the machines were being fuelled up, we were offered würst, cigarettes and even ice cream – pure things that we on the Eastern Front knew only from hearsay. Anyway, there was everything for the crews – things that we had not seen for a very long time.

Today was the first mission organised under Operation 'Sternflug'. The Kommandeur assigned me as wingleader, and we went to 8,000 metres above Mizil and flew a northerly course. There! Under us was a flight of Mustangs, heading eastwards. We were in a great position, being 1,000 metres higher, and they had not spotted us or seen us yet. I told the boss about the Mustangs and drew his attention to exactly where they were, but he gave no instructions to attack the US fighters crossing beneath us, more's the pity. In my time as a fighter pilot in Romania and subsequently in the defence of the Reich, I never again experienced such a good starting point with which to attack a Mustang unit. After landing in Zilistea I spoke with the Kommandeur, who had not seen the Mustangs and had therefore not taken my observation seriously.

In Schlachter circles there was still an aversion to aerial fighting. According to the guidelines our main task was to battle against ground targets. But there were still some of the old 'SG 1' Gruppe around who had a fighter pilot's blood running through their arteries. To be a good fighter pilot, you have to be born that way.

On Friday 23 June 1944 there was another 'Sternflug' mission. We took off from Zilistea and, after reaching an altitude of 8,000 metres, were led to the area round Bucharest. Over the city we encountered our first US bombers of the mission, apparently without fighter protection. We flew the first attack as a Gruppe (twenty FW 190s), closing in on the B-17s from behind, as we had practised against our Ju 88s. My aim was good and I think that the bomber was hit. I positioned myself to hit the same bomber again and opened fire. It appeared to have some effect and the bomber began to hang back from the rest. Unfortunately I was too preoccupied with the B-17 and forgot to keep an eye on my group, although I was actually of the opinion that my Schwarm would remain near me. Unfortunately, this view was mistaken. My young flock flew onwards with the rest of the 190s, who had given up the attack and flown back to Zilistea. My pilots were not yet ripe for operations and the leader of the group was no fighter. Pity.

There were no enemy fighter protection aircraft in the sky – at least I couldn't see any. My B-17 had already lost altitude and hung back far behind the group, so I wanted to settle the matter. It would

A cheerful Oberfeldwebel Hermann Buchner at Zilistea in June 1944. He now sports the German Cross in Gold, awarded on 17 October 1943.

Pilots of 4./SG 2 in Zilistea, Romania, in July 1944, about the time that Oberfeldwebel Hermann Buchner was appointed Staffelkapitän. Few of the pilots shown here had had any combat experience, and quite a few were still only partly trained.

be my first four-engined aircraft. On the third attack I opened fire on the rear gunner with my 13mm machine gun from 1,000 metres away, and at 500 metres I added the 20mm cannon. The hits were good; the rear gunner was no longer firing and the way to success was open. On the fourth attack I aimed for the inside engine and the shots were just as good as the previous ones; the rear gunner was still not firing. Some of the crew jumped with their parachutes one by one from the rear gunner's position, six or seven men. The bomber signalled and had already lost a great deal of height. I no longer had to worry about its defensive fire, so flew up to its left side and signalled to the pilot that he should get out. He looked at me, but made no move to leave the plane. After another attack both the left engines were on fire, the B-17 tipped over to the left and began to spin. I circled it, and at an altitude of about 1,000 metres the tail broke in two. Only then did both pilots take to their parachutes. The bomber[35], or at least its parts, crashed to the ground in the vicinity of the Mizil fighter airfield and both pilots also landed near the airfield. My joy was great and I landed at Mizil, where II. Gruppe JG 77 was stationed. I searched out the command post for the confirmation of the aerial victory and my machine was refuelled and I took care of the necessary formalities.

After a stay of about an hour I took off to return to Zilistea. My Kommandeur was not exactly overjoyed at my report, since my Schwarm had been broken up. I said that the leader of my Staffel was still very inexperienced and was also no fighter. During this enemy encounter, we had the chance to teach the Americans a lesson. Unfortunately my colleagues had flown only one attack and had then departed for the journey homewards. The opportunity of catching a group of bombers without fighter protection was rare. On top of that, we had tactically approached them from behind, and finally we were over our own area. It was a shame, because this operation could have become a proper shooting party. Pilots like Otto Dommeratzky, Lambert, Stollnberger and Erich Müller just weren't around any more. After a discussion with the Kommandeur over the fighter operation, we transferred to Bakau again, and again we flew operations against Russian positions and troop concentrations, proper Schlachtflieger operations. Slowly the young pilots of 4 Staffel learned to fight, they became tougher and even took the fight to the Russians. They learned to fly and learned to value the 190. It was a joy to see how the lads came along, how they remained with the group during operations. With that attitude they would have remained with the Schwarm during the attack on the B-17 group over Bucharest.

Hauptmann Hans Stollnberger was one of the first 'Schlachter', with II.(S)/LG 2 in the Battle of Britain. From November 1942 he was Staffelkapitän of 8./SchG 2. This picture was probably taken shortly after he was awarded the Knight's Cross on 14 October 1942 for 460 combat missions and twenty air victories.

Leutnant August Lambert of 6./SG 2, shortly before he was awarded the Knight's Cross on 14 May 1944. In 350 missions he shot down 116 enemy aircraft, the highest score by any Schlacht pilot.

Today was another big flying day, the weather was good and again 'Sternflug' was ordered. Away to Zilistea! Again, when we landed there were cigarettes for the smokers and würst; again we chatted with mates from the other Staffeln, and again news of all the crews was exchanged. Hardly had the machines been refuelled when the order to proceed came through, and we had no time to linger at Zilistea. Time was pressing and already the Gruppe was taxiing to the start. Together we took off and climbed to an altitude of 8,000 metres over Bucharest, as ordered. We were led westwards and could already see vapour trails from bombers in the distance. The Kommandeur gave the order to attack and the Schwarm took up its attack formations. Today we were unlucky, for the bombers had long-distance fighter protection, which attempted to interfere with our attacks. They were lucky as well, and we had to break off our attack and became caught up in a fighter battle. For the first time my Schwarm had P-47 Thunderbolts as opponents when the fun started. The bomber group flew eastwards and, after carrying out its task, would fly on to Uman in the Ukraine to land; this method had been used several times.

Meanwhile my Schwarm was still occupied with the P-47s. My young pilots acquitted themselves well and I had not yet recorded any losses. But nevertheless I had not succeeded in eating up any of the Thunderbolts. We were already over the coast at Konstanza and the turning battle was still in progress. My colleagues and those of the American were no longer to be seen or, for that matter, heard on the radio. To my regret I had to accept that the pilot of the P-47 must be a shrewd fellow. He was obstinate and wanted to have me unconditionally, but I was also not prepared to break off the fight. I tried to get myself into a good position to shoot or to break off the fight. My supply of fuel was a problem, so I had to break off the fight. The US fighters had a good 5-6 hours' flying time against 2 hours for the 190. Alone with a P-47 at 8,000 metres over Konstanza there was no chance of success. The battle was still undecided.

I had to decide. A quick decision – break off circling and dive down at full speed. Suddenly out of a tight curve into the depths – that was a surprise for the American. I turned my 190 on its nose and full pelt on a crash course. The American dived after me, shooting from all his barrels. If I wanted to live I had to stay out of his line of fire. The throttle was out as far as it could go and the ASI was at its limit as well. The engine howled, but it was my last chance to get away from the American. He was certainly a tough, hard-boiled so-

and-so, who wanted to have my scalp. To get out of his line of fire I turned my 190 around longitudinally. That was too much for the American, for we had lost a lot of altitude by this time. We were now at about 5,000 metres and I had to slowly pull out of my dive, but it had lasted too long for the American as well and he had to leave his intended booty. He left me and flew back to his assembly point. Or was he of the opinion that I had crashed? The American was a tough opponent and still had a long way to go back to Bari in Italy.

After anxious minutes I ended my dive and pulled the throttle back, my trusty 190 having done a lot in the last few minutes. A deep breath – keep calm. Now I tried to fix my position, exactly 2,000 metres altitude over Konstanza. Returning to Zilistea, I landed there with my last drops of fuel. Again I was the last of our Gruppe to drift in to the airfield after a wild encounter with the enemy. Again I was another experience richer. Again I got the usual telling-off from the Kommandeur. Again there followed a lecture about the duties of the Schlacht pilot. He didn't want to hear my report of the aerial battle with the P-47 at all. The old story – we are not fighters and our duties lie elsewhere. This mission was far too difficult for the young pilots of 4 Staffel. Nevertheless, they made the effort to keep up, and succeeded, managing to get away from their opponents without any casualties and land safely at their airfield. Anyway, I was one of the few pilots of II./SG 2 who, without ending up as a casualty, had aerial battles with Mustangs and Thunderbolts and managed to shoot down a four-engined bomber over Romania.

Word got around, and one day I had to carry out a comparison flight with a Romanian fighter pilot, Lt Fladerano, in an IAR 80[36] in the presence of Romanian and our own Generals. The programme was established jointly by Lt Fladerano and myself. We started as a Rotte and climbed together to 4,000 metres over the airfield. In the climb I had no problems against the IAR 80 and, after reaching the altitude, we separated and flew in opposite directions for 3 minutes. That was the starting position and now the game could begin.

We flew towards each other at the same altitude and I could soon make out my opponent for this exercise. Now the game was open. How would the Romanian begin the game? The starting position had been the same for both of us. Already he was rushing past on my left side. Now it was up to me to bring the battle to him. I circled to the left and tried to gain height at the same time. My opponent turned in as well and the circle was closed. Who could get more from his

Curious Luftwaffe and army troops inspect a Romanian IAR 80 fighter similar to the one against which the author flew in mock combat. Seen near Tusow in August 1942, the location must presumably be close to the front line as all the men are armed. Based on the engineering technology of the Polish PZL 24 parasol-winged fighter, which the Romanians had built under licence, the IAR proved to be a useful supplement to the Romanian Air Force and took part in many actions against Allied bombers attacking the Romanian oilfields.

A similar view of another IAR 80A. No 211 shows some useful details of the markings employed on Romanian aircraft. Of particular note are the yellow wing crosses (known as Michael's crosses to the Romanians) and the fuel and oil filler details on the forward fuselage. On the top of the fin is the trademark of the IAR factory.

machine, or which machine had more performance available? One thing was clear to me: I had experience in a turning battle, and I had to try to display my ability. In spite of the tight turns, I had to get my 190 in a higher position. After two or three rounds I had done it – I had him in my sights, about 30 metres behind his IAR 80. He no longer had a chance. I had out-turned him and I was breathing down his neck.

The battle was broken off by a radio message from the ground, then restarted. After a short time I decided that round two was also in my favour. The Romanian with his IAR 80 had no chance; his machine was more manoeuvrable, yes, but I flew my 190 to the limits of its performance. During the past weeks I had been involved daily in hard aerial battles, so I was in top form. Daily I had brought myself and also my 190 safely to the ground again at our airfield.

The test was broken off by radio and we landed as a group in front of our Generals. After we left the cockpit at the parking place and reported back to our superiors, we shook hands. The Generals congratulated me on the presentation. The game was over, and we, the actors, chatted a bit about our personal flying histories: flying school, training, enemy missions and aerial victories. Lt Fladerano was definitely good, but he should have flown a few times as second to Dommeratzky. Then he would have learned or would have had to learn the skills of a fighter pilot. It was a shame that the pilots of the Romanian Air Corps had had so little experience on the front. Their training also left something to be desired.

For the afternoon the officers of the Gruppe and myself were invited to a tour of a Romanian Fighter Group in Baniasa/Bucharest and to a gala meal. The unit had IAR 80s and Lt Fladerano was a pilot in this Gruppe. For us there wasn't a great deal new to see. More interesting was the celebration in a castle near Bucharest. It was quite fantastic and I found the whole thing unbelievable. We had lost the Crimea and had just returned to the mainland – the Ukraine had also been lost – and here was a festival taking place as if it were the depths of peacetime. Women in elegant dresses, the officers in dress uniform with many medals, and me, a little Oberfeldwebel in working uniform with a pilot's insignia. I think I was the only one who wore a normal uniform in the chambers, but I was the actual cause for this exhibition. They had probably hoped that in the turning battle the IAR 80 would have had the advantage.

It was a great party, and late that night we drove back to Zilistea. After sleeping in, the day returned to its normal routine. I instructed my pilots about the opportunities of being successful in turning battles. The pilots had to get through a bit of coaching, for they were now ready to take advantage of my experience. Since taking over the Staffel I had only lost Wolfgang Richthofen, but it was still not ready for hard aerial warfare. The 4th Staffel of the Gruppe was coming along nicely; the pilots knew what they could do and they flew happily in the Schwarm. In spite of everything, we were trusted by the men of JG 77. They instructed us not only in their attack experiences in battle against the US fighters, but also in battle against the bombers. I understood that these lessons were very important for the pilots. We were already respected by the fighters and we were taken seriously. Unfortunately, our Kommandeur was not enthusiastic about the fighter pilots.

In July 1944 the Inspector of the Schlachtflieger, Oberst Alfred Druschel, came to Zilistea to inspect our Gruppe. The Gruppe had a good name and was gladly presented. Many years previously the General had been a Staffelkapitän with SG 1 and I knew him from that time. He was very happy with the performance of the Gruppe. He also viewed 4 Staffel and interested himself especially in the rate of achievement of the young pilots. We talked for a considerable time and he also knew of my enthusiasm for taking on aerial battles and of my success. He was absolutely amazed that my Staffel, in spite of the last tough missions against the US bombers, had come out of the rounds without any casualties. The fact was, that I, along with Oberleutnant Beutelspacher, was the oldest 190 pilot in the Gruppe. Oberst Druschel made me two offers: either I could remain with 4 Staffel as Staffel leader with a field promotion, or I could leave and go back to an Erganzungsgruppe in Prossnitz at home. Druschel was of the opinion that I could go to Prossnitz at the same time as Major Frank, who was also of the opinion that I had been at the front long enough. This was a very difficult decision for me. I was just at the peak of my flying success. I had been lucky and successful. Now it was hard to know what to do. A week after this talk with Oberst Druschel I was asked by the new Kommandeur what my decision would be, as the General of the Schlachtflieger wanted an answer.

In July 1944 I had done the most missions on the 190 of anybody in II./SG 2. I had now thought long enough about my future and had made my decision. Back home was my answer. If they wanted to promote me to an officer, they could also do it at the Erganzungsgruppe in Germany. Meanwhile I continued to lead my

An exhausted mechanic sleeps under the wing of a Focke-Wulf FW 190, allegedly from Gefechtsverband Druschel, an ad hoc unit led by Major Alfred Druschel, who was also the commander of SchG 1 during the pivotal Battle of Kursk in July 1943. Unusual on a ground-attack aircraft, the horizontal bar markings indicate a Stab machine, but whether this is Druschel's own is not known.

4th and waited until my replacement from Germany arrived. With nostalgia I gave up my Staffel – the pilots had been good lads and useful pilots, trusty fellows, and could fly.

My replacement arrived, but to my horror it was my good old friend Ohm Kruger. We had been together at the Fighter Pilots' School, the Erganzungsstaffel and at 8. Staffel of SG 1. About a year previously Ohm had been detached from the front because his wife had been blinded and their small children needed to be cared for. Had I known this sooner, I would have done without the posting. In spite of everything, the joy of seeing Ohm again was great and we well and truly celebrated seeing each other again, and my leaving. Ohm got a good Staffel from me and good pilots, and I could only wish him lots of luck and many happy landings.

My effects were quickly packed and, after a year at the front, I was on my way home again. At the hangar in Zilistea stood an Arado Ar 66 from a night-fighter Gruppe, which was waiting to be taken back to Germany. Better flying an old banger like this than spending a week on the train. I soon had a passenger as well, a

Viennese mechanic from our Gruppe who had leave to go home. The weather was favourable and my things were soon stowed away, but the mechanic had a lot to stow away – the observer's position was crammed full with his things.

We took off for Germany early on a lovely summer's day. I lectured my passenger that during the whole journey he was to watch the skies carefully and immediately inform me of anything he saw. The flight path was from Zilistea via Buzau, the Buzau Pass, Kronstadt, Arad and Stuhlweissenburg to Malatzki (north of Pressburg). The machine was definitely overloaded – we only reached the necessary altitude to fly over the Buzau Pass with great effort – so I flew, after a fashion, at an altitude of 200-300 metres above ground in the direction of home. Our first interim landing was at Arad and we spent the night there as well; I did not want to fly for the rest of the day because of the many US fighters in the area, not with me in an old Ar 66. We were accommodated with civilians; my billet was lent by a butcher, who was very pleasant and provided me with enough food for several weeks. Early the next day I took off over the Pussta in the direction of Stuhlweissenburg. Here, we were refuelled and on we went to Malatzki. After landing, I gave up the machine in the hangar there, my task fulfilled.

The machine was now in Germany and I set about getting a flight to Vienna. From now on I was on holiday. I said goodbye to my passenger, who was going to see how he could get himself and his things to Vienna. That evening in the camp canteen I met a Ju crew who were flying to Vienna/Seiring the next day and had a place for me. In two days I had made it from Zilistea to Vienna. After a 30-minute flight we landed in Seiring and, after saying goodbye to the crew, I took the tram to the Western Railway Station in Vienna, where I caught the train to Salzburg and, that same day, was able to hand over a package of sausages to my mother. From the train station in Salzburg I took the trolleybus home and there was great joy when I walked in to see my parents. Even greater was their surprise when I told them of my transfer back to Germany. Naturally, the donation of sausages was very welcome. I passed a week in Salzburg and then went off to the Erganzungsgruppe in Prossnitz. Either I was very lucky or, as was often the case, had a good nose – hardly had I left Romania when the putsch took place and Romania changed sides. Several days previously six of my friends had been shot down by US Lightnings shortly after taking off during an alarm start in Zilistea.

These ex-pilots of 6./SG 2 in Prossnitz, Bohemia, are now serving as flying instructors with SG 152; it is after August 1944 as Hermann Buchner (left) wears his Knight's Cross. The other two pilots remain unidentified; however, the man in the middle has obviously seen much service as he wears the German Cross in Gold, the Iron Cross 1st and 2nd Class, a Wound Badge and the Schlachtflieger's Combat Clasp.

Erich Müller, Ernst Beutelspacher and some young pilots fell. I had made it away from that disaster, spending some days at home with some school friends who were still there.

Naturally, the time at Salzburg was soon past and the time came to take my leave of my loving parents, my friends and my beloved mountains. Again, as so often before, I tramped to the train station and went to Vienna – this time not to Lemberg, but to Olmütz via Lundenburg. In Prossnitz I met many old acquaintances from my time with SG 1 who had been detached from the front at some time and had stayed on here as instructors. After reporting to the Kommandeur, old 'Allan' Frank[37], who was happy at my posting here, I took over my accommodation and we celebrated and exchanged news again.

Chapter Eleven

A flying instructor again
July 1944-October 1944

O ver the next few days my assignment as Gruppe Flying Instructor began. Naturally I also visited the city and made my first observations; the deepest feeling of peace prevailed and I had no idea how wonderful living back at home could be. I had money and no worries. There were several hospitals in the city and therefore lots of nurses. For me there was so much that was new that I simply could not overcome my amazement.

In Prossnitz there was time to relax. Here pilots from SG 152 find time to soak up some sun – and as always with fighter pilots there were girls!

My comrades explained the peculiarities of the job. I made two to three practice missions daily with my students in Schwarm formation. It was child's play for me to fly with the young pilots, to make them ready for the front. They had no idea what one could pull from the 190. Every day the missions were tougher and what they involved was more difficult. Well, it was my task to train these pilots and to put the finishing touches to them. They should not be able to say that they had not yet learned the necessary lessons.

Something was always going on in the evenings and we instructors were always on our way to town. I was a regular at the 'Drei König' coffee bar and got to know a lot of people. Some of them were Czech, whom I took a liking to and got on well with. I was often out with Jonny Zeitner; he had been with me in 1941 at the Schlacht-Erganzungsgruppe in Lippstadt. Jonny was a natural talent – he danced and tap-danced at every opportunity. Nevertheless, I was more than rewarded for the lost time that I had spent in Russia. We also got to know some of the nurses, including my future wife. At the beginning of our acquaintance it was a very casual friendship and we only occasionally saw each other at the 'Drei König'.

In July I was awarded the Knight's Cross. The Geschwader was assembled and Oberst Druschel, the General of the Schlachtflieger, did the awards ceremony. It was a wonderful day for me; my friends were pleased, as was my Kommandeur, Allan Frank. Again, another huge festival was on the cards. In August there was to be a large Staffel party and I was tasked with its organisation. It was to be a wonderful event. Because I had always organised the parties on the front, I had been tasked with carrying out this one in Prossnitz. Jonny declared himself ready to help me and at the same time to appear as 'La Janna'. I hastily assembled a band from some soldiers so I could draw up a programme. I visited the Kommandeur and he gave his blessing for the party to go ahead. For three weeks I worked only on the party. An amazing beer tent was erected by buttoning together one-man tarpaulins[38], a job requiring a lot of effort – after the day's work was done the soldiers had very sore fingers. We had put together a variety programme and the Kommandeur was full of praise for the preparations we were making. Now came the hardest part – who should be invited? We had not only officers and soldiers from the hospitals, and Red Cross sisters in mind, but also girls working in nearby camps and also some Czechs.

At Prossnitz in August 1944 Hermann Buchner, in parade uniform with full decorations, receives the coveted Knight's Cross from the hands of Oberst Druschel. Major Frank, newly appointed commander of the base, is on the right, holding the presentation case for the decoration.

Accompanied by Oberst Druschel, the newly decorated Hermann Buchner is saluted by the assembled members of his new unit. Note how, since the attempt on Hitler's life in July, all members of the Wehrmacht were required to use the Nazi salute.

A portrait of Hermann Buchner
wearing all his medals and
decorations and the 1943
model field service cap.

The invitations were on their way and the weather was also co-operating – at least the meteorologists had forecast good weather for us. For those who had helped and given up several weeks of their free time, the anticipation was great. Certainly the weather was on our side – it was beautiful. The first visitors drifted in, soldiers from the hospitals, medics, the nurses with Matron, the working girls with their leaders and many civilian guests. Our house was full, and the programme could begin. Our Kommandeur, Allan Frank, opened the Staffel's Summer Festival with some witty words. The performance received the approval of the guests, as well as the soldiers in our Gruppe. However, the star of the show was our Jonny with his performance as 'La Janna', which received a lot of applause. The festival had reached its climax, the atmosphere was terrific, and it was a really successful show. Long after midnight the first guests began to leave the party and the last visitors did not leave until dawn. The effort put into the preparation had paid off, and the Kommandeur was happy with how it had turned out. Now there was a great deal of work to do over the next few days to remove all traces of the event and take down all we had built. Within a week the whole thing had passed into history. Naturally a lot of friendships were made during this Staffel party.

Major Alfred Druschel is seen in February 1943, just after he won the 'Swords'.
Kommodore of Sch/G 1 from March to October 1943, soon afterwards he became
Inspector of Day Ground Attack Units, with the General der Schlachtflieger,
before taking command of SG 4. He went missing during the massive Luftwaffe
operation on 1 January 1945.

A lighter moment for ex-pilots of 6./SG 2 in Prossnitz, Bohemia, now serving as flying instructors with SG 154. Hermann Buchner sits third from right. The two men to his left also appear in the picture on page 206. The identity of the Oberleutnant third from left wearing the Knight's Cross is not known.

For us instructors, our normal duties returned to the forefront the next day. We flew our practice missions in order to perfect the pilots that the front-line units urgently needed. We had to fly the necessary number of hours with the students. I was with a Schwarm flying in the Olmütz area, simulating a low-level attack on a group of trees. On the second attack at about 100 metres above ground there was a bang in the engine and the machine was ablaze. A quick decision – I pulled on the stick, opened the cockpit canopy, unfastened the harness and was out of the machine. Everything happened very quickly and already I hung in my parachute, a pine forest under me. I had no chance – I was going to land in the woods on the tops of the pines. My machine crashed nearby in a field and I fell into the woods between the tips of the trees. I was lucky, for my parachute caught in the trees and I, poor thing, hung about 10 metres above the ground between the tree trunks, like a puppet. I couldn't reach any tree trunk, and was also unable to grab the branches above me. The parachute was entangled in the crowns of the trees and I hung over the forest floor like a Christmas decoration.

Again, as so often in my flying career, I paid for my decision. My attempts to pull myself upwards using the parachute lines failed due to a lack of strength in my arms. Then I tried to reach a tree trunk, but this came to nothing as well. Finally, I let my pistol fall to the ground and counted the time it took to fall. My reckoning that I was about 6-8 metres up appeared to be correct. I thought about it again, then undid the harness with both hands and fell to the ground. I lay there and my first attempt to stand up failed. Unfortunately, my right knee and foot would not play, and I just could not stand up. Meanwhile I looked for my pistol, crawled to it and stowed it away in my 'Kanalhosen'[39], and also straightened up my uniform.

I knew that I was in Czech territory, but did not know who would find me first. In any case, I wore no epaulettes on my brown leather vest and I hid the Knight's Cross. I crawled laboriously through the woods towards a clearing. My right foot had to be dragged and it was a painful undertaking. After a short while I reached the clearing and saw a farmer ploughing a field with horses. I plucked up the courage and crawled towards him; he spotted me and came towards me. He asked whether I was an aviator, speaking in Czech. I moaned and made no other sound, especially not a word of German. The farmer was very helpful; he took me to his wagon and loaded me on top of some potatoes already there. Then he took me to his village, telling the people he passed on the way that he had found an aviator and was taking him to the Gendarmerie. There were a lot of curious people on the way and everybody wanted more details from the farmer. I was already worried about how the thing would turn out, but one thing was clear to me; the farmer was taking me to the local police station.

We arrived there near the post office and he carried me into the office at the station and explained to the Czech officials present where and how he had found me. He also told about the aircraft that had been flying in the area. I did not break my silence, even for the police officials across from me. I first of all wanted to know exactly what they intended to do with me. They laid me on a bed and offered me cigarettes and a policeman tried to make a telephone connection with another police station. My pain stayed within limits and I continued to follow the silence tactics. I wanted to allow the Czechs to keep their belief that I was an Allied pilot. My brown leather clothing as well as the lack of rank insignia, and my moans of pain, contributed to their assumption. After an hour, perhaps more, the solution arrived – the door opened and on the threshold stood two

officers of the SS security service. They inquired of the police where
the pilot had been found. They were also of the opinion that I was a
US pilot. I quickly clarified the situation and greeted them with
'Heil, Hitler!', telling them of the course of events leading to my
jump. They were somewhat disappointed that I was one of their own
pilots, but were happy that I had been rescued, thanking the police
chief and giving him cigarettes.

I went by car with the SS men back to Prossnitz, where they took
me to a hospital. There word got round quickly that nurse Käthe's
friend had been brought in. After a close examination I was
discharged back to my unit. The unit doctor organised my admission
to my home town hospital in Salzburg for further treatment and
convalescence. So, after only a short while I returned home to
Salzburg, where I was admitted to the Liefering Residential Hospital.
My right knee needed a support bandage and rest. After four weeks I
was back at my unit in Prossnitz. Again I had been lucky, as the day
before my return the airfield had been bombed and destroyed by a US
bomber group, then attacked by their accompanying fighter escort.
The fighters had caught a slow-moving group of students as they
were moving and shot down seven machines in an aerial battle. This
was easy for the US fighters since the 190s weren't armed and were
thus handed over to the attackers powerless.

On 25 August 1944, the day before the author returned from a spell in hospital in
Salzburg, Prossnitz was raided by bombers from the US 15th Air Force. Here
aircraft on the field burn fiercely.

The entire field at Prossnitz is covered in thick smoke as installations burn out of control.

Aftermath: on 29 August 1944 the survivors of the raid four days previously prepare to bury their friends who were shot down by the US fighters escorting the bombers. The German armed forces always placed great importance on due ceremonial for their fallen comrades.

The same day my old friend and comrade Otto Dommeratzky fell in battle. He was on his way in a 190 from Silesia to the Eastern Front in the region of Hungary. The US had attacked Mährisch-Ostrau and on this occasion Otto encountered the Mustangs. He had his mechanic in the tail, and was on leave so that he could acquire the papers to get married. In an aerial battle he took a direct hit in the engine and had to make an emergency landing. He did not want to take to his parachute out of consideration for his mechanic. During the emergency landing he struck high-tension electricity cables and the crash was complete – both burned. Otto had more than 600 missions, around sixty aerial victories and wore the 'Oakleaves', one of the most successful Schlachtflieger on the Me 109 and FW 190. He was buried in Prossnitz with pilots of the Erganzungsgruppe who had been shot down.

During this time two more of my comrades fell on the Eastern Front. Bruno Schultze was shot down over his home in East Prussia, and Jonny Zeitner also fell during a low-level attack in East Prussia. He got a direct flak hit and went straight into the ground. He had always wanted to have a good crash and burn.

Of the old ones, the old instructor guard, nearly all fell within fourteen days. An even worse blow took place. My Kommandeur, Major Frank, was shot at in the casino (the officers' mess) during a function and subsequently died in hospital; Hauptmann Smola took over the Gruppe. On 20 July 1944 the assassination attempt on the Führer took place and subsequently the Wehrmacht was ordered to carry out the Nazi salute. In the course of supplying aircraft and unit leaders from the Staff, our Gruppe had forty trainee officer pilots transferred to us, who had to be schooled for use at the front in a very short time. I got them as students and at the same time twenty 190s were available to me.

Now things were happening fast and we flew four or five practice operations per day. Punctually at 0800hrs there were flight and Schwarme assignments. Every second day there was a meeting of the five Schwarme. At an altitude of 4,000 metres above ground the circling would begin – it was not low-level attacks we were practising, but aerial combat. The men were learning quickly. Many of them had flown no operations for a long time and had been away from the front for too long. Some of the Staff Officers complained to me and also to Hauptmann Smola about the way the flying was being carried out. They were of the opinion that Schlachtflieger should not be fighter pilots. The demands on the Schwarm leaders were too great, too difficult. After fourteen days our first pilot was posted away. Some had had enough of the whole thing, but there were also those who did not want to go to the front, at least not so quickly. The actual situation at the front meant that the pilots of the Schlacht groups had to learn the tactics of the US fighters. On the whole it was a good job and the pilots learned how to handle the 190; previously many of them hadn't known what the 190 was capable of.

In spite of everything, I had had my fill of schooling groups and I wanted to get back to the front. My talk with the Kommandeur about a transfer to a front-line unit met without success. He said that it made no sense and that for a while I would not be free for a transfer. Something had to happen – I wanted to get to an operational Gruppe, I was looking for aerial battles, and I wanted to fight against the Americans. There was a field post box, No 2000, where every front-line soldier and every member of the Wehrmacht could deposit his troubles; the number was publicised on the radio request programmes, and the listeners were recommended to write in with all their requests and inventions and they would always receive an answer. I had nothing to lose – I was hoping to be lucky – so I wrote a postcard. My request was: 'A transfer, please, as a pilot in the Reichsverteidigung.'[40] My comrades at the school made bets as to whether I would receive an answer or not.

After about five days I was ordered to report to the Kommandeur in Service Dress for the first time in my entire service. What was going on? He greeted me in a friendly manner and asked me to take a seat. He asked me about my note to the General der Jagdflieger. He also asked me whether I knew that I had bypassed the usual channels. At first I was of the opinion that he was making a joke – seven years' military service without any punishment, awarded the Knight's Cross, and here I was about to be punished. I was not prepared to take such a punishment. After a bit of discussion, we came to an agreement of three days' house arrest, with the key on the inside of the door; I would be 'locked up' and the transfer would be authorised.

Some way, any way, I wanted to be away from the heap. After four years I wanted to be back with the fighter cadre. Naturally, they weren't exactly saying good things about me, but they had had enough time to fulfil the promise they had given me. The old Kommandeur was gone and the new one did not want to keep the promise. In Romania they had promised me a field promotion, in

Prossnitz they had promised me a Staffel and so on and so forth.
With my comrades Heinz Drefahl, one of the last, and Ohm, who
had meanwhile returned home from the front, I celebrated my
departure from Prossnitz. A good time was coming to an end for me.
I also celebrated my birthday with Käthe and we announced our
engagement at the same time. Another segment of my life was over.

The author and Heinz Drefahl
enjoy a stroll in Prossnitz in
August 1944.

Chapter Twelve

Reichsvertidigung
November 1944-December 1944

On 2 November 1944 I reported to the Command HQ of the General der Jagdflieger at Berlin-Gatow. A new era of flying had begun for me. By the order of Fighter Command many pilots had been summoned, including former bomber and transport pilots, and I knew many of them from the Eastern Front. They asked me what I was doing there, where I had been assigned and so on. They also told me that I should be on my guard that I did not get transferred to the Waffen-SS or to a tank troop. This was new territory for me – I only wanted to go to a fighter unit at the front.

I finally reached the head of the queue, reported to an Oberleutnant in the office and gave him a short account of my flying career. He listened attentively and then said that I should go to a D-9 unit. Since I had never before heard of a D-9[41], I turned down the offer – I did not want to be sent to the slaughter. A solution presented itself when a Hauptmann came through the door who knew me from my time in Romania, greeted me and asked what I was doing. The Oberleutnant explained and the result was a decision most favourable for me; I was going as a novice to Lechfeld. For me, the whole matter was wrapped up. I announced my departure and took the train to Lechfeld. A pilot I knew asked me again where I would be going, and was astonished that I was going to the Messerschmitt 262. I myself had never heard anything about the Me 262 aircraft before, but now I was going to experience it.

On 4 or 5 November I arrived in Lechfeld and reported to the HQ and an Oberleutnant Wörner. He looked at my papers and explained what was going to happen. For the moment I had to go to Landsberg am Lech to fly some hours on twin-engined aircraft – I think 5 hours was necessary – then I would return to Lechfeld. The next day I again took the train, this time to the airfield at Landsberg, but the process was not at all as easy as I had envisaged it would be. There were about a hundred pilots on this airfield, all of whom had to be or wanted to be converted to twin-engined aircraft. I had to find another way, otherwise I would be in Landsberg for weeks. As an old hand, after my accommodation had been secured, I made enquiries around the airfield. In the hangar I chatted up an aircraft inspector and asked about the work and how many pilots he had to do test flights and the like. We worked out an agreement: he was happy to have found a pilot to do test flights and I thus got my required flying hours. In this manner I got the necessary flying hours in only a few days and the inspector was happy that the flights had been carried out. He was sorry when I took off after a few days – the arrangement had been of service to both of us and I had jumped the hurdle in a very short time. So, it was back to Lechfeld.

Oberleutnant Wörner was amazed that I had been able to acquire the necessary flying hours in such a short time, but I was assigned to a basic course. There were several NCOs who were being instructed. An engineering officer gave lessons about the power plant, about starting up and switching off; we had to carry out the whole sequence of events blindfolded. After two days of basic instruction we began to practice starting up an Me 262 parked on a field in front of the hall. After a thorough instruction in the cabin, taxiing in the Me 262 began. Taxiing with the two engines was somewhat difficult; one first had to have a good grasp of how the engines operated and the revs. A course had been built using pine trees and one had to taxi through these. In between a flying instructor explained again and again the starting procedures, the flight and the preparations for landing. On 19 November 1944 I had my first flight in a 262. Everything went like clockwork. It was a magnificent feeling and after 20 minutes an equally exemplary landing followed. The spell was broken – it was easier than expected. I have to say, though, that the instruction and the preparations had been logically and intensively carried out. In truth, nothing could go off the straight and narrow.

The following days passed with flights lasting from 30 to 50 minutes. There were problems with the flying assignments, for there were many higher-ranking officers present on the conversion course, so we NCOs hardly got a look in. But we easily solved this problem: we were always at the start at 0800hrs and the flying instructors assigned us the first flights. The gentlemen officers didn't arrive until about 0900hrs, and by then we had already had our first go. After eating, we were again the first there, so there was, without actual assignment, a clear division between us. It was my third or fourth flight, I think, when I flew to Salzburg, to fly over my parents' house and to see if it was still standing. It was a lovely flight along the Bavarian Alps, over the Untersberg, the Gaisberg, a left turn and at low level over my parents' house in Itzling. A wonderful flight! The house was not damaged, so I was reassured. The return

The Me 262 was a formidable aircraft but was not invulnerable. This complete frame from the gun camera film of Lieutenant James W. Kenny of the US 357th Fighter Group, taken on 8 November 1944, shows the Me 262A-1a, Werk Nummer 110404, of Kommando Nowotny flown by Oberleutnant Franz Schall after Kenny had shot it down and Schall had been forced to bale out. It can be seen that the canopy is missing and the port engine is smoking. Schall had just shot down Warren Corwin of the 357th before being hit himself.

In a picture taken at Lechfeld showing him perched on the wing, the author makes last-minute checks prior to a flight in 'White 7', a Messerschmitt Me 262A-1a of Kommando Nowotny. According to his logbook Hermann Buchner made only two flights in an Me 262 numbered '7' from Lechfeld, both on 20 October 1944. Judging by the shadows this may be just prior to the early-morning flight at 0820, before the 'gentlemen officers' arrived.

was over the Chiemsee and Ammersee to Lechfeld. Slowly I began to come to grips with the machine – it was a lovely bird and a joy to fly. The fear of its speed abated and we flew more freely and made more demands of the machine. Landings also were a joy – the tension was past, and I was now fully fledged to fly it.

On 22 November came the first flight as a Rotte and, unintentionally, the first encounter with enemy Mustangs. We followed them from south of Lechfeld to the southern Tyrol near Bozen, but could not achieve any successes. We broke off and flew back to Lechfeld. A marvellous flight – finally a hunter and not the hunted in an excellent machine! It had all the prerequisites for success. Already we wanted to be employed against US groups, but when the alarm went the 262s were put under cover of the woods and the crews had to go into air raid shelters. We were not happy with this. A man on the conversion course, Major Sinner[42], was of the same opinion, and he organised it so that when the alarm went a Schwarm of 262s would be kept available.

By 26 November things were ready for us on the conversion course to begin the Defence of the Reich with jet aircraft. The alarm went! The Schwarme were assigned and my 262 had a tactical number – a gold '8'. The weather was not exactly ideal, for there was a huge cloud bank pushing towards us from the west. This would be my first enemy mission in the 262. Around 1000hrs the order to take off was given, the engines were started and the turbines roared. I was assigned to intercept US Air Force reconnaissance aircraft in the Munich area. It would be my first flight being led by instructions from a ground-based Fighter Control Officer using radar.

The 262 rolled forward and the speed increased meteorically. Just before the end of the runway I lifted the machine and operated the undercarriage lever. After the undercarriage and the flaps stopped moving, I made a quick check of the engine instruments, especially the temperature of the turbines. My 262 picked up speed and climbed upwards. I turned on my FuG 16[43] and found the fighter frequency 'Bavaria'. A short call, 'Bavaria from Schwalbe 8, please come in', a few seconds pause, then 'Bavaria' came on and gave the first instructions clearly and exactly. Meanwhile, my 262 had reached an altitude of 5,000 metres. I was assigned the Munich area, looking for US Air Force reconnaissance aircraft who were checking out the effect of their bombing. It was my first live mission in the 262.

The speaker from ground control spoke very calmly and radiated an atmosphere of confidence. A further order: 'Course 340, height 7,000, distance ahead 20km.' My 262 had quickly reached the altitude, I was on course and the distance was diminishing rapidly. The weapons were loaded and the safety released, and the engine instruments checked again. I was ready to begin the battle. 'Bavaria' came through with new instructions: 'Distance ahead 5, 4, 3, 2, 1 – you have made contact – the highest concentration.' I looked around to see if I could catch sight of my target. Unfortunately it must be said that this first attempt was a complete wash-out. I could not acquire the target; consequently there followed another attempt on a different target.

The second attempt also met with no success. Unfortunately I could not catch sight of any enemy aircraft. Something wasn't right – it could not be right. I had experience as a fighter pilot, was in control of the Me 262 and was otherwise OK. Feverishly, I checked over my flight and engine instruments and the fuel supply. All indicators were in the green area.

A new instruction from ground control – 'Course 270' – and a few minutes later: 'Handing you over to Leander.' 'Leander' was the Stuttgart Fighter Control Centre. Just after Augsburg a cloud bank pushed eastwards and I flew over a sea of cloud. I was alone, nothing but a cloud bank under my 262, above me the blue sky streaked with vapour trails, the only contact with earth my radio. 'Leander' called and gave me an instruction: 'Course 270, reconnaissance, distance ahead 70km.' The altitude was 8,000 metres and my 262 shot there like lightning. Hopefully, it would work out this time. The engines were running normally, the instruments were showing the correct readings and 'Leander' let me know the narrowing range. I had already been under way for 35 minutes and still had not had sight of the ground. The decision should – no, must – soon be made; the target was still 10km away. Once again I checked my weapons and the tension mounted. 'Leander' continued to count down the time to the target, then from the right there appeared a point. This point must be my target.

The seconds felt like an eternity, then I could identity him – a Lightning from the US Air Force returning to France. The target in my sights, my right hand grasped the control column and the weapons handle. A push on the cannon button and the first projectile left its barrel and sought its target. The first shot lay too high, so I let the altitude control drop a little and the projectile hit the aircraft's fuselage. A lick of flame shot out of the mid-right section and my 262 flew over the Lightning and away. I circled and saw how the Lightning tipped over on its left wing and went over, spinning.

I could see how the burning Lightning dived into the cloud bank lying beneath us. Now my tension abated somewhat and I reported shooting down the aircraft to 'Leander', and asked at the same time for instructions for the return flight to Lechfeld. 'Leander' congratulated me on my success and ordered: 'Course 090'. Again, I checked all the instruments, especially the engine indicators and the fuel supply, and everything was in the best order. My 262 flew calmly through the air. General Galland once said of the 262: 'It's as if the angels were pushing.' My reverie was broken when 'Leander' came through with, 'Handing you over to Bavaria, have a good trip.' The flight still continued above the cloud bank, but the fuel was visibly less.

'Bavaria' took over and informed me: 'Course 090, leave your flying altitude and begin descent.' The weather at Lechfeld was also reported. The lower edge of the cloud was 500 metres above ground, visibility 10-15km. Now everything happened very quickly. My 262 dived into the cloud cover and it was murky. I held the speed to 650kmph. At an altitude of about 600 metres I shot out of the clouds, exactly over my home airfield at Lechfeld. Now everything was routine: cut the speed to 300-250kmph, flaps out, undercarriage out and an orderly landing approach. The tyres squealed and the 262 smoothly set down after a flying time of 80 minutes (1135-1255hrs). After taxiing out, I turned at the end of the runway and rolled to the dispersal. It was finally time to get back on solid ground. Radio off, weapons secured and engines shut down. Now my tension dissolved. I undid my parachute harness and climbed out of my 262.

The machine I had shot down was an F-5E (photo version of the P-38 Lightning) of the 7th Photo Recon Group, 27th Photo Squadron. The F-5E-2-LO, serial number 43-28619, was being flown by Lieutenant Irvin J. Rickey[44]. He was able to take to his parachute near Spesshardt around 1215hrs German time and was taken captive at Moetlingen, 8km north-west of Calw.

A line-up of Messerschmitt Me 262A-1s of Kommando Nowotny at Lechfeld in November 1944. 'White 10' and 'White 11' (Werk Nr 170061?) are being prepared for flight by mechanics while the pilots discuss tactics. Hermann Buchner flew a number '11' just once, on 29 November. The contrast between the upper-surface colours suggests that they might be in a grey and green scheme.

In the second week of November the 'Nowotny' unit at Achmer was disbanded after Nowi[45] fell during an aerial battle on 8 November 1944. The rest of the unit was transferred back to Lechfeld. There were now pilots already available with their first operational experience and slowly the troop was forming. We, the Lechfelders, actually flew a great deal, especially we NCOs, on account of our simple solution of being present at the start in good time. Early one morning we flew a practice operation in Rotte formation, but were soon called back over the radio because of approaching bad weather. From a great distance we could already see the snow showers approaching the airfield at Lechfeld from the north. Ground control gave us instructions to land immediately. As we approached the airfield from the south, the snow shower was already on the northern edge. We reduced speed and began the descent. However, we still had too much speed – the flaps had not come out. Again and again I tried, but I was still doing 300kmph. We were simply going too fast and had hardly any more time available. Landing gear down and again flaps out – and it was high time, for the landing strip was just in front of us. We were just about to set down and the snow shower had now reached the middle of the airfield. I slammed my 262 onto the landing strip doing 260kmph and suddenly saw a wheel running in front of me. I had broken off the end of the axle during the hard landing and the wheel had now separated. The aircraft swerved to the left but, with a great deal of effort and additional help from the left engine, I succeeded in keeping the machine going more or less in the right direction and steered past a parked fuel truck. After a few frightening seconds I brought my jet to a standstill. All went well, and the machine only needed a new undercarriage. It did not go as well for my number two. He was also too fast and broke his nose wheel on landing, the machine skidding across the runway on its nose and engine nacelles. The petrol-fuelled starter motors immediately caught fire. After the machine came to a standstill the fire brigade put out the fire in the engine pods.

This flight had been a very good and useful learning experience for us; only the end had been a complete wash-out. Everybody, the instructors, the ground control and the pilots, had learned something of value. The time at Lechfeld was a great time for me, we had the opportunity to get to know and fly a new aircraft. I was able to fly proper sorties, at times with success, and I got to know new friends. Altogether, I was again several experiences richer.

At the beginning of December 1944 the Erpropungskommando Lechfeld was disbanded and JG 7 was set up. The Kommodore of the Geschwader was Oberst Steinhoff[46], the Gruppe got Major Hohagen[47], and I was assigned to 9 Staffel. My Kapitän was Hauptmann Eder[48], a holder of the 'Oakleaves'. We also had two Knight's Cross-holders, Major Grotzinger and Hauptmann Gutmann from the bombers, who

Hermann Buchner, second from left, and comrades from JG 7 clown for the camera. All these pilots wear the black leather two-piece flying suits adopted by the Luftwaffe late in the war.

were going to be schooled in our Staffel. The Staffel was transported by train to Parchim in Mecklenburg. The 10th Staffel was transferred to Oranienburg while the 11th and the Gruppenstab went to Brandenburg-Briest. The III. Gruppe was now fully established.

December was occupied with the collection of 262s from the works. On 16 December myself and three other pilots picked up four 262s from Obertraubling. The weather was very bad, so for several days we were unable to make the flight northwards. After a great deal of to-ing and fro-ing from the weather station, on Christmas Eve 1944 we were given the go-ahead by the weather men and could fly north on our own responsibility. I drew up a flight plan for a Schwarm of 262s to Brandenburg-Briest and started around midday. Because the weather deteriorated en route, I decided to land the Schwarm at Egger on the factory airfield. The weather was extremely poor, but the landing went smoothly. The civilians were amazed at our machines and were also curious, wanting to know what kind they were and where we were going. We answered all their questions. They themselves built Heinkel 177 bombers in the factory, a creature unknown to us. We were given a veritable feast in the factory canteen. I made the necessary reports to Flight Control and made sure about the weather conditions over the next few days. My Kommandeur in Brandenburg-Briest was happy that I had the machines safely on the ground.

The weather was also very bad in the north, so my decision was approved. In good weather conditions I would have been able to carry out the trip. My colleagues and I were invited for Christmas celebrations with Sudeten German families, and we celebrated in the circle of very nice families. They also gave me the opportunity to phone my fiancée at the hospital in Prossnitz. The members of the factory also took good care of us. As the weather situation was so gloomy we remained in Egger until 29 December. When the weather improved we said our goodbyes to our hosts and started on the flight to Brandenburg-Briest. Over the Thuringer Forest lay a cover of stratus cloud and one could only reckon on a view of the ground from Magdeburg-Dessau. So, after taking off we pulled up to flying altitude (8,000 metres), also to save fuel, and headed north. We did not use the radio, unless there should be an emergency. The flight went off like clockwork. Unfortunately, our number four had problems with his nose wheel on landing[49] It broke and the intakes of the engine nacelles began to burn; again there was work for the fire brigade. The damaged 262 and a companion stayed in Brandenburg and I flew with my Rotte further on to Parchim. After twelve days' absence I was again with my Staffel. They were still celebrating, so we also celebrated the New Year with a wild party in the mess. We were still mad, even considering the war situation. But perhaps it was just the pilots' black sense of humour.

Chapter Thirteen

The new year, the last year, begins
January 1945-May 1945

During the first few days of January we were unable to fly because of thick fog. The time was used for instruction and for accounts of pilots' experiences.

From 15 January 1945 I was given leave. The base Kommandant, Oberst Kamphausen, gave me a clothing sack full of spirits and cigarettes for my wedding reception. I took the train to the Ruhr area. The Reichsbahn only took soldiers on leave from the front as far as Mülheim in the Ruhr; beyond, no more trains were available, as the lines had been destroyed and the air supremacy of the Allies was total. Well, as an old hand from the Russian Campaign, I tried to catch a lift with an Army supply vehicle from a passing column of Waffen-SS; the driver of a self-propelled 20mm gun took me as far as Frechen. Without exaggerating, our column was the last that drove across the bridge over the Rhine near the cathedral in Cologne, and behind us the bridge collapsed from a direct bomb strike. At least I had now reached Frechen; now I had to get to the next town, Bachem. I had never been in either before.

Something quite amusing happened when I arrived at my fiancée's parents' house and introduced myself. My fiancée, Käthe, was not yet there. Up to this time she had wartime employment as a Red Cross nurse in a reserve hospital in Prossnitz in the Protektorat (Czechoslovakia). My future in-laws were very nice to me, but didn't quite know what to do with me. After two days on my own Käthe drifted in and the necessary preparations were made at the local administrative office and with the priest.

The registry office wedding took place on 18 January and the church ceremony took place the day after. After the wedding in church, we went back to my wife's parents' house, where the postman brought me a telegram with orders to immediately return to my unit. This news naturally dampened spirits at our wedding table, but we had a modest celebration in the circle of family and relatives. Naturally, I wanted to start the return journey to Parchim the next day, and my wife was fully determined to break off her holiday and travel with me, so this sojourn was actually a disappointment for us both.

On the 20th we said goodbye to the parents and, with our modest belongings, left for Cologne, then Dortmund. From there a troop train was running (railway connections between Cologne and Dortmund no longer existed). By early morning we were in Dortmund, waiting for the train to Stendal via Hagen and Hannover, where we changed for Parchim, going via Perleberg and Ludwigslust. The train was absolutely full of soldiers returning from leave to the front, and because of my Knight's Cross the railway policeman found us two places in a compartment. The train began to move, and I was actually happy to be returning to my Staffel. The soldiers were travelling from their homes, from their destroyed flats, returning to their units on the Eastern Front. Their mood was negative and most of them were quite unhappy.

On the heights at Bückeberg at about 1000hrs the train was attacked by cannon from US Lightnings and the locomotive was damaged. The train stopped and remained still, while soldiers ran to the windows and sprang from the train, each running for his life. Käthe wanted to retrieve her suitcase, but I left it standing, took my wife by her hand and headed for the open. After 10 minutes the US pilots ended their handiwork and flew away. We moved back to the train and looked for our belongings. After about 3 hours a replacement locomotive arrived and on we went.

We arrived in Perleberg in the early hours of the morning, after a long train journey. There we got a bit of breakfast and I was able to phone my Staffel thanks to the area railway manager at Parchim. We arranged that a vehicle would pick me up that afternoon at the railway station at Parchim. Preparations were also made to provide for my wife. Once this matter had been settled, the Staffel – the officers and the boss – sorted everything out for my arrival. Our journey from Cologne to Parchim had taken nearly a full two days with all the interruptions. In Ludwigslust we had to change trains again and, after a journey of 40 minutes, we reached Parchim. The driver was there on time, presenting flowers to my wife on behalf of the Staffel. Now we were safe again – no low-level enemy aircraft, no need to worry.

I reported to Major Krötzinger at the Staffel. Hauptmann Eder was no longer there; he was in hospital in Wismar. Krötzinger offered me his apartment in Ledigenheim for the duration of my wife's stay. At the same time he disclosed that, with effect from 14 January, I was to be entrusted with the leadership of the Staffel on the flying side. The schooling of the pilots was continuing, as ever, in between duties, but because of the bad weather there were no missions. The intensive training finished with a large exercise in

With 'White 7' in the background, Oberfeldwebel Hermann Buchner, with his
flying helmet hanging from his belt, is in discussion with an unidentified
member of Kommando Nowotny on 20 October 1944 at Lechfeld. The dog seems
remarkably unconcerned by the noise from the jets.

central Germany in the area of Launa and Leipzig. During the return
journey above the clouds near Magdeburg, ground control ordered
us to make visual ground contact. The lower level of the clouds was
100 metres and visibility was very bad. The ground was covered in
snow. We were flying northwards at low level at 700kmph, over the
Elbe near Perleberg, and would soon emerge at Parchim.

I heard ground control very faintly over the radio, but he could
offer me no navigational help. To my astonishment, instead of Parchim,
the Elbe appeared again and now I had really lost my bearings. We
then found ourselves flying over heathland and I tried to make contact
with a ground position, but was unsuccessful. We had already been
under way for 50 minutes and my number four lost his nerve and made
a belly landing on the heath. I circled to watch his landing: there was a
short burst of flying snow and the 262 lay on its fuselage on the
ground. The pilot climbed out of the cockpit and waved to us.

We flew onwards, heading south, and tried to find a prominent
point or make radio contact with a ground station. Then our three
262s reached a railway line, and I could make out the Ülzen railway
station in the Lüneburg Heath. I had really lost my bearings. Things
were slowly getting a bit dicey and we needed to find an airfield at
which to land. Lüneburg was the next airfield, but it had no starting
runway, only a grass field, but nevertheless it was the obvious

choice. For the time being I ordered the other two pilots to shut down one engine, which both succeeded in doing. After flying for a total of 65 minutes we reached Lüneburg and its airfield. The engines were started again and we landed individually. I made the first landing and gave the others the necessary instructions over the radio. All three of us made orderly landings and taxied to the marked parking place in front of the control tower.

We were the first 262s to land in Lüneburg, and the excitement, as well as the curiosity, was very great. Unfortunately, as already related, my number four had landed too early on the heath, having lost his nerve. I therefore used the telephone to report back to our Kommandeur at Parchim, and the message from my boss was not pleasant. Well, he had not experienced the situation with us – he had been sitting on the ground. I was the one who had had to make the decision. I explained that, first of all, we had to find some fuel and that we would fly back the next morning after refuelling. The reproach that followed worried me less than finding accommodation that night. On 18 February, in the morning hours, the Kette returned to Parchim without any incident of note, and the machines were again available for operations over the coming days. After reporting back to the Kommandeur, life was again rosy – he was happy that we were back with the Gruppe. I, however, was older and wiser yet again.

In the middle of February 1945 there was a change in the occupation of the Kommandant positions; the new Kommodore was Major Weissenberger[50], the Gruppe got Major Sinner and 9 Staffel got Oberleutnant Wegmann as the new boss on 12 March. I was again a veteran and kept my Schwarm, for the reason that I had not lost any pilots. Wegmann was no great flyer and there were different opinions about the methods of attacking the four-engined bombers. During the weeks of February and March we were operational and were trialling the newly delivered R4M[51] rockets. The launch racks were fitted under the wings by the groundcrews.

In preparation for an operation, Oberleutnant Wegmann gave us a talk. We, the pilots, wanted to fly, but Wegmann was of the opinion that the weather was too bad. The discussion was very lively and he was simply not prepared to take note of our argument. After a repeated discussion with only the two of us present, I asked to be transferred to 10 Staffel. Wegmann declared that he would think about it. During the next mission I found myself assigned as number two to Wegmann, but I declined the assignment as his Rottenflieger (wingman). As a result,

Wegmann took away my 'Black 11' and flew the operation in this machine. During this operation, on 17 March, Wegmann and his Rottenflieger were shot down by Mustangs; Wegmann took to his parachute but his Rottenflieger was killed. The problem had sorted itself out and my transfer to 10 Staffel subsequently took place.

10 Staffel was located in Oranienburg near Berlin, and once again I was on my way there by rail. In Berlin, during the night of 17-18 March 1945, I experienced a bombing attack. At Lehrte Railway Station I was inspected by the Military Police, because of my Knight's Cross. After proving my identity, I was free again. I spent the night at the destroyed 'Fatherland' pub and the next morning took the tram and the train to Oranienburg. On my arrival at the airfield at around 0900hrs, the Staffel was just ready to take off. At the same time the alarm was given, and we barely had time to leave the airfield. The Staffel had just made it into the air and we had just left the airfield when it was turned into a pile of rubble, and ruined for jet aircraft traffic for several days. I spent exactly one whole day at Berlin-Oranienburg – on the 18th I went back to Parchim with the ground elements.

I could have been spared this little holiday. 10 Staffel was led by Oberleutnant Schall, an Austrian from Graz. Schall was an old pilot from JG 54 with aerial victories, but all the others were younger pilots. One thing must be added: Schall was a proper fighter, he had guts and a knack for a good formation. There was a place for me, I got to know the new faces, was again assigned as Schwarm leader, and everything was back in its proper place once more.

On 19 March I again flew missions from Parchim to the Berlin area. We met Mustangs, but we had no successes; you could not defeat Mustangs unless you surprised them. After the turning battle had ended, one of my engines failed, so I was glad that we were able to make our return journey without the enemy. My Rotte colleagues remained near me and brought me back to Parchim. The subsequent landing with one engine went off with no problems.

On 22 March there was a mission against US bombers in the Leipzig-Cottbus area. We had caught the bombers at 6,000 metres altitude and were able to fly our first attack. I was scoring good hits, but I could not discern any effect. During the return flight, at 5,000 metres I saw a well-loaded B-17 that was clearing off eastwards. On the first attack I was able to make sustained hits to the right inside engine, starting a fire, which led to an explosion. After another go, the crash followed, and moreover the gun camera had taken a picture of the aerial victory. My Schwarm and I could land united at Parchim. After landing I reported to the command post and was loudly shouted at by the Kommandeur present there, Major Sinner, because no one was to go to the command post. I had no idea whatsoever about the whole thing, as I had only just landed. The times during those weeks in March were very turbulent.

Leutnant Karl 'Quax' Schnörrer was shot down by Spitfires over Hamburg and had taken to his parachute. After his return, using the pilots' special rations, he made coffee and cakes for the pilots and their wives. After returning from operations there was always coffee and a snack laid on in the dining room. In between operations we were schooled in blind flying, for which Siebel 204s were assigned to our Gruppe at Parchim from the Blind Flying Schools. During the early morning hours and in the evening the blind flying instructors taught us instrument flying; during these flights I was occasionally in Ludwigslust. The weather was nearly always good, although even when it wasn't we were still forced to go up through the clouds.

In March we were continually on the go. I think that on the 3rd we flew an operation with ten machines against a US unit near Hannover. At 8,000 metres we came into the attack position on a unit of B-17s without any fighter protection. We closed up into battle formation and opened fire using the R4M rockets at a distance of 1,000 metres. Hauptmann Gutmann flew on my right-hand side, and was fatally hit about 800 metres away by the defensive fire of the rear gunner, crashing from this altitude directly into the ground. We carried on with the attack and scored a few good hits, but were unable to see if we were successful. There were five confirmed aerial victories for the Staffel during this operation, and these were granted by the Division. Unfortunately we lost our friend Gutmann, a former bomber pilot.

Gutmann had fallen and Major Orbtzinger died on 15 February of polio. The old ones were becoming ever fewer: Russel had fallen over the Baltic, Oberfahnrich Schnur had crashed doing a test flight in my 262, Wegmann was wounded, and Oberleutnant Wörner had taken to his parachute, wounded, as had Schnörrer, also wounded. My friend Oberfeldwebel Arnold of the 11th Staffel had been killed. Missions were increasingly more difficult, and the pilots were becoming increasingly nervous. The Staffeln were evacuated to nearby villages and our Staffel went to Malchow. When we were in the air with the 262s the last mechanics departed from the airfield and left it empty.

Helmut Lenartz and I were quartered with the Pingel family, who were very nice to us and we were allowed to sleep in the family bedrooms.

On 31 March there was something new for us – an early scramble. We were still at breakfast in the dining room and the weather was not very good with a cloud base 150-200 metres above the ground. We flew with seven 262s led by Oberleutnant Schall, one Schwarm and one Kette. Our mission was against US units in the Hannover region, with take off at 0900hrs. We climbed in tight formation into the clouds, heading westwards.

The clouds just weren't coming to an end and Schall asked the ground station guiding us whether we should make 'Luzi-Anton'[52]. A brusque answer came back over the radio: 'First of all make Pauke-Pauke.'[53] At 7,500 metres above ground, we had just come out of the clouds when Schall got the order: 'Assume course 180, Dicke Autos[54] course 180!' At the same moment someone from our unit cried, 'To the right of us, nothing but bombers, to the right of us!' Schall, as well as the rest of us, saw the bombers, flying north in a formation that was new to us. They flew staggered, about 1,000 metres deep and 2,000 metres wide. They were not US bombers, however, but Tommys in night-flight formation, doing a daytime attack on Hamburg. Schall ordered us to take up attack formation, already having long forgotten the order 'assume 180'. We were lucky to reach the band without fighter protection and Schall, a fighter with real heart, was not going to pass up a chance like this.

As we got closer we could clearly see what kind of bombers they were – RAF Lancasters – on their way to attack Hamburg, but still 50km away over the Lüneberg Heath. On our first attack seven Lancasters were shot down with the R4M rockets. Now the large unit dissolved somewhat and the Rotten flew a renewed attack on the bombers. I made a right turn and lined up for another attack, using the nose cannon. My Lancaster lay directly in my sights and I only had to get a bit closer. I opened fire, the hits were good, but the pilot of the Lancaster must have been an old hand. He turned his Lancaster steeply over on its right wing, making a tight turn around the main axis. With my speed I was unable to follow this tight manoeuvre and was also unable to see if my shots had had any effect, or to see how he flew on. I shot through the pile and had to think about returning home. The other pilots were also having the same problem. We had a shortage of fuel and had to get back to our own garden. At the same time, all called to the ground control 'Autobahn', for the course number for the direction back to our home airfield.

Only one of us could be handled by 'Tornado' ground control, but all of us wanted to be given a course. We were still all in the tangle of RAF bombers, but none of us had visual contact with each other. We all had to go back down through the cloud layer. I thought to myself, 'Go back down alone!' At 7,000 metres I dived into the cloud layer, laying on a course of 090, 700kmph and the engines running at 6,000rpm. Over the radio I could still hear my colleagues calling 'Autobahn' to 'Tornado' – they were all still in the air. My altimeter showed that I was quickly losing height, and at 1,000 metres it was already dark – I had to get out of the clouds soon.

My altitude was diminishing, the gauge showing 500, 400, 300 metres – the ground must surely soon appear. Yes, there it was. Doing 700kmph I shot out of the clouds and found myself over fields and clumps of trees. Unfortunately I didn't know quite where I was. On my left side I could make out the sea – was it the Baltic, or where was I? Anyhow, I flew eastwards with a normal turbine rpm and at 800kmph. In the distance I could see the silhouette of a town. I quickly thought about it, then I was sure that the town had to be Lubeck. I had recently seen a film called *Die Budenbrocks* in which the silhouette of the town had been shown. Flying over the harbour, I came under fire from light flak, but I was too fast – they had no chance of hitting me. Now I knew how I could get back.

My other comrades were also on their journey back to Parchim, and now the traffic with 'Tornado' was quieter, so I could also call up and ask for instructions, giving him my location. I was the last 262 to call in after the mission at 7,000 metres. Now he had his flock together. By the time I reached Ludwigslust I had already been given permission to land, as well as the comforting news that there were 'no Indians on the airfield'. After 65 minutes flying I landed without difficulty in Parchim, the last of the seven. My list of aircraft shot down was extended: one Lancaster confirmed and one definitely damaged. Altogether we had certainly shot down ten Lancasters and five others had been damaged.[55] The seven 262s on the mission had landed without problems after 60-70 minutes flying time in bad weather conditions. The reported aerial victories were confirmed by Jagd Division, and the bombers had offloaded their cargoes over the heath, far from their target. Around sixty flying personnel were taken prisoner on the heath. At midday another mission was flown against US units.

The days were hectic and we were really in demand. Our mechanics were loyal souls and they worked tirelessly. During this time I was flying with Leutnant Sturm and we were assigned against a unit of B-24s in the Stendal area. On the first attack Sturm shot down one using his R4M rockets. The hits were so good that the Liberator fluttered from the sky. Again, we were bothered by US fighter protection, but landed smoothly at Parchim.

On 2 April, early in the morning, I flew a Rotte mission against US units in the Hamburg area. After my Rotte had reached 8,000 metres over Hamburg, or at least the destroyed city of Hamburg, I spotted a Spitfire. We were actually supposed to be fighting against US pilots, but there it was – an RAF Spitfire. It was about 1,000 metres below, flying northwards towards Denmark. In my Rotte I flew at the same altitude, onwards towards Heligoland, in expectation of US bombers. From the ground station came the instruction to stay in the Hamburg area, and we were over Hamburg when back came the Spitfire again at the same altitude. Over the city it turned away to the north-west; it must have been an RAF reconnaissance aircraft. Now I was ready. From an excessive height I began the attack. Unseen I came towards the Tommy fast, too fast. At the last moment I thought that he would hit me head-on. Then I made a mistake. Instead of shooting, I pulled the 262 hard away to the left – too hard, as the air stream was broken off and the machine tilted over on its wing. Momentarily I was very shocked at the flight situation, and had both hands full trying to bring the machine under control again. Because of this unintentional manoeuvre, I had not only lost a great deal of altitude, but my wingman as well. After I got my machine under control again, I looked for my wingman and also for the Spitfire, but could find neither of them. The fuel supply demanded that I begin the journey back. Once more an experience richer, and an adventure richer, I flew back to Parchim and landed smoothly – hardly profitable, but enjoyable, nonetheless.

My wingman had landed shortly before me, sure that I had rammed the Spitfire and had been wiped out. A day full of effort and still no success. That evening in the dining room the details of the aerial battle were again dragged up. Unfortunately, there were fewer and fewer of us old ones and even the young ones had to bear their share of the losses. From the old days at Lechfeld you could count on one hand the number of people still left.

Parts of our airfield were badly destroyed, the accommodation was unusable and the landing strip was being repaired by the engineers again and again, a feat that required their maximum effort. Our operations were almost always now flown only as a Rotte or Schwarm. Two to three operations were flown against the US bombers and RAF pilots. The Allied pilots had absolute air superiority over Germany and were able to fly their attacks at altitudes from 4,000 metres. Our sanctuary was the mess at Parchim, where all the pilots would gather together, all who were still with us from the party. Talks were given, battles fought, and we tried to make the best of the defeat. Photographs of our fallen comrades hung on the walls and the young pilots had already put nails in, so that their pictures could be hung there. In spite of all this, the mood was not bad – we would pull through.

On 4 April Sinner was with us at Parchim and led a mission from here. In accordance with assignments, he led the first Schwarm and I was to lead the second. The weather was not exactly good – we had a total cloud base of about 150 metres above ground, and above it US Mustangs were already waiting for us. Sinner told me that he would immediately go through the clouds. I replied that it would be better first to pick up speed, then go through the clouds, but he did not share my opinion.

We were ready. The order to take off came and we taxied to the start, the first Schwarm in front and my Schwarm behind. Sinner rolled away and, just after lifting off, he disappeared behind the clouds. I then took off my brakes and we started. Just after my Schwarm lifted off I heard Sinner's radio traffic. He was already entangled in battle with the Mustangs. I was still under the clouds with my Schwarm, and with the best will in the world I could not help him. As we came out above the clouds there was not an aircraft to be seen. Sinner had taken to his parachute and his wingmen had landed in Garz and Parchim. In accordance with orders from ground control, I flew against four-engined bombers in the area south of Hamburg and made a few good hits when we attacked.

Basically, we were on the go daily, in every kind of weather. The enemy superiority was very great and the possibility of success was, for us, slight. Even so, I was still always able to bring my Schwarm back to Parchim or any other available airfield without any casualties.

On 7 April we took off again against US units in the Hannover-Magdeburg area. Enemy fighter units hung over our own airfields, especially over Brandenburg-Briest and Parchim. Only with a lot of cunning and luck could we leave our own base without incurring casualties. The US bombers now only flew at heights from 4,000 metres – they had hardly anything to fear any more. After we managed to push through the umbrella of fighter support aircraft, I made an attack using the R4M rockets. The defensive fire was so strong that we didn't have time to worry about whether we had possibly hit them, and a second attack was simply not possible because of this defensive fire. We started our flight back to Parchim, but about 100km away I received instructions from the Parchim Ground Control not to fly there, but to change and go to Wismar on the Baltic. I changed course and steered northwards towards the coast. Our altitude was about 3,000 metres and we were actually not really pestered by anyone.

Contact with Wismar airfield was established and was good. We still had about another 6 minutes' flying time when I made out aircraft coming from the west. Now the matter was critical – I had determined that they were Thunderbolts, also flying towards Wismar. The matter was clear to me; they wanted to intercept us. No matter what, our Schwarm had to land at Wismar before the Americans. We still had a small lead. Coming from the south, we flew over the concrete runway at low level, pulled up, reduced speed, then lined up to land from the north. We did without the landing strip and landed on the grass. Our friends the Thunderbolts were already over the south-west part of the airfield, but we still had a small advantage. I slammed my 262 onto the grass, just on the edge of the airfield, hardly a metre away, and we taxied at high speed southwards over the airfield. With both feet on the brake pedals, the tiger profile of the racing tyres stripped the grass in places. On the south side of the airfield Ju 52 transport machines were parked, and my machine came to a standstill right beside them. Engines off and out of the machine just in time – the Ju 52 was already in flames as I leapt into a trench. We were lucky, my colleagues and I, to have just reached cover; we had got away from the horror. We now sat in trenches, worried about our 262s as the Junkers were already burning brightly. The rest of the Jus were shot up in flames when the Thunderbolts came around for their second attack. Because of the huge clouds of smoke the Americans were unable to make out our 262s and were content with the destruction they had already caused. After three attacks they regrouped and flew away westwards.

For us the show was over and our machines remained undamaged. Now I could find flight control, organise our landing at Parchim and receive any further orders. My pilots saw to it that the machines were refuelled. Everything worked wonderfully, and we would be able to land in Parchim at 1700hrs. We still had time to talk to the Ju crews in the canteen and, together with the Ju coachmen, we celebrated a birthday. The crews of the transport machines were not really upset that their machines had been shot up in flames. They could not now fly back to Kurland (Latvia), for they had been relieved of their task. I think they ended the war in Wismar.

That evening, around 1730hrs, we started our 262s, this time on the runway, and returned to Parchim, flying as a unit. Our mechanics were very happy that we had returned, and told us that the airfield had been attacked by US bombers and the runway had been damaged. The engineers were once again busy at their work, doing makeshift repairs.

On his return Oberleutnant Schall could not land on the airfield and, having too little fuel, was forced to land outside. He tried to do a belly landing outside the airfield, but was killed when his machine rolled, crashed and burned. In the confusion of the last days of the war he was buried without the presence of colleagues from the soldiers of the base command. Leutnant Sturm took his Knight's Cross from the gravediggers and, in spite of his imprisonment by the Czechs and later by the Poles, brought it back to Oberleutnant Schall's family. The airfield and the accommodation was partly destroyed, although the runway was made operational again by the engineers and American prisoners. The crews and the rest of the personnel had been accommodated with villagers in the area for some time now. One could hardly believe it, but our mess in Parchim was still undamaged and remained operational. In the evenings the few remaining trusty pilots would gather there to talk over their aerial battles. But the crowd was becoming ever smaller.

On 8 April my Schwarm and I were again operational; the weather was not bad and visibility was good. We started around 1100hrs, deployed against a group of bombers. We flew towards the bombers in the Bremen area while, on the ground, English troops had already penetrated part of the area. After getting over the US fighter protection, we flew an attack on the B-17 bombers and our hits were good. In spite of the enemy superiority, we attacked another group of B-17s with again some good hits, but unfortunately we were not able to linger among the bombers. We were unable to see the effect of our attack, although some bombers were trailing smoke and hanging back from the group. The situation in the air was not suitable for us to remain in this Mustang-infested area. The defensive fire was very strong, the Schwarm collapsed, and the Rottenflieger could not follow my flying movements or had some problems. Several of the pilots in the group were still too young and had few hours on the 262.

It needs to be remembered that, taking part in a single raid by the 8th Air Force, there could be up to 900 bombers and 800-900 Mustangs and Thunderbolts. In addition to our propeller-driven fighter aircraft, of which there were a hundred, there were twenty to thirty Me 262s, but often only four or six Me 262s against the enemy.

We stayed too long with the enemy, and I had to break off and start on the return flight to Parchim. Because I had problems with fuel, I tried to find a place on the heath. First I broke away from the enemy fighters and searched for a suitable place. The first attempt to land at Archim near Bremen came to nothing because the airfield, or at least the surface I made out to be an airfield, was occupied by armoured vehicles. I went up to my flying altitude again and flew further eastwards. There was still time to find a field for the landing, and in Rothenburg an der Wimme, in the Lüneburg Heath, I found it. Whatever it was didn't matter, it had to be there. With my last drops of fuel I lined up to land, convincing myself that there were no enemy fighters in the area, that the air was clear. Diminish speed, undercarriage and flaps out, and turn to land in from the west. Actually, everything went like clockwork, then just before I set down something blazed from my right wing, and I could also make out hits on the ground in front of me. As I landed the enemy fighter made further shots at the engine mounts. My machine began to burn. The Mustang or the fighter had surprisingly appeared from nowhere. He was too fast, or he had only seen me at the last moment, so he had no more time to take good aim. In spite of the flames on both sides, I was able to bring the machine to a standstill at the end of the runway. Now it was time to leave the cockpit – the flames were already joining together above the cockpit canopy. In my haste I forgot to undo the harness. I forced myself to be calm, then undid the harness and left the cockpit.

I went over the wings onto the grass and away from the burning machine. In my haste I still had my parachute on and it hit the backs of my knees hard. After about 50 metres I came to the end of my strength and collapsed, unconscious. I was rescued by the medics and finally taken to the sick-bay. It wasn't bad; it was only the initial shock that gave me problems. I was lucky – again I had got away. My opponent had definitely been too fast, or perhaps he had seen me too late. It was also possible that he himself was surprised to see a 262 in such a favourable position in front of his weapons. Anyway, he was unable to use his chance. It was unbelievable luck for me – I had survived and it was my last combat mission in the Second World War. From accounts of the soldiers at the tower, the Mustang[56] flew over again after I had landed and fired on the already burning machine.

On the airfield itself they were breaking up and it was all I could do to get into contact with my Staffel in Parchim to make my report. They were very happy that I had reported in, congratulated me on my luck and were already looking forward to my return. After I had taken care of the formalities, I went in search of the canteen and got some food and something to drink. There I met an Obergefreiter of the Flak. He told me that he had to take a train of munitions to Hamburg that evening, and to my question as to whether he would take me along with him, he replied, 'Of course', if I met him at the canteen at 2000hrs. I wasn't going to pass up this opportunity. Tensely I waited at the arranged place and time and punctually the train came towards me. I climbed into the driver's cabin and away we went into the night. The driver told me that he had been carrying ammunition for the flak units in Hamburg for days. He was actually happy to have a passenger, for up to now he had always been on his own. Around 0200hrs the following morning we arrived in Hamburg and he took me close to the main station. Hamburg was totally destroyed, and only the main railway station was in some kind of working order. There I stood in the dark night, unable to give the driver a little gift. I had nothing, only my flying suit, my helmet, the parachute and my RV (Reichsverteidigung) identification. I had a few Marks in my pocket, but I needed those myself. A handshake and best wishes, that was all, then his train disappeared into the darkness.

At the damaged railway station – but still running – the only people in the middle of the night were careworn soldiers, women and children … and me, a shot-down pilot carrying a sack in which there was nothing worth mentioning. There was a train going to Ludwigslust at 0400hrs. Some women spoke to me; they thought I had come from Denmark and wanted to know whether I had anything to eat or cigarettes with me. Unfortunately I had to disappoint them, for I did not have even a single cigarette – I was really a pauper. So the time passed and I talked with soldiers who were travelling like myself. Meanwhile the train came in and the travellers boarded. The coaches were partly damaged, the windows without glass and only paper or cardboard used to repair them. Punctually, at 0400hrs, the train departed and we steamed through the night. The conductor was not happy about my presence. I had no travel documents, no battlefield, only my RV identification. He did not want to believe my account of being a shot-down pilot. At that time the people, as well as the German Luftwaffe in general, did not believe that there were German fighter pilots still flying.

I finally managed to convince him. Not being pestered by Allied pilots, we reached Ludwigslust around 0600hrs, and after a short time I caught the connection to Parchim. Again I had problems with the conductor about a ticket, but he found my explanation plausible. After 40 minutes I reached Parchim and informed them that I could be picked up at the railway station. They were happy that I had made it back in such a short time, and after a short wait our old driver appeared to pick me up. He told me the latest news, but also wanted to know who had shot me down. After my arrival at the Kommandeur's office and reporting the details of the operation, I got myself something to eat and had a few little Cognacs, then off to a bed to catch up on last night's sleep. That evening we celebrated my return in the mess and I was given a new task. The next day I was to take a vehicle and two pilots, Oberleutnant Schrangl and Leutnant Heckmann, and drive to Brandenburg-Briest, pick up three 262s and fly them back to Parchim. The night was another long one and the stories made their rounds. I soon had my things together and around 0400hrs we clattered away for Brandenburg-Briest in an Opel P4 truck, arriving at the command post there around 0900hrs.

I was back with the Gruppe again and the Technical Officer greeted me with the words, 'Hurry up, Buchner – there is an operation starting any minute.' We had just arrived and hadn't even reported back. Meanwhile there were vehicles loaded with people on their way to the exit, in the process of leaving the airfield. I was too much of an old hand not to know that things were serious. I immediately said to both the officers, 'Quickly, into a vehicle, get away from the airfield!' We threw our parachutes onto a tracked vehicle and jumped in. As we left, the western side of the airfield erupted under a hail of bombs; the buildings were already in flames, and the runway was a thing of the past. Everywhere things were burning, clouds of smoke billowing – the sky was 5/8ths or 6/8ths covered by it. With a great deal of effort we reached the Havel and looked for cover. After the thick smoke had dispersed somewhat, the fighter-bombers appeared and shot at anything on the ground that moved. Schrangl and I crawled into a canal duct and lay in this 'heroes' cellar' for at least a half an hour. It was terrible, for our 262s were definitely under the wreckage, and the pilots who had already been sitting in their machines had possibly been caught as well. It was unclear to us why the possible take off of 11 Staffel at Brandenburg had been ordered so late, but it had. After an hour the whole thing was over. We could leave our position, and were happy that we had survived the whole mess.

Back we went to the still burning airfield, on foot this time. Near the gate, by a 20mm four-gun flak position, stood a riderless moped. We took possession of it and were motorised from now on. At the buildings we tried to help, but unfortunately without success. Schrangl tried to help the signals girls rescue their belongings from the burning accommodation, but there was only fire and crying girls everywhere and, among them, a few soldiers who had also lost their heads.

Now it was hard to know what to do. Our 262s were only fragments, having been destroyed in the hail of bombs. For the moment we considered what we should do first of all. The situation was not very good for us, and we had not seen any officers or even Unteroffizier from our Gruppe – they had all disappeared off the face of the earth. Near the control tower there stood an undamaged Siebel 204 that belonged to a transport Staffel. We had a word with the boss of the Staffel as to whether it would be possible to use the Siebel on the condition that we brought it back again. I promised the Major everything he wanted to hear, for I wanted to have a machine above all else. After we had loaded the machine and started the engine, we had some difficulties with the tank switch – no one had any idea how it functioned. After a short conference about the situation, we came to one conclusion – we had no idea how it operated, therefore we had to give up our plan. I gave the aircraft papers back to the Staffel.

The time dragged and it was hard to know what to do. The runway was badly damaged, but some of the grass parts could still be used. In any case it was possible to make a landing, for a Bücker Bestmann taxied towards the place where we were standing and an Unteroffizier detached himself from the machine. We immediately asked him where he had come from and where he was going. He told us that he was a flying student at the Flying School at Magdeburg East. The Americans had just taken Magdeburg and the flying students were told to fly the aircraft north and eastwards. Since he lived near Brandenburg, he had flown his Bücker here. He readily agreed to our suggestion that we trade his aircraft for our quick moped. The exchange quickly took place and we now possessed a Bü 181 complete with papers. After a short time we saw the brave pilot leave the airfield; he had definitely made it home, but we still had a longer journey ahead of us.

Anyway, we had an aircraft that we could use. After all the events of the day, a return flight to Parchim during daylight hours was no longer possible, so we decided to stay overnight with the machine.

First, Hans Schrangl made another inspection of the take off runway, looking for possible stretches between the bomb craters; it was obvious that he, being the largest of us, should pilot the Bücker. I sat in the jump seat without a parachute and little Heckmann sat on my lap. We put the parachutes in the luggage area. Early in the morning, still by lamplight, we started on our latest undertaking.

The weather was OK and the start went smoothly. We flew north-west at about 150 metres altitude. Admittedly, with three pilots on board, there were different opinions about the accuracy of the course, but Schrangl was convinced of his navigational abilities and forbade us both to speak. After about an hour's flying time we flew over the bombed-out Parchim airfield. Hans made several circuits over the airfield to try and make out a suitable stretch on which to land. The concrete runway was not suitable, but by the side of the runway he found a stretch that appeared suitable to land the Bücker. In between the bomb craters Schrangl taxied towards the destroyed flight control barracks. It looked wretched – the airfield and the accommodation were totally destroyed. Of our unit, only a rear party remained. The flying portion no longer landed at Parchim after their operation, but in Alt-Lönewitz instead. The ground element had moved to Prague and to southern Germany on the same day of the attack. Hans wanted to fly the Bücker to Fürstenfeldbruck by night, but I didn't really want to.

The matter was soon decided for me, since I was tasked with leading the rear party back via Dresden, Aussig, Prague (reporting in Ruzyne), Pilsen and Deggendorf, reporting at the main command post there. That evening we left in a column and drove swiftly through the night to gain as much distance as possible so that we were not pestered by low-flying aircraft. Around midnight we passed through Zossen, Jüterbog and Königswusterhausen. The sky over Berlin was alight with searchlights looking for enemy aircraft. Before noon the next day we stopped for a rest in a place near Grossenhein. The vehicles were camouflaged and the soldiers had a well-earned sleep on the ground near their vehicles. Doing anything during the middle of the day was avoided because of low-flying enemy aircraft, so the troops rested.

After a discussion, at about 1600hrs we started on the next leg of the journey via Dresden, the Erz mountains and Aussig. Between 1800 and 1900hrs we drove through Dresden, possibly the last unified unit to do so. The vehicle column rolled past piles of bodies from the air raids, a terrible sight for us pilots and also for our mechanics. After Dresden we made a mistake. We did not drive along the Elbe, but over the Erz mountains towards Teplitz-Schonau. The road became increasingly steep and settlements fewer and further apart. We stopped at one village and I enquired where we were and whether we could get some kind of accommodation. The people were very friendly Sudeten Germans and naturally were prepared to accommodate soldiers. In the morning we had a proper breakfast, something we had not had for a long time. After heartfelt thanks – we were unable to give anything else, since we ourselves had nothing – we went onwards to Aussig on the Elbe. The column was on its way again, initially uphill, then finally into the valley again, rolling through Teplitz-Schonau before noon and on to Aussig. We wanted to get as far as possible towards Prague before noon, and put as many kilometres as possible between us and the low-flying aircraft. At midday we would put the camouflage covers up and rest again.

At the exit from Aussig towards Theresienstadt a Luftwaffe column stood on the side of the road, and an officer was trying to stop passing vehicles. As we got closer I recognised Oberleutnant Grünberg of the I. Gruppe at Kaltenkirchen, who was on his way to Prague with his unit. I stopped my column and, after greeting him, asked whether he needed anything. To cut a long story short, he was stuck there without any fuel for his vehicles. We could help him there, for, in the column, I had an Opel Blitz carrying Otto fuel.[57] The men from Kaltenkirchen were duly provided with fuel and went on with their journey towards Prague. There was still time for us to get there as well before the fighter-bombers were due to appear. As we drove through the city the streets were empty and there was a tense atmosphere, as it was shortly before the Czech uprising.

Around 1300hrs I was able to report to the Kommandeur and also inform him of the destruction of Brandenburg-Briest. The Kommandeur was happy that I had the rest of the unit in Prague already, but at the same time he ordered me and my group to immediately leave Prague-Ruzyne and try to reach southern Germany. He wished my soldiers and I lots of luck and every success in getting back. I don't think I was in Ruzyne for even an hour, so I had no opportunity to talk to my friends in the Staffel, which presumably is what the drivers of the various trucks and tracked vehicles had hoped to do. We drove and drove, with no warm meals, eating out of tins and having little sleep. In addition the threat from the Czechs returned and we were ready, weapons in hand, to fight as a unit. Our goal was to get to Bavaria. We did not want to surrender to the Czechs, so we had voted to fight if we had to. We had already passed Pilsen and were now heading southwards over Klattau, the Bavarian Forest and Deggendorf. We were unfortunately one vehicle less; a meteorologist had wanted to drive on ahead, since the journey was too slow. I warned him and pointed out that he should stay with the unit, but he was not to be told. We never saw him again, nor did we ever hear anything about him; we lost him in the confusion of the retreat, and he was driving a BMW 326 Cabrio.

In the region of Klattau we were spotted by some fighter-bombers and attacked. The Jabos shot up in flames our two trucks with trailers; one of the trailers was loaded with R4M rockets. We tried to rescue some of the luggage that was on the trailer, but there was too little time for this. It was time to leave the burning truck and trailer and to find cover. After a few minutes the R4M rockets on the burning vehicle exploded. The explosions were massive and our vehicles, including their freight, were destroyed, and some of the houses nearby were damaged. After a short break in the journey, we resumed our trip southwards. Around 1800hrs we reached Zwiesel in the Bavarian Forest. We had reached our target of Bavaria and we were all very happy about it. In Zwiesel we stopped for a rest and the people provided us with tea and sandwiches. We received a very friendly welcome – they wanted to put us up for the night, but we did not have time to stop there. We had to go onwards – this single route in the southern German area had to be kept free for the next army columns that would be coming through. Reluctantly, the inhabitants let us go and we departed, thanking them gratefully, having nothing else to give.

Near the exit to Deggendorf we had another accident when the driver of an Opel Blitz was unable to control the speed of his vehicle any longer, and it rolled and crashed into a ravine. Because it rolled and finally lay in the water, it crushed the soldiers who were in it, killing an Oberleutnant, five Obergefreiter and one of the female news reporters. After an eventful, even adventurous, journey of more than 900km, we had lost seven men and two trucks with trailers. Late that evening we reached Deggendorf and our main headquarters. After reporting in, I was happy that I had fulfilled my duty to myself and my soldiers by leading my column back and sparing the soldiers certain imprisonment. Now began the old routine of looking for accommodation and something to eat – and what was going to happen now? According to the rumours, we were going to move to Fürstenfeldbruck. But, initially, these were only rumours.

On 21 April we experienced another Jabo attack on the airfield and on the cigarette factory at Deggendorf. During this operation five Lightnings were shot down by flak. In retaliation the airfield and the town were bombed the next day by a group of US Marauders. The people were quite indignant and were of the opinion that we had caused the attack by shooting down the Lightnings the previous day.

On the next day, or possibly the day after, the ground element of JG 7 moved to Fürstenfeldbruck at dawn. The journey was chaotic, and the streets were clogged with army vehicles. In spite of this, our unit arrived as a whole at Fürstenfeldbruck, unmolested by low-flying enemy aircraft. The airfield had been evacuated and our flying sections were still in Prague. We again looked for accommodation for a few days with farmers in the area. This wasn't difficult, for the inhabitants were very friendly and were happily prepared to take us in. Here in Fürstenfeldbruck, my friend Schrangl appeared again; he had actually flown the Bücker here at night from Parchim. He was still of the opinion that we should don civilian clothing and go into the mountains. To this end we needed some commodities, things that we could exchange for civilian clothing. Among others we visited the Officers' Mess and acquired there some fine blue and white curtains, which, in Schrangl's opinion, were suitable for trading. Schrangl and I each left a suitcase full of personal belongings with the farmers at Fürstenfeldbruck, saying that if we had not appeared within a year to pick them up, the farmers were to do with them what they wished. We thanked them for their friendly reception and took our leave.

We were off to Mühldorf in Bavaria, ordered to drive there with the Kommandeur in his car, a BMW 327 Cabrio. The driver set off and arrived in a totally destroyed Munich where, on one of the streets, we were stopped by a military patrol and asked if we could take a lady with a small babe in arms along with us to Mühldorf. The Kommandeur declared himself prepared to take the lady along; she was a Viennese woman who wanted to return to Vienna, so we gave her a place in the back of the vehicle. From Munich we made good time and were lucky as well, since we were unmolested by Jabos and unhindered by columns of vehicles. On arrival in Mühldorf we said goodbye to the lady from Vienna and her child and the Kommandeur asked me if I could first find definite quarters for our Gruppe. For the Kommandeur I found a very nice place with the wife of a director in a single family house, who placed a newly furnished bedroom at his disposal – rather too good for us beaten soldiers, although in the air, in our element, we were still undefeated. I also confirmed accommodation for the rest of the members of the Gruppe with the mayor.

The next day we drove to the airfield. There were quite a few pilots there who explained to us that they would be belonging to JG 7. Our Kommandeur told them that only the remaining parts of the Geschwader would be here; the flying element was still in Prague-Ruzyne. He could not imagine that there would be any more operations flown from Mühldorf, hearing which the pilots present there were very disappointed. The situation was fundamentally hopeless and very turbulent, with rumours buzzing through the area. What I gathered from the Kommandeur's speech was that the Geschwader in Mühldorf would officially be dissolved and the soldiers released. In Mühldorf I also met our signals officer from Parchim, Leutnant Pantlischko, a Viennese. He told me that, in the next few days, he was going to drive a truck to his wife in Salzburg. We quickly agreed that he would take me along with him, and we arranged a meeting point for the next day in the camp at 1600hrs. I reported to the Kommandeur that I had organised the journey; he gave me his blessing and officially let me go.

After being in existence for hardly six complete months, the Geschwader was disbanded and each could go his own way. Unfortunately, during the last days I did not see Hans Schrangl. There were loud rumours that the Americans were already in Regensburg and Munich. I packed my belongings into a kit bag and looked for the meeting point with Pantlischko. I arrived punctually, but my dear Leutnant was nowhere to be seen. A radio-man told me that he had left for Salzburg in a radio truck before noon. So there I stood, poor fool, and had no idea what to do next. There were vehicles galore, so I asked a driver whether he would take me to Alt-Otting. Naturally he agreed, and dropped me off at the main airfield there, where I stood among many soldiers, all of them wanting to get to Traunstein. The vehicles rolled by, but none of them would stop; most were overloaded. It was evening by now and there was still no chance of getting transport. After several hours a group of towing vehicles stopped, and in a trice all available places were quickly taken. I got a place on the tank behind the cab – definitely not first class, but I was on my way to Salzburg.

Away went the post and our jalopy rattled through sleeping villages, unmolested by low-level enemy aircraft. At dawn, just before Traunstein, one of the soldiers tried to open the tarp on the trailer using his side weapon and saw there that the load consisted of cartons of food. Without further ado, a carton was opened and examined, and there it was – a carton of lovely tinned sausage. In turn we climbed onto the trailer and filled our sacks with tinned food; I emptied my kit bag of everything unnecessary and filled it full of cans. At least I would take food home with me if I managed to get to Salzburg.

Because of the disturbance caused while the sacks were being filled, it was difficult to keep one's seat on the tank, but after our men had been provisioned with tinned food it fell quiet again, and just in time, for towards morning we reached Traunstein. The column halted for technical reasons at the town limits near the base. We passengers climbed out and, for the first time, stretched our legs. I confirmed that the vehicles belonged to the Kriegsmarine and that the supplies would be transported to a fortress in the mountains. For me this business was finished, so I left and tramped towards the motorway. It was clear to me that I had to get to Salzburg before the US troops, and on no account did I want to be taken prisoner.

When I reached the motorway to Salzburg, without having been intercepted by a patrol, I stopped for a rest. It was also time to stop for food and I had some sausage, thanks to my midnight journey. The amount of traffic on the motorway increased and it was time for me to try to catch a lift. I was lucky – one of the Steyer cars stopped ahead of me, and the driver asked what I wanted. Naturally I said that I would like to be taken along with him to Salzburg. It was now going well for me, for the driver had barrels of Otto fuel on board and was taking them to his divisional headquarters at Bad Ischl. I was able to go along with him as long as I watched the air carefully for enemy aircraft. Well, it was the least I could do, but how far I had come from being a fighter pilot to an air observer on an army truck! The trip to Salzburg passed without any special incidents – perhaps the enemy pilots were still having breakfast. In any case, our vehicle was not bothered.

Now, it was a good thing that the driver had me on board, because the motorway bridge over the Sallach near Salzburg had already been blown, so I was able to show him a detour. We drove via Freilassing over the Sallach bridge, then we were in Salzburg – through Lehen, past the railway station to Itzling, then onto Maxstrasse, hardly 100 metres from my parents' house. The driver stopped and I explained the route to his destination and gave him many thanks for taking me along; for the first time I was able to give him a little gift of a 1kg tin of sausage. He was very happy with this, but I was equally happy to be standing right near my parents' house.

Just before 1100hrs I was home. I had done it, made it to my parents' house before the end of the war. The first people I was able to greet were Wehrmacht officers who were quartered with us. As my father appeared, I called, 'Father, the war is over!' The officers present were not very impressed with my statement, being of a different opinion. But more important was the greeting I received from my mother and my Käthe, for I had kept my word. As we had said goodbye in March at Parchim, I had said to my wife, 'It doesn't matter what happens, at the end of the war we will meet again at my parents' in Salzburg.'

In all probability I arrived in Salzburg on 3 May 1945. On that day some 262s landed at Salzburg airport and I was curious. On the 4th, wearing civilian clothing, I cycled to the airport, accompanied by my Käthe. I wanted to know who was there from the old ones. At the airport, near the 'Kugel Hof' inn, there stood ten 262s parked in a row. The HQ was in the inn, where the officers of JV 44 were present, among them Major Hohagen, my former Kommandeur. The Staffel had transferred from Munich-Riem to Salzburg and wanted to end the war here. Unfortunately, apart from Hohagen and Major Bär[58], there was nobody there I knew. My wife and I and the two men talked about my experiences of the last few weeks and about the return journey from Parchim via Prague to Salzburg. Hohagen said to me in the presence of my wife, 'Buchner, you've got it good. You have a wife, but who would like me with my face injury?' Hohagen and Bär were of the opinion that my wife and I should go back home again, since the war was over and so that I could avoid captivity.

On 5 May 1945 the Americans marched into Salzburg. During the afternoon, just before they took possession of the airfield, the mechanics of JV 44 set fire to the parked Me 262s. The smoke clouds climbed into the sky, marking the end of the 262. Some days later my friends, who were accommodated on the Riedenburg base, were taken in cars to France as prisoners of war. As the flames from the burning aircraft on the Salzburg airfield died out, the triumphal march of the 262 came to an end – a machine that had made history and one that could, possibly, have changed the course of the war.

Tragically for the Luftwaffe, the most advanced flying machines in the world were so much scrap by the end of May 1945. This one, whose yellow fuselage band suggests that it may have once served with Kommando Nowotny, was found abandoned at Munich-Riem.

Appendix

Documents

Close study of the facsimile documents that follow, in chronological order, will give the reader some idea of the way in which Hermann Buchner's career developed. Following the invasion of Czechoslovakia, the acquisition of the pilots' licence takes eighteen months. There is then a lull as he concentrates on his instructional duties. Once he reaches an operational unit, the frenzied pace at which Luftwaffe operations were taking place in Russia in 1942 quickly become apparent. Within six weeks he has earned the Combat Clasp in Bronze, then in Silver, and the Iron Cross both Second and First Class. Three weeks later he has completed sufficient sorties to be awarded the Combat Clasp in Gold. In August 1943 he reaches 300 missions. Two months after that comes the Honour Goblet. He then settles down to the grind of relentless combat sorties. In October 1943 comes the German Cross in Gold, but two weeks later he is severely wounded, for which he receives the Wound Badge in Black. Back in action once more, by January 1944 he has completed sufficient operational missions to be awarded the Combat Clasp in Gold with Pendant. More missions follow as the Luftwaffe withdraws from the Crimea and retreats to Romania; then in July, as he is at last posted away from the front, comes the award of the Knight's Cross. But the times of greatest trial are yet to come, and the only documents for those are in his logbooks and his memoirs...

The award certificate for the Medal and Bar of 1 October 1938. Known as a 'flower medal' in the Wehrmacht, it was given for the unopposed occupation of Czechoslovakia. The bar features a silhouette of Prague Castle.

The permit authorising Hermann Buchner to fly the different types of aircraft as listed. It is dated 18 September 1939, while he was training at Neustadt-Glewe.

The award certificate for the Pilot's Badge, dated 24 May 1940.

The award document for the Fighter Pilot's Combat Clasp in Bronze, dated 7 June 1942 while the author was with I./SchG 1.

The award document for the Fighter Pilot's Combat Clasp in Silver, dated 22 June 1942 while with I./SchG 1.

The award document for the Iron Cross 2nd Class, dated 24 June 1942 while a Feldwebel.

The award document for the Iron Cross 1st Class, dated 18 July 1942 while a Feldwebel with 8./SchG 1.

The award document for the Fighter Pilot's Combat Clasp in Gold, dated 2 August 1942 while with SchG 1.

Jd) verleihe
dem

Feldwebel
Hermann B u c h n e r
in Anerkennung seiner hervorragenden Tapferkeit
und der besonderen Erfolge als Schlachtflieger

den Ehrenpokal
für besondere Leistung
im Luftkrieg

Hauptquartier des Ob. d. L., den 2. Oktober 1942

Der Reichsminister der Luftfahrt
und Oberbefehlshaber der Luftwaffe

Reichsmarschall

Die erfolgte Verleihung wird beglaubigt:
Der Chef des Luftwaffenperfonalamts

General der Flieger

The award document for the Honour Goblet. This was usually the first sign that the recipient was being considered for the German Cross. It is dated 2 October 1942 while the author was a Feldwebel.

The tradition and Gothic imagery (two eagles in combat) of the silver Honour Goblet date from the First World War.

The award document for the German Cross in Gold. This was normally a prerequisite for consideration for the award of the Knight's Cross. The original certificate is an impressive 255mm wide. It is dated 17 October 1943 while the author was with 6./SchG 1.

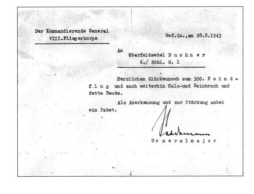

A congratulatory telegram from the Commanding General of VIII Fliegerkorps to Oberfeldwebel Buchner of 6./SchG 1 after he had completed 300 combat sorties, dated 28 August 1943.

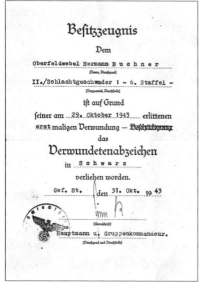

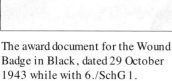

The award document for the Wound Badge in Black, dated 29 October 1943 while with 6./SchG 1.

The award document for the Fighter Pilot's Combat Clasp in Gold with Mission Pendant, dated 11 January 1944.

The signal sent to Oberfeldwebel Buchner on 29 July 1944 while he was in Prossnitz with SG 152, notifying him that he had been awarded the Knight's Cross. It had been sent from SG 2.

4.15.4.2

Vorläufiges Besitzzeugnis

Der Führer
und Oberste Befehlshaber
der Wehrmacht

hat

dem <u>Oberfeldwebel Hermann B u c h n e r</u>

das Ritterkreuz
des Eisernen Kreuzes

am _____20. Juli 1944_____ **verliehen**

Hauptquartier d.Ob.d.L. ___,den__1. August 1944__
Der Chef der Personellen Rüstung und
National-Sozialistischen Führung der Luftwaffe
I.A.

Oberst

The award document for the Knight's Cross, dated 20 July 1944, curiously the same day as an attempt was made to assassinate Adolf Hitler.

Notes

1 The so-called Austrian Legion was an organisation of Austrian National Socialists formed in the 1930s to press for 'Anschluss' – the unification of Austria and Germany. Heavily armed and living in camps, and given covert support by the Germans, in effect they made war upon their own government. Complaints by the Austrian government to the German Foreign Ministry were brushed aside on the grounds that it was 'an internal affair'.

2 There were three grades of glider pilot proficiency certificates in line with FAI requirements. The 'B' required 60 seconds of free flight with an 'S' turn manoeuvre.

3 The 'C' grade proficiency certificate entitled the holder to the Official Soaring Licence. The test itself consisted of both a flight test and an oral examination.

4 Alexander Löhr (1885-1947) was the commander of the Austrian Luftstreitkräfte at the time of the Anschluss. He later commanded Luftflotte 4 over Poland, the Balkans and Russia before returning to Yugoslavia to lead German attempts to quell the partisans. He surrendered there at the end of the war and was later executed by the Yugoslavs.

5 This was the day that German troops, unopposed, occupied Austria and the annexation became a reality.

6 20 April was Hitler's birthday and was a favoured day for the swearing-in ceremony for new recruits.

7 'Fips' Philipp is the twelfth ranking Luftwaffe fighter ace, with 206 victories. He was commander of JG 1 when he was killed in action near Nordhorn on 8 October 1943 while attacking a USAAF bombing raid.

8 The term 'Gruppe' is normally associated with the main Luftwaffe tactical unit, roughly equivalent to an RAF Wing, but is frequently used for smaller German military formations. Here it would approximate to 'squad' or 'section'.

9 The bad weather severely hampered the German invasion, and, unknown to outsiders, exposed many weaknesses in the organisation and equipment of the Germany Army.

10 It is indicative of the lack of planning for a long-term war by the Germans and a measure of his over-confidence in his control of the international situation felt by Hitler at this time that leave could be so freely given.

11 The 11,700-ton 'pocket battleship' Deutschland carried floatplanes for spotting purposes. Crews for the aircraft were provided by the Luftwaffe, although under the control of the Kriegsmarine. The vessel was used extensively before the war for training, including participation in the Spanish Civil War 'non-intervention patrols'. Renamed *Lützow* in February 1940 to avoid any embarrassment should she be sunk under her previous name, she was scuttled at the end of the war. Until 1943 or so maritime aircraft based at coastal stations flew with mixed Luftwaffe and Kriegsmarine crews. The units were commanded by a Luftwaffe general who reported to the naval High Command. By 1943 the system had proven too unwieldy and all units were taken into Luftwaffe control.

12 A shallow lagoon close to the base giving access to the Baltic and forming an ideal situation for maritime aircraft and small boat training.

13 Captured from the French, who had received 214 of 230 ordered from North American by the time of the French collapse.

14 Theodor Weissenberger later served with JG 5 and 7 and scored 208 victories. He won the 'Oakleaves' to the Knight's Cross in August 1943 and survived the war, only to be killed in a motor-racing accident in 1950.

15 Armin Köhler flew with JG 77 and gained the Knight's Cross and sixty-nine victories. Captured by the Russians at the war's end, he managed to escape while on his way to Siberia, although he did not reach home until 1953.

16 Albert Brunner flew with JG 5 in Finland and scored fifty-three victories before he was killed in 1943 when forced to bale out of his aircraft too low for his parachute to open. He was awarded a posthumous Knight's Cross.

17 Junkers Ju 90Z-2 D-AVMF *Brandenburg*, of DLH, crashed near Kamenz on 8 November 1940. The aircraft, WNr 9000010, was only six months old. All twenty-nine people on board were killed.

18 Theodor Osterkamp (1892-1975) won the 'Blue Max' as a naval lieutenant in 1918 after scoring twenty-three victories. He joined the Luftwaffe in 1935 and commanded JFVS 1 until 1940 when he was given command of JG 51 with whom he scored six more victories and gained the Knight's Cross. While Commander of Fighters in northern France and later Sicily, his outspoken criticism of the conduct of the war by the senior Luftwaffe commanders led to his enforced retirement in 1944.

19 A 'Schwarm' was the basic four-aircraft formation used by the Luftwaffe and later adopted by almost all other air forces. A 'Rotte' consisted of three aircraft, while a 'Kette' was a pair.

20 Spanish volunteers in the German Wehrmacht were so called on account of the dark blue shirts (indicating the Falangist Party, led by Franco) that they habitually wore.

21 Better known as 'the one that got away'. He was killed on 25 October when his aircraft crashed into the sea off Holland.

22 An expression that originated during the First World War to denote a large formation of, usually, fighter aircraft, as in 'von Richthofen's flying circus'. In the event, experience led the Schlachtgeschwader to generally operate in formations only as large as a Schwarm, ie four aircraft, as any more than that were too difficult to co-ordinate over the battlefield without the possibility of dangerous confusion.

23 Otto Dommeratzky, born 1916, claimed thirty-eight aerial victories in two years. In that time he gained the Knight's Cross and the 'Oakleaves' before his death in action against US P-51Ds on 13 October 1944. Rather than abandon his mechanic, whom he was carrying in the rear fuselage of his FW 190 (a fairly common practice) when he was shot up over Germany, he tried to force land but both died in the ensuing crash.

24 'Indians' was the Luftwaffe codeword for enemy aircraft, akin to 'Bandits' in the Royal Air Force.

25 Leopold Steinbatz, born in Vienna on 25 October 1918, joined the Austrian Air Force in 1937. In the Luftwaffe he served with 9./JG 52 as Hermann Graf's wingman in late 1940. Following action over Crete and the Balkans he went to the Eastern Front in August 1941. There he was awarded the Knight's Cross after forty-two victories, the 'Oakleaves' in June 1942 after ninety-one victories. On the 15th of that month, shortly after claiming his ninety-ninth victim (all in the East), he was posted missing after his aircraft was hit by flak. Subsequently he was posthumously awarded the Swords to his Knight's Cross.

26 The Ritterkreuz or Knight's Cross came in five different grades: the Knight's Cross itself, then with, in ascending order, the 'Oakleaves', 'Swords', 'Diamonds' and 'Golden Oakleaves'. The last-named were awarded only once, to Hans-Ulrich Rudel, the famous Stuka pilot.

27 The higher grades of the Knight's Cross were indicated by small metal brooches attached to the suspension ring of the Cross, which hung around the neck. The author was nominated for the award of the 'Oakleaves' but the war ended before the process was completed.

28 Panje horses were the small and hardy animals used throughout the steppes of Russia as mounts and beasts of burden. It seems that the term was applied to similarly utilitarian motor vehicles.

29 French-speaking Belgian volunteers in the German Army were formed into the 'Walloon Legion' in August 1941 and employed in Russia from November of that year, where it was known as 'Infantry Battalion 373'. Flemish-speakers were regarded as being more 'Germanic' and were inducted into the SS. In June 1943 all Belgian volunteers were transferred to the SS. Many of these fought well for the Germans, suffering heavy losses in the process, but at the end those who survived were regarded as traitors by their home country and treated accordingly. Most were court-martialled and given prison sentences; not a few were executed.

30 Hans-Ulrich Rudel (1916-82), the most highly decorated man in the Wehrmacht, was almost a one-man army, with more than 2,500 operational missions to his credit and more than 500 tanks, a Russian cruiser, a destroyer and a battleship destroyed as well as hundreds of other vehicles, armoured trains, artillery pieces and naval vessels. He was in command of SG 2 by the end of the war, and despite losing a leg he continued flying until the end, lastly in an FW 190. Almost incidentally he was also a fighter ace with nine Russian aircraft shot down.

31 Gerhard Barkhorn was the first German airman to complete 1,000 operational missions. He was also one of only two men ever to be credited with more than 300 confirmed kills, with 301. The other man was his long-time friend Erich Hartmann, with 352. Both served in JG 52.

32 Known as the 'Cementer' to the Germans and 'Ilyusha' to the Russians, the Ilyushin Il 2 was tantamount to a flying tank. It was the scourge of German ground forces, attacking with cannon, bombs and rockets, despite appalling losses. It has the distinction of being produced in greater numbers than any other aircraft in the world.

33 Italian Savoia-Marchetti SM 82 tri-motor transports were seized by the Germans when Italy collapsed. Used in the Crimean evacuation by III./TG 1, their extremely capacious fuselage, considerably larger than that of the Junkers Ju 52, meant that they made a significant contribution to German airlift capacity.

34 Probably from NJG 6, which was the only Luftwaffe unit based at Zilistea equipped with the Messerschmitt Bf 110. The pilot was perhaps not very happy as that was the day his unit began evacuating to Otopeni.

35 The veteran Boeing B-17F-95-BO, 42-30267, 'Hustlin' Huzzy', of the 341st Bomb Squadron, 97th Bomb Group, 15th USAAF, flown by 2nd Lt Lyle Fleener, is believed to have been the aircraft shot down by Buchner on 23 June 1944 during the raid on Ploesti.

36 IAR 80 fighters were the first such type to be designed and built by the Romanian aircraft industry. Based on the experience gained while licence-building the PZL 24, 240 were built and the aircraft proved to be a useful stop-gap until the Germans were able to supply Messerschmitt 109s. IAR 80s were some of the first Romanian aircraft ever to engage the USAAF when the latter raided Ploesti on 1 August 1943.

37 'Allan' Frank flew Hs 123s in the Polish and French campaigns with 5th Staffel of II.(S)/LG 2. By October 1943 he had worked his way through the ranks to command II./SG 2. He was awarded the 'Oakleaves' in January 1943 after 700 operational missions. By April 1944 he had reached 900. He was Kommandeur of IV./SG 151 at the time of his death.

38 Zeltbahn, the camouflaged waterproof poncho issued to all members of the Wehrmacht, could be buttoned together to form tents capable of accommodating several men.

39 'Kanalhosen' was the slang term given to the trousers of the special two-piece leather flying suits worn by Luftwaffe fighter pilots and meant to give protection from exposure if immersed in water. The reference dates from 1941, and their anticipated usefulness in the event of the wearer being shot down in the Kanal, ie the English Channel.

40 Reichsverteidigung was the Luftwaffe home defence fight force.

41 This refers to the 'long-nosed' Focke-Wulf FW 190D-9 with the Jumo in-line engine.

42 Rudi Sinner was a thirty-nine-victory ace who served with JG 27, JG 54 and JG 7.

43 The FuG 16 ZY was the standard radio transmitter/receiver fitted to the Me 262.

44 The speed of the attack and the devastating impact of the cannon fire from the Me 262 was so great that Rickey believed he had been hit by flak.

45 Austrian Walter Nowotny (1920-44) was the fifth-ranking Luftwaffe fighter
ace. Known to all his friends as 'Nowi', he was a daring if undisciplined pilot
who had gained the 'Oakleaves', 'Swords' and 'Diamonds' by the age of 23.
Appointed to command the first operational Me 262 unit, his ability to fly was
not in doubt, but he was probably not the right choice to be given the
responsibility of developing both the new equipment and training in a new
form of air warfare. Lack of technical and tactical skills meant that Kommando
Nowotny suffered heavily in the few months of its existence. After his death in
action on 8 November 1944 after 258 official kills and thirty-one unconfirmed,
the unit was pulled out of the line for re-training by order of Adolph Galland.

46 Johannes 'Macki' Steinhoff (1913-94) was probably one of the most versatile of
Luftwaffe pilots, serving as a day, night and jet fighter pilot. He served on every front
with the Luftwaffe, and in more than 900 missions he shot down 176 enemy aircraft,
six of them while flying the Me 262. A severe landing crash in the jet left him with a
badly burned face requiring numerous skin grafts. After the war he joined the new
Bundesluftwaffe, which he eventually rose to command before his retirement.

47 Knight's Cross-holder Erich Hohagen flew variously with JG 2, JG 27 and JG 51,
mostly over the Western Front. He was wounded several times and scored fifty-six
victories, twenty on the Eastern Front. After Kommando Nowotny was disbanded
Hohagen was given command of III./JG 7 until the end of December 1944 after
suffering a serious head wound. His last kill was his one and only on the Me 262.

48 Georg-Peter Eder was legendary for his courage and chivalry. After flying with
JG 1, JG 2 and JG 51, during which time he claimed fifty-three aerial victories,
he joined Kommando Nowotny in October 1944. Credited with twenty-five
kills on the Me 262, he was one of the most successful jet fighter pilots of all
time. He commanded 9./JG 7 until, low on fuel, he was shot down on 22
January 1945 and broke both legs, which ended his wartime flying career.

49 The novel undercarriage gave trouble during the early days due to
manufacturing difficulties and a tendency for the tyres to burst.

50 Theodor Weissenberger took over command of JG 7 in early 1945. He had
spent much of his early career with JG 5 and ended the war with 208 victories,
including three B-17s, on the Me 262.

51 In a bid to increase the likelihood of a hit against the US bomber formations,
55mm R4M rockets were fitted under the wings of many Me 262s. Fired in a
spread pattern, a single rocket was sufficient to destroy a bomber.

52 Presumably this meant to return to base.

53 'Pauke-Pauke' – literally kettle-drum – meant 'I am attacking'.

54 'Dicke Autos' – 'fat cars', ie heavy bombers.

55 RAF Bomber Command lost at least six Lancasters to Me 262s on 31 March
1945. Unused to flying in the mutually protective box formations of the
USAAF bombers, the usually nocturnal Lancasters were easy targets for the jets.

56 It was believed to be an RAF Mustang from either 130 or 403 Squadron.

57 Synthetic fuel.

58 'Heinz' Bär was the Luftwaffe's eighth-ranking ace with 220 victories,
sixteen on jets. He ended the war as the last commander of JV 44.

Index

Other titles available in the Crécy Classic series

Albert Ball VC
Chaz Bowyer
Fascinating story of the Royal Flying Corps' first
celebrity ace with 44 kills.
280pp soft cover
Over 75 b&w photographs
9 780947 554897 £10.95

Enemy Coast Ahead – Uncensored
Leader of the Dambusters
Wing Commander Guy Gibson VC DSO DFC
One of the outstanding accounts of WWII seen
through the eyes of one of its most respected and
controversial personalities.
288 pages, soft cover
b&w photographs and illustrations throughout
9 780859 791182 £10.95

Fist from the Sky
Peter C Smith
The story of Captain Takashige Egusa the Imperial
Japanese Navy's most illustrious dive-bomber pilot
272 pages, soft cover
Over 75 B+W photographs
9 780859 79122 9 £10.95

Janusz Zurakowski
Legend in the Skies
Bill Zuk and Janusz Zurakowski
A rare combination of skilled engineer, painstaking test
pilot and unparalleled display pilot.
336 pages, soft cover
Over 75 b&w photographs
9 780859 79128 1 £10.95

In the Skies of Nomonhan
Japan versus Russia – September 1939
Dimitar Nedialkov
A new perspective on this interesting and largely
unknown pre World War II encounter.
160 pages, soft cover
Over 50 b&w photographs and 20 colour profiles
9 780859 79152 6 £10.95

The Luftwaffe Fighters' Battle of Britain
Chris Goss
An insight into the experiences of the German fighter
and bomber crews from the attacker's viewpoint.
208 pages, soft cover
Over 140 photographs
9 780859 791519 £10.95

Pure Luck
Alan Bramson
An authorised biography of aviation pioneer Sir
Thomas Sopwith, 1888-1989
Foreword by HRH The Prince of Wales
288 pages, soft cover
Over 90 b&w photographs
9 780859 791069 £10.95

Thud Ridge
Jack Broughton
F-105 Thunderchief missions over the hostile skies of
North Vietnam
288 pages, soft cover
79 photographs plus maps and plans
9 780859 791168 £10.95

Sigh for a Merlin
Testing the Spitfire
Alex Henshaw
The enthralling account of Alex Henshaw's life as a
test pilot with the Spitfire.
240 pages, soft cover
b&w photographs throughout
9 780947 554835 £10.95

Spitfire
A Test Pilot's Story
Jeffrey Quill
The autobiography of an exceptional test pilot and
RAF and Fleet Air Arm fighter pilot.
336 pages, soft cover
b&w photographs throughout
9 780947 554729 £10.95

We Landed By Moonlight
Hugh Verity
Secret RAF Landings in France 1940-1944
256 pages, soft cover
b&w photographs throughout
9 780947 554750 £10.95

Winged Warfare
William Avery ('Billy') Bishop VC, DSO MC
A unique autobiographical and contemporary account of
one of the highest scoring fighter aces of World War I.
224 pages, soft cover
integrated b&w photographs
9 780947 554903 £10.95

Order online at
www.crecy.co.uk
tel +44 (0) 161 499 0024

Crécy Publishing 1a Ringway Trading Est,
Shadowmoss Rd, Manchester, M22 5LH
enquiries@crecy.co.uk